*Evolution of a
Missouri Asylum*

Evolution of a Missouri Asylum

FULTON STATE HOSPITAL, 1851–2006

Richard L. Lael, Barbara Brazos,
and Margot Ford McMillen

UNIVERSITY OF MISSOURI PRESS
COLUMBIA AND LONDON

Copyright © 2007 by
The Curators of the University of Missouri
University of Missouri Press, Columbia, Missouri 65201
Printed and bound in the United States of America
All rights reserved
5 4 3 2 1   11 10 09 08 07

Library of Congress Cataloging-in-Publication Data

Lael, Richard L., 1946–
  Evolution of a Missouri asylum : Fulton State Hospital, 1851–2000 / Richard L. Lael, Barbara Brazos, and Margot Ford McMillen.
       p. ; cm.
  Includes bibliographical references and index.
  Summary: "Traces the history of Missouri's first state mental institution, the Fulton State Hospital, founded in 1851. This institutional history examines a century and a half of changing attitudes toward mental illness, evolving treatments as medical and psychiatric science sought cures and the continuing administrative challenges of overcrowding and chronic underfunding"— Provided by publisher.
    ISBN-13: 978-0-8262-1689-2 (hard cover : alk. paper)
    ISBN-10: 0-8262-1689-7 (hard cover : alk. paper)
    1. Psychiatric hospitals—Missouri—History. I. Brazos, Barbara, 1947– II. McMillen, Margot Ford. III. Title.
    [DNLM: 1. Fulton State Hospital (Mo.) 2. Hospitals, Psychiatric—history—Missouri. 3. History of Medicine—Missouri. 4. History, 19th Century—Missouri. 5. History, 20th Century—Missouri. 6. Psychiatry—history—Missouri. WM 28 AM8 L158e 2006]
  RC445.M83L34 2006
  362.2'109778'335—dc22
                                                      2006031773

♾™ This paper meets the requirements of the American National Standard for Permanence of Paper for Printed Library Materials, Z39.48, 1984.

Designer: *foleydesign*
Typesetter: The Composing Room of Michigan, Inc.
Printer and binder: Thomson-Shore, Inc.
Typefaces: Baskerville and Nimbus Sans

To all those patients and staff who have occupied this place, living the mission, vision, and values and looking for a hopeful future for all of us.

Contents

Preface ix

Part I, *by Richard L. Lael*

1 From Idea to Reality, 1844–1850 3

2 Overcoming Obstacles
   The First Decade, 1850–1860 17

3 Disaster and Rebirth, 1861–1872 36

4 Administration Gridlock and Recovery, 1869–1897 55

5 "To the Victors Belong the Spoils"
   Asylum Patronage, 1872–1923 71

6 Search for a Cure
   Treatments in Transition, 1905–1940 83

7 Bursting at the Seams
   Growing Pains, 1890–1940 103

Part II, *by Barbara Brazos and Margot Ford McMillen*

8 Three Early Residents 119

9 Dramatic Changes in Treatment, 1940–1949 132

10 Missouri's Mental Health Care Comes
of Age, 1950–1959 150

11 Enlightened Leadership, 1960–1969 165

12 New Strategies, New Challenges, 1970–1979 178

13 The Challenge of Youth, 1950–1991 196

14 Deinstitutionalization, 1980–1989 204

15 New Missions as the Century Turns, 1990–2000 218

16 An Uncertain Future 228

Fulton State Hospital Administrators 239

Index 241

Preface

Anniversaries are for celebrating past successes, reflecting on lost opportunities and failures, and looking forward to the promises of the future. For organizations and institutions, centennial and sesquicentennial celebrations hold special meaning. Groups marking a century or more of existence have survived the rigors of creation, adapted to stresses and strains, and reached a maturity that many never attain.

In 2001, Fulton State Hospital celebrated its sesquicentennial, marking 150 years of treatment of the mentally ill. Its success at its founding was far from certain despite the optimism shared by the legislators, administrators, and staff whose efforts led to its opening in 1851. Mental illness was imperfectly understood in the decade prior to the Civil War. Influenced by European physician-authors and by successes of institutions on the continent and in the northeastern United States, in 1847, the Missouri General Assembly authorized the erection of the first state asylum for the mentally ill west of the Mississippi.

Just as its name evolved from the State Lunatic Asylum, to State Lunatic Asylum No. 1, to State Hospital No. 1, to Fulton State Hospital, so too did its quest for a cure. The optimism that characterized debate in the middle of the nineteenth century—the belief that most patients could be cured—gave way to a deepening pessimism by century's end, as the institution increasingly focused on custodial care. In the early twentieth century, new approaches and techniques, coupled with increasing reliance on scientific investigation and the resulting new practices, rekindled the earlier optimism. Then, by midcentury, the end of political patronage in Missouri meant that the institution could search outside the state for professionals with the highest degree of training, knowledge, and skill.

Managing an effective treatment facility required more than the latest medical theories or therapies. It required a dedicated staff of administrators, physicians, nurses, and support staff. The facilities and other infrastructure required ongoing effort and expense. Once the buildings were finished, they required constant maintenance, repair, renovation, or replacement. Wells had to be dug. A boiler plant had to be kept on line while being enlarged to meet institutional growth. For much of its history, the hospital strove for self-sufficiency; thus the fields had to be plowed, cattle, hogs, and chickens fed, orchards planted and harvested, food stored, clothes sewn, and mattresses fabricated. It was only in the last half of the twentieth century that the goal of self-sufficiency was surrendered.

Accomplishing all these tasks required a significant expenditure of money, even though the regular use of patient labor helped contain costs. No matter how many patients worked in the sewing rooms and workshops or provided agricultural labor, state appropriations and county payments for patient care were essential. Unfortunately, whether in 1851, 1921 or 2001, money always seemed in short supply. As they tightened their financial belts, administrators admirably pursued the most modern medical techniques despite the challenges, but understaffing and underfunding for training meant that at times treatments were carried out in substandard conditions. Indeed, for the most helpless patients—segregated African Americans, the poor, the anonymous, or the most violently delusional—life in the institution was frequently anything but therapeutic.

Stakeholders in the institution, as defined in its 2001 and 2004 strategic plans as "those who share in our mission to provide services," include constituencies—clients, families, courts, law enforcement agencies, hospitals, legislators, and other high-ranking Missouri elected officials—that would have been equally familiar in 1851 or 1901. Other twenty-first-century stakeholders would have been unheard of in the nineteenth century: the Department of Mental Health, Community Mental Health Centers, the Missouri Protection and Advocacy Services, the Missouri Mental Health Consumer Network, and the state's higher-education institutions. The growth of the number of stakeholders during Fulton State Hospital's 150-year history reflects the growing awareness of, and attention to, the needs of the mentally ill in Missouri—a trend that current and past stakeholders would celebrate.

In the past 150 years policies toward stakeholders have changed most significantly for the "client" group. Late- nineteenth and early-twentieth-century administrators would undoubtedly be surprised by the language of recent hospital strategic plans. Clients have become important players, along with their treatment teams, in the development of policies. The 2004 strategic plan, for example, called for including greater participation by clients. Its goals include: "Seek input from client councils on creating a culture of non-violence; have clients help develop orientation packets; survey clients as

So that they could produce their own food, early state institutions were located in rural settings. The Fulton State Hospital was self-sufficient in food production until the mid-1980s (Kingdom of Callaway Historical Society).

to how participation in treatment team meetings could be redesigned to be more positive and client-friendly."[1] This is a far cry from the warehousing and drugging of patients at the turn of the preceding century.

In 2001, reflecting on how historians might assess his hospital's legacy, its practices, and its relationship to patients and clients, Dr. Felix Vincenz, chief executive officer of the Fulton State Hospital, cautioned against historical smugness:

> Before we look too smugly upon our past, its primitive science and its atrocities, and question with a sense of superiority "What were they thinking?" we must realize that no one who served at this hospital believed that they were doing harm, and all believed they were providing the best available treatment with the clients' ultimate interests at heart. What will they think of us in another 150 years? At what primitive practices will they shake their heads in wonder? Pride must be mixed in equal measures with humility, with a sense that we have come far but have far yet to go. Only then can we take satisfaction in our ac-

---

1. Master Strategic Plan, January 7, 2004, Fulton State Hospital Archives, Fulton, Missouri (hereinafter cited as FSHA).

complishments and in our history, only then will we honor the sacred and make restitution for the profane.[2]

The history of Fulton State Hospital reveals noble aspirations—the desire to create a restorative environment for the mentally ill, to treat them with kindness, sensitivity, and respect, and to develop and apply therapies that will allow them to return whole to their families and communities. But historical analysis also reveals the darker sides of an institution that was throughout much of its history racist and one that sometimes too readily engaged in questionable therapies, one that too frequently lost sight of the best interests of the patients.

To gain some perspective, then, we must ask if U.S. asylums comparable to the Fulton facility have functioned primarily to protect, uplift, and hopefully cure the mentally ill or if instead they became coercive institutions used by the dominant portion of society to repress and isolate the social, political, moral, or even economic "deviant." Should those who entered the asylums be considered patients or inmates? The words used to describe institutions, their constituents and their practices carry powerful images. An "inmate" and a "patient" may both be housed in an institution, but the image that each word evokes is dramatically different. Choosing a descriptive verb such as *protect* or *coerce* again conveys immense meaning. As to which vision of the asylum and its constituents, if either, is more accurate, historians disagree.

In 1949, Albert Deutsch characterized the asylum movement as a triumph of enlightened values that addressed the needs of the mentally ill, who had too often been seen and treated as subhuman.[3] While mistakes and misjudgments occurred, the movement to shift the mentally ill into state and private asylums was worthy of praise, not condemnation. Deutsch's analysis reflected the historical interpretation of the U.S. asylum movement that dominated until the early 1960s. For historians who adopted this "progressive" interpretation, verbs such as *protect*, *uplift*, and *cure* were the correct ones.

By the 1960s, as debates intensified about race, war, and gender, a generation of historians emerged who began to question older interpretations of many aspects of American history. Howard Zinn, writing in 1970, vigorously argued for a "value-laden" historiography, using history to "intensify, expand, [and] sharpen our perception of how bad things are for the victims of the world," to "expose the pretensions of governments," to "re-

---

2. Felix Vincenz, remarks at Secretary of State's Fulton State Hospital Sesquicentennial Celebration, Missouri State Archives, May 2, 2001, Jefferson City, Missouri.

3. Albert Deutsch, *The Mentally Ill in America: A History of Their Care and Treatment from Colonial Times* (New York: Columbia University Press, 1949).

By financing a new plant to generate electricity, the state showed its commitment to the hospital in the 1940s (Fulton State Hospital).

capture those few moments in the past which show the possibility of a better way of life than that which has dominated the earth thus far," and to "show how good social movements can go wrong." Embracing such a revisionist approach and rejecting the "fog of righteousness which has enveloped and nearly smothered past efforts to come to terms with the treatment of the insane," academics such as Michel Foucault, Thomas Szasz, and Andrew Scull reexamined long-held perceptions of the asylum movement in both the nineteenth and twentieth centuries and found them wanting.[4]

4. Howard Zinn, *The Politics of History* (Boston: Beacon Press, 1970), 35–55; Michel Foucault, *Madness and Civilization: A History of Insanity in the Age of Reason*, trans. Richard Howard (New York: Vintage Books, [1965] 1973); Thomas Szasz, *Cruel Compassion: Psychiatric Control of Society's Unwanted* (New York: John Wiley and Sons, 1994); Andrew Scull, *Museums of Madness: The Social Or-*

Such scholars continue to describe asylums as institutions used by dominant elites to coerce or contain those whom they deemed disruptive, objectionable, deviant, or unproductive. Szasz, writing in 1994, argues that "the history of civilization [is] a catalog of the various methods man has developed to dispose of unwanted persons and the pretexts with which he has justified doing so." He condemns U.S. mental health policies in particular: "I view our statist-institutional psychiatric practices not as specialized medical technics for treating mental diseases, but as socially approved procedures for disposing of unwanted persons."[5] For him, the deinstitutionalization movement of the late twentieth century is just as flawed as its institutionalization predecessor. In both cases, Szasz points out that the state is equally coercive of the mentally ill and equally blind to treating them as responsible persons.

Bridging these two schools of historical thought are the postrevisionists. Richard Fox, for example, revealed that California's asylums from the very beginning had as their goal both the treatment and improvement of the mentally ill *and* the detention of the social outcast. Edward Shorter and Gerald Grob accept neither the progressive nor the revisionist images without reservations.[6] Drawing from the research and perspectives of both schools, they acknowledge both the successes and the failures of the asylum movement in the United States and paint a portrait in shades of gray, not in absolute black or white.

Other postrevisionists, including Marvin Olasky and Lewis Thomas, directly attack the revisionists' condemnation of mental hospitals, arguing that these institutions still can serve an important and humane function in American life. Adding to the ongoing debate about the validity of revisionist criticism and analysis, newer studies are contributing to our understanding of mental health history. Examining the history of insanity in South Carolina from the colonial period to the Progressive era, Peter McCandless focuses not only on life inside the asylum, but also on the life of the mentally ill outside its walls. John Hughes, utilizing the letters of a woman housed in Alabama's state mental institution between 1893 and 1920, pro-

---

ganization of Insanity in Nineteenth-Century England (London: Allen Lane, 1979). The "fog of righteousness" quotation is from Scull, *Museums of Madness*, 256.

5. Szasz, *Cruel Compassion*, 9–11.

6. Richard Fox, *So Far Disordered in Mind: Insanity in California, 1870–1930* (Berkeley and Los Angeles: University of California Press, 1978), 17; Edward Shorter, *A History of Psychiatry* (New York: John Wiley and Sons, 1997); Gerald Grob, *The Mad among Us: A History of the Care of America's Mentally Ill* (New York: Free Press, 1994); Gerald Grob, *From Asylum to Community: Mental Health in Modern America* (Princeton: Princeton University Press, 1991); Gerald Grob, *Mental Illness and American Society, 1875–1940* (Princeton: Princeton University Press, 1983); Gerald Grob, *The State and the Mentally Ill: A History of Worcester State Hospital in Massachusetts, 1830–1920* (Chapel Hill: University of North Carolina Press, 1966).

vides a patient's view of institutionalization. Gregg Andrews's *Insane Sisters* describes a fascinating case study in Missouri of how the admissions process into an asylum could be manipulated for economic gain. Some new histories reach well beyond an academic audience. For example, Lynn Gamwell and Nancy Tomes, in *Madness in America: Cultural and Medical Perceptions of Mental Illness before 1914,* combine a lively narrative with etchings and photographs that appeal to the general reader as well.[7]

Like *Madness in America,* the present volume is written with the general reader in mind. It acknowledges both the noble aspirations of Fulton State Hospital as well as its failures to consistently transform those aspirations into realities.

• • •

Researching 150 years of Fulton State Hospital history posed significant problems. Few institutional records of the first hundred years have survived. Indeed, staff shortages throughout its early history may well have curtailed extensive record keeping. Financially strapped administrators also may have viewed archival storage as an unnecessary expense that took away time, money, and space that could better be spent elsewhere. No administrative procedure seems to have existed for the regular transfer of nonpatient files from a superintendent, matron, steward or Board of Managers to successors in the nineteenth and early twentieth centuries, and any files that might have been transferred may have turned to ash in the spectacular administration building fire in 1956. As if this was not daunting enough for historians, the records most likely to have survived the passing of the decades—patient files—are not available to researchers due to the state's privacy policy.

One set of records that did survive were the biennial superintendent and Board of Managers' reports submitted to the Missouri General Assembly. Bound as part of the Senate and House Journals, and housed in the Missouri State Archives, these documents are uneven in quality, depending largely upon the style, forthrightness, and comprehensiveness of their authors. Supplementing these official reports are other documents: trial records, letters, gubernatorial papers, county documents, one rare set of

---

7. Marvin Olasky, *The Tragedy of American Compassion* (Chicago: Regnery, 1992); Lewis Thomas, *Late Night Thoughts on Listening to Mahler's Ninth Symphony* (New York: Viking Press, 1983); Peter McCandless, *Moonlight, Magnolias, and Madness: Insanity in South Carolina from the Colonial Period to the Progressive Era* (Chapel Hill: University of North Carolina Press, 1996); John Hughes, ed., *The Letters of a Victorian Madwoman* (Columbia, S.C.: University of South Carolina Press, 1993); Gregg Andrews, *Insane Sisters: Or, the Price Paid for Challenging a Company Town* (Columbia: University of Missouri Press, 1999); Lynn Gamwell and Nancy Tomes, *Madness in America: Cultural and Medical Perceptions of Mental Illness before 1914* (Ithaca: Cornell University Press, 1995).

board minutes, workshop ledgers, blueprints, construction contracts, newspaper articles and editorials, and supply catalogs.

The nature and quality of sources has significantly shaped how the institution's past comes alive. Richard Lael's analysis of hospital history prior to World War II (Part I of this volume) relies upon traditional archival sources, records, reports, personal letters, gubernatorial papers, legislative investigations, court records, and newspapers. On the other hand, Margot Ford McMillen and Barbara Brazos, who continue the analysis for the hospital's last sixty-five years (Part II), were able to draw heavily from a rich collection of recent oral histories of workers, clients, and neighbors. As a result, the second half of this volume benefits from livelier, more detailed, and more personalized information than the first. Drawing from a broad spectrum of personal insights and reflections, it examines not only the hospital's day-to-day operations but also the memories and emotions of current and former administrators, employees, clients, and neighbors. Unfortunately, few such personal reminiscences exist that address the institution's first one hundred years.

The problems of access to historical materials and their preservation and storage do not lie simply in the past—these remain current issues, if we hope to preserve the experiences of those who lived, worked, and interacted with the hospital throughout its history. Staff shortages, budget cuts, lack of time or expertise, and the absence of temperature- and humidity-controlled storage continue to threaten the long-term preservation and classification of the hospital's documents and photographs. Equally important is the ongoing identification and collection of information and materials relating to the hospital's history that are privately held, whether in the form of letters, diaries, artifacts, or memories. We have been fortunate that two agencies devoted to historic preservation have been generous in their assistance throughout this project. We encourage any of our readers who have letters, diaries, or memories of the institution to contact either the Kingdom of Callaway Historical Society or the Missouri State Archives to discuss how their materials and information may be preserved for the future and how these may be made accessible to future researchers.

...

This study would not have been possible without the generous and enthusiastic assistance of Fulton State Hospital administrators, staff, and patients, both past and present. Like us, they wanted to explore the long-neglected history of the institution. They wanted to understand the trials, tribulations, triumphs, and failures of those thousands of men and women who worked at or who were served by the hospital. To list all those to whom we owe a great debt of gratitude is not possible in this limited space, but we acknowledge the following special contributors: Chief Executive Officer Dr. Felix Vincenz and Business Manager Ken Lyle not only enthusiastically made available records and photographs but also enabled us to explore buildings and tunnels as well as to talk to current hospital personnel. Former Volunteer Coordinator Joyce Glover worked diligently to assemble dispersed records and materials and served as our hospital concierge, answering innumerable questions, establishing contacts with other personnel in the hospital, clearing the way for us to wander where we wished, under guidance and escort of course. At no time have hospital administrators or staff tried to influence our conclusions and interpretation of events. Rather, they willingly provided us the research data and allowed us to analyze the data as we found suitable. For that assistance and for that noninterference, we are extremely grateful.

This study would also not have been possible without the assistance and cooperation of other groups, institutions, and individuals. The staff of the Kingdom of Callaway Historical Society (KCHS), the staff of the Missouri State Archives, Cassidy Rohrer at the *Columbia Daily Tribune*, and the large number of current and past employees of the hospital who agreed to be interviewed deserve special mention. Barbara Huddleston at the KCHS was especially helpful. She gladly answered our questions and filled our numerous requests for materials, exceeding the call of duty by seeking out material in the collections that we didn't know existed. Greg Olsen and the Main Reading Room personnel at the Missouri State Archives generously gave of their time and advice as we sought relevant records in that facility's extensive holdings. Special thanks also go to Westminster College and to the Lane Harlan History Fund for financial support of this project. There are other organizations not listed here that also deserve recognition. To all these individuals and organizations, we extend a most enthusiastic *thank you!*

*Evolution of a
Missouri Asylum*

I

by Richard L. Lael

1
From Idea to Reality, 1844–1850

Missouri governor Thomas Reynolds, disturbed about the "slanders and abuse" he faced from his political enemies, began to place his affairs in order. On January 6, 1844, he drew up a will, leaving his property to his wife. Although during the next few weeks he continued the routine duties of Missouri's chief executive, he obviously remained troubled. On Friday, February 9, he rose, ate breakfast, walked into his office in the executive mansion, wrote a short note, tied a piece of twine around his rifle's trigger, twisted the other end around his thumb, and pulled the trigger. He died instantly.[1]

Lieutenant Governor Meredith Marmaduke, a Democrat elected in 1840, assumed the reins of state government. Since 1844 was a gubernatorial election year, Marmaduke had only months in office before the August elections. Although as a willing candidate and sitting governor, he would normally be the first choice of his party to pursue the governorship, Missouri Democratic leaders were divided between supporters and detractors of U.S. Senator Thomas Hart Benton and rejected Marmaduke as their nominee. Recognizing his chances of winning were remote, Marmaduke withdrew his name from the race before the state Democratic convention met during the summer. Therefore, on November 18, two days before Democrat John C. Edwards was inaugurated, Marmaduke delivered his first and only biennial message as governor to the legislature.

In that message, he reviewed the status of past legislative directives. He stated his belief that the Iowa-Missouri boundary dispute was nearing resolution. Meanwhile, the survey of the southern boundary of the state, or-

[1]. Buel Leopard and Floyd Shoemaker, eds., *Messages and Proclamations of the Governors of the State of Missouri* (Columbia: State Historical Society of Missouri, 1922), 1:442–44.

dered by the legislature in 1841, had not gone well and now, three years later, only sixty miles had been surveyed. The governor then outlined the fiscal health of the state treasury. While the government currently had a surplus of over $48,000, having paid out during the past two years $348,615.40, the future state of the treasury was not rosy. Over $900,000 in state bonds previously issued would start to come due in 1846, and in Marmaduke's judgment, Missouri did not have the money to meet those obligations, together with its regular expenditures. The legislature had two choices—issue new bonds to service the payment of the old bonds, or raise taxes. Marmaduke favored the latter.[2]

Marmaduke could have used his address only to review the status of previous legislation and to comment on the current situation of the state. But, as with his recommendation on a tax increase, he had decided to use the address to spur the legislators into action on issues he cared strongly about. He seemed particularly passionate about two issues. He vigorously supported the annexation of Texas, which had declared its independence from Mexico in 1836 and whose request for annexation by the United States had twice been rejected by the federal government. That he addressed the "Texas Question" was perhaps not surprising, since it had already become a major issue in the 1844 presidential campaign between Democrat James K. Polk and Whig Henry Clay. His second proposal, however, was mirrored in neither national nor state politics in 1844: "I feel it to be my duty," Marmaduke declared, "to recommend . . . the erection of a lunatic asylum in this State."[3]

Erection or purchase of an asylum in the state capital of Jefferson City, he reasoned, could be supported on both humanitarian and pragmatic grounds: "It is our duty as a Christian people," he argued, "to treat these miserable beings, for whom, for some wise purpose, doubtless, our Creator has withheld the noblest one of his gifts, as fit subjects for our compassion and not as objects of our punishment, and to regard their calamity as an appeal to our protection and not as an incentive to our inhumanity." The current absence of adequate care deeply concerned the governor. Using the findings of the 1840 census, he estimated that in 1844 Missouri was home to at least fifty insane persons for whom no acceptable method of treatment existed. Missouri law simply confined such persons in county jails, along with thieves and murderers and other criminals. If the families of the insane wished for better treatment, they, at their own expense, had to identify institutions in other states that might be suitable, had to transport their patient

---

2. *Journal of the Senate of Missouri*, 13th General Assembly (1844/1845), 15–27. The journals of the Senate and the House will hereinafter be cited, as appropriate, as *Senate Journal*, *House Journal*, or *House and Senate Journals*.

3. Ibid., 22.

to that facility, and had to pay for the care and treatment of their relative while at that institution.[4]

The governor did not believe that county jailers were by nature mean, brutal or hard-hearted; but the fact remained that the purpose of county jails was to house criminals, not to provide an atmosphere where insane patients could be treated effectively. Having read about the treatment of the insane in other states, Marmaduke made it clear to the legislature that, given a proper environment and assistance, the insane could be cured, at least if the insanity was treated within the first year of its emergence. "It is true," the governor noted, "that a kind Jailor may sometimes ameliorate their condition, but it can scarcely be supposed that his attention, distracted by his other prisoners, can be rendered very serviceable, or that his efforts can tend much to the recovery of the lunatics in his custody, when he has neither the skill nor time to use the only means that have been found effectual in their cure. The consequence is that the future restoration of the lunatic, if not rendered wholly impossible, is made a matter of great doubt and difficulty." Marmaduke stated that the response to this condition was obvious—establish a Missouri asylum for the insane.[5]

Almost as an afterthought, the governor closed his remarks on this topic by raising a practical reason why the establishment of an asylum in Missouri would be desirable: "The plea of insanity has become a very common one, in cases of homicide, and when it is used successfully, the offender is turned loose upon the community, perhaps to repeat the offence for which he was arraigned. Would it not be well by making this plea a special one, one on which the jury must specially determine on the fact of madness, to imprison the accused in the Asylum until he has been pronounced, by competent authority, entirely cured of his homicidal propensities?"[6] Perhaps, by adding this argument, the governor hoped to convince legislators who might not otherwise be swayed by his humanitarian rhetoric.

Had Marmaduke not risen to the state's highest office in 1844, would another prominent antebellum Missouri official have embraced the plight of the states's mentally ill? Almost certainly. The three decades before the Civil War witnessed an agitation for reform that was unprecedented in Missouri's short history as a state. During those years, state leaders agreed to provide educational opportunities to citizens who were deaf, dumb, or blind. They voted to support and regulate internal improvements, including construction of railroads, bridges, and water projects. They agreed to fund a state library. They passed legislation that authorized county governments to

4. Ibid.
5. Ibid.
6. Ibid., 23.

establish a special tax to support poorhouses. In response to temperance pressures, they also allowed voters, through local elections, to revoke liquor licenses. Despite vigorous debates, other reforms, including adoption of a ten-hour workday and recognition that married women should control all property they owned prior to their marriage, failed passage in the General Assembly.

So, amid this reform fervor, undoubtedly some state leader would have embraced the cause of the mentally ill. But according to Robert W. Wells, a U.S. district judge and former Missouri attorney general to whom the General Assembly turned for advice on the asylum proposal, Marmaduke was not only the first governor, but also the first person, in Missouri to appeal to the state legislature to address the plight of the state's insane population.[7] While Missouri would have eventually turned to the status of its insane, the tragedy leading to Marmaduke's accession as governor in 1844 sparked that debate sooner rather than at some vague future date.

Within weeks of the biennial report, the state senate established a committee to investigate the asylum proposal. In response to a request from that committee's chair, Judge Wells submitted on January 3, 1845, his evaluation of issues relating to the establishment of an asylum in Missouri.

Governor Marmaduke erred in his report to the legislature in 1844, according to Wells. The number of insane persons in Missouri, both white and "colored," far exceeded the figure he had cited. There were 270 Missourians, according to the 1840 census, not 50, who needed assistance. Even that figure, Wells warned, was much too low. The difficulty, he noted, was that census takers in 1840 did not see the need to pursue data on the number of insane in Missouri—so the 270 insane persons actually identified at that time were far too few.[8]

To calculate more accurately the number of citizens in need, Wells assembled data from six New England states—Maine, New Hampshire, Massachusetts, Rhode Island, Connecticut, and Vermont—that had already established insane asylums and that had published statistical data on the number of insane persons in relation to the population of their respective states. Based on those figures, he found that, on average, there were 1.66 insane persons per thousand population. "The same research and investigation in Missouri," he concluded, "would, in all probability, show the same, or nearly the same result as that shown in New England." Applying these findings to the free and slave population of Missouri, he reported that approximately 1,280 people would be labeled as "insane" or "idiotic." Even if

---

7. R. W. Wells to General Assembly, January 3, 1845, *Senate Journal Appendix*, 13th G.A. (1844/1845), 71.

8. Ibid., 71–72.

the legislators were unconcerned about the slave population, there were still approximately 1,102 persons in those two categories. Although admitting that not all such persons would likely be institutionalized, he felt that many of them would be "fit subjects for an asylum."[9]

Having addressed the question of need based on the numbers of persons afflicted, Wells then examined the question of need based on the current treatment of the insane in Missouri. Observing that no survey of the condition of the insane in the state had ever been made, he once again turned to comparative data to make his case. Evaluating the condition of the insane in both Europe and in the United States in the period immediately preceding the decision to establish asylums in those locations, he cited example after example of inhumane, appalling treatment.

His discussion revealed an official who was well read on the dramatic rethinking of treatment of the insane that had seriously begun in Europe seventy-five to one hundred years earlier. Wells had drawn most heavily upon the thought and writings of Philippe Pinel, a Paris physician who, during the French Revolution, had led an assault on the existing perceptions about treatment of the insane. Pinel rejected the contemporary practices of confining insane persons in jails, pens, cellars, and garrets, areas often without sufficient air and light; restraining them in chains, straitjackets, camisoles, girdles, and chairs; feeding them only bread and water; and hiring attendants based on their strength and not on their sympathy or medical training.[10]

Although not cited by Wells, other Europeans, who either preceded Pinel or were his contemporaries, had also argued for the establishment of asylums where custodial care would be replaced by treatments aimed at returning patients to their families and communities. Leaders of the asylum movement included William Battie in England in the 1750s, Vincenzio Chiarugi in Italy in the 1780s and 1790s, and Johann Reil in Germany in the first decade of the nineteenth century.

Stimulated by local circumstance and by external examples, colonists in Williamsburg, Virginia, in 1773 established the first psychiatric hospital in the British colonies. The New York Hospital, founded in 1791, opened its own "lunatic asylum" in 1808, acknowledging the need for a special center for the treatment of the mentally ill. Pennsylvania Hospital opened its own asylum in 1817, borrowing from English models.[11] By 1844, Wells's task was

---

9. Ibid., 73.
10. Ibid., 73–76. See also Philippe Pinel, *A Treatise on Insanity*, trans. D. D. Davis (New York: Hafner Publishing Company, [1806] 1962); Grob, *State and the Mentally Ill*; Charles Goshen, *Documentary History of Psychiatry* (New York: Philosophical Library, 1967); and Emil Kraepelin, *One Hundred Years of Psychiatry* (New York: Philosophical Library, [1917] 1962).
11. For a discussion of the leadership of Chief Physician Thomas Kirkbride at the Pennsyl-

to demonstrate to legislators the relevance of the European and eastern U.S. experiences to frontier Missouri.

By focusing on Pinel and the conditions in France, and by using the reports produced by insane asylum directors and by state legislatures in the late eighteenth and early nineteenth centuries, Wells attempted to demonstrate that Missouri was not likely to be very different when it came to the numbers of persons in need or when comparing these persons' previous treatment. Citing the reports of asylums in England, Pennsylvania, Massachusetts, New Jersey, Ohio, New York, Vermont, New Hampshire, and Connecticut, Wells concluded that the mistreatments described by Pinel in France were not unique to that nation. Wells pointed out similar examples from the United States before the introduction of asylums, describing American patients: "[He] had been in one prison for fourteen years; he was naked; his hair and beard had grown long." "[He] had been chained for twenty-five years, and had his chains taken off but once in that time." "[She] had so long been chained with a short chain, as wholly to lose the use of her lower limbs. . . . She had not walked for years." "[He] had been ten years without clothes." "[He] had a wreath of rags around his body and another around his neck; this was all his clothing. He had no bed, chair or bench. A heap of filthy straw like the nest of swine, was in the corner. . . . The air was so impure as to produce vomiting."[12] Based on his own experience, Wells reported that he had himself seen individuals who were confined in both winter and summer in log pens, without fire or light, or who were kept naked or who were allowed in their confinement to live in a filthy condition.

Having demonstrated need based on numbers and described the mistreatment many patients had endured previously, Wells then laid out the advantages of having a state asylum. Drawing on the prevailing opinions in both Europe and in the eastern part of the United States, Wells claimed that 90 percent of those patients who were diagnosed within the first three months of their insanity "would be cured and discharged after being in [the asylum for] one year." How could such success be possible? An 1838 report of a Connecticut legislative committee attributed success to the removal of patients from their former companions and associates, including family members. Transferring such patients from those attics and cellars and jails to an asylum, hiring medical and staff personnel who were committed to curing the patients, and providing the insane with a safe, healthy environment were all critical. Each asylum, in Wells's opinion, should also have at least 150–200 acres of agricultural land suitable for the patients to plant

---

vania Hospital between 1841 and 1883, see Nancy Tomes, *A Generous Confidence: Thomas Story Kirkbride and the Art of Asylum-Keeping, 1840–1883* (Cambridge: Cambridge University Press, 1984).

12. R. W. Wells to General Assembly, January 3, 1845, *Senate Journal Appendix*, 13th G.A. (1844/1845), 76–78.

and harvest, thus ending the "tedium" of constant confinement with nothing to do:

> Out of 100 or 120 patients in an asylum, there would always be enough willing to labor to cultivate 150 acres in the very best manner. This 150 acres, thus cultivated, would produce enough or nearly enough of the grain and vegetables, hay and provender, milk and butter, and, after a few years, fruit sufficient for the whole establishment. The labor thus bestowed, would not only greatly diminish the costs of the establishment, but would greatly improve the health, both of body and mind, of the patients. . . . A few shops could also be erected, and nearly all the utensils and furniture necessary for the establishment, [could] be made therein by the patients. [Such a] system of moral management and treatment consists in kindness and indulgence; in recreations and amusements, and CONSTANT EMPLOYMENT. This soothes the patients, and prevents that everlasting brooding over their misfortunes or supposed misfortunes, which caused and continued their insanity.[13]

What would be the likely cost for such an asylum? Drawing on data from other states, Wells estimated that an asylum capable of handling 100 patients could be built for between $20,000 and $28,000. While acknowledging that Missouri did not have such monies in its treasury, he concluded: "Nearly every State in the Union has one or more Asylums—and several of them, two, three or four. If THEY could build them, so could WE."[14]

Motivated by pleas of Governor Marmaduke and Judge Wells, in January 1845 the senate committee drafted "an act to provide for the erection of a Lunatic Asylum." That bill authorized the government to borrow $30,000, to be repaid in six years, to build an asylum. Preferably, the commissioners who would oversee construction—the governor, the state auditor, the state treasurer, and the state attorney general—would identify a five- to fifty-acre site for construction that the state already owned "at or in the suburbs of Jefferson City," excluding, however, locations next to the state capitol, the state house, and the state penitentiary. The structure should also be "of convenient size and as far as practicable fire proof, inside and outside." The act also specified that the building was to be constructed "of brick or stone and covered with lead[,] tin or copper." Read twice in the Senate on February 4, the bill was not passed by the Senate until several weeks later. On February 5, the Senate received notice that a bill with the same objective had been introduced into the House. On March 27, however, without explanation, the House referred the Senate bill that it had received to the

---

13. Ibid., 79; 81–82.
14. Ibid., 84; emphasis in original.

next meeting of the General Assembly, which was scheduled to open in the fall of 1846.[15]

Perhaps one factor accounting for the House's delay was unhappiness about the proposed location. Whatever the logic, asylum supporters in St. Louis used the extra time to circulate a petition that drew well over two hundred signatures. That petition, submitted to the legislature when it reconvened in 1846, enthusiastically supported creation of an insane asylum since it would provide a "superior chance" for the "rapid and permanent cure" of many of the insane in the state. It did not, however, support Jefferson City as the site for the institution: "We would beg leave to represent and propose St. Louis for its location, as we believe that greater advantages are here afforded than at any other place in the State."[16]

On Wednesday, December 9, 1846, the Senate agreed to establish a select committee of seven to determine "the propriety and expediency of erecting a lunatic asylum at the expense of the State." By the following Monday, the committee had not only concluded that erection was appropriate but also approved a document that would, if passed into law, accomplish that objective.[17] The same day, the Senate read the bill twice and sent it to the Committee of the Whole—the entire Senate—for the third and final reading. The Senate, meeting as the Committee of the Whole on January 6, 1847, could not reach a decision. Its members agreed to postpone further discussion until January 13. That meeting, however, did not result in approval; on January 15, the Senate, by a 27–4 vote, approved creation of a state insane asylum. Almost a month later, on February 13, the House concurred with the decision and sent a formal bill to the governor, which he signed on February 16.

Under that act, the Senate and the House jointly chose three commissioners to select a site for the asylum. The law made clear that St. Louis would not be a viable choice. For it to be accessible to all in the state, it must be located in one of eight mid-Missouri counties: Callaway, Howard, Boone, Chariton, Saline, Cooper, Moniteau, or Cole. Gone was the 1845 language that commissioners would select a site of between five and fifty acres. Instead, the legislature required between 100 and 500 acres for the facility. Unable to pay for the construction or purchase of the land directly,

---

15. Capitol Fire Documents, reel S-404, folder 11276, Missouri State Archives, Jefferson City, Missouri (hereinafter cited as MSA).

16. "Memorial," Capitol Fire Documents, reel S-413, folder 12012, MSA.

17. The disastrous fire that destroyed the Missouri State Capitol on February 11, 1911, consumed or severely damaged many of the archival records of the state legislature, including this senate bill. The remaining fragments of this handwritten document, however, may still be seen in the Missouri State Archives. "A Bill to Establish an Asylum," Capitol Fire Documents, reel S-413, folder 12071. For a printed version, see *Laws of the State of Missouri* (Jefferson City: James Lusk, 1847), 60–63.

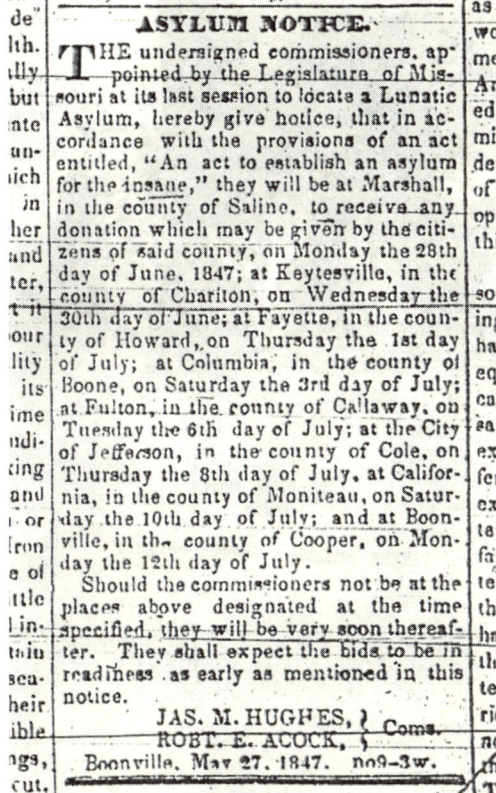

The notice that the state was seeking a site for the asylum ran in the *Boonville Observer* on May 27, 1847 (State Historical Society of Missouri, Columbia).

and concerned about borrowing additional money for state projects, the legislature instructed the commissioners to consider in their site selection the amount of land or money that each county would pledge as an incentive for the facility. Such site-selection criteria were not unique. Insistence on a mid-Missouri location was consistent with the guidelines used to establish the state penitentiary in Jefferson City in 1833 and the University of Missouri at Columbia in 1839. It also was a criterion for the placement of a school for the deaf in Fulton in 1851. Likewise, pledges of land and money were also often critical determinants in site selection for such state institutions.

Nor did the legislature leave the timing of events to the commissioners. It requested that the site selection be finalized by April 5. Since the legislature also stipulated that the commissioners visit each of the eight counties to solicit pledges, and since it required them to give at least two weeks' notice to the counties before those visits occurred, the new commissioners had to begin their duties very quickly. To avoid spurious pledges or a change of heart by local governments and private donors, the state required that "at least fifteen responsible individuals" guarantee, collectively and in writing, the entire amount pledged to locate the asylum in a particular location. That pledge would, of course, be binding only on those individuals in the county ultimately selected.

The timetable set by the legislature proved unrealistic. The commissioners were unable to meet at all between February and April. Although they had agreed to meet in Jefferson City in April to decide how best to proceed, only two—Jas. M. Hughes and Robert E. Acock, attended. Beginning on June 28, those two men traveled by horseback to each of the county seats to receive the sealed proposals as to what monies and lands each county would make available in order to secure construction of an insane asylum within its boundaries. The counties of Chariton, Saline, and Moniteau, clearly uninterested in or unable to compete for the asylum, made no financial promises. Of the remaining proposals opened at Boonville on Tuesday, July 13, none proved as attractive as that from Callaway County. Callaway promised indisputable title to 500 acres of land together with $11,500 in cash.[18]

In January 1849, Commissioners Jas. Hughes, M. Horner, and William McElheney described the asylum's location in Fulton, as well as Fulton itself, in almost idyllic terms:

> The location is made in a rich, fertile and healthy county, and the lands upon which the Institution is to be erected, is well adapted to the growth of corn, wheat, grass, vegetables, etc., together with a great abundance of timber for building and other purposes, as well as a great abundance of stone coal of a fair quality. The county of Callaway contains a population of about 14,000 souls, who are mostly engaged in agricultural pursuits, and therefore provisions of all kinds are abundant, and can be had at a very cheap rate. . . . There is a stream of never failing water running through the south end of said tract of land, about half a mile from where it is proposed to erect the building, and on the premises, there is a great abundance of building rock of the finest quality and well adapted for all the stone work that may be required for said building. . . . There is also on the premises a large two story frame dwelling house in first rate repair, containing five comfortable rooms, kitchen and other necessary out buildings, etc., also a first rate well of water.[19]

"The town of Fulton," they continued, "is a beautiful village, containing a population of about 700 souls, the principal streets of which have been

---

18. Report of the Commissioners to Locate Lunatic Asylum, January 3, 1849, *Senate Journal Appendix*, 15th G.A. (1848/1849), 105–9. See "Asylum Notice," *Boonville Observer*, May 27, 1847, 1, for the text of the request for bids and the dates the commissioners would visit each county.

19. Report of the Commissioners to Locate Lunatic Asylum, January 3, 1849, *Senate Journal Appendix*, 15th G.A. (1848/1849), 107–8. The site advantages attributed to Fulton reflected traits of the ideal location being advocated across the nation. See Grob, *Mad among Us*, 71–72.

graded and macadamised, and has also within it 4 churches, one male and female academy, besides other schools."

The legislature had not only authorized the commissioners to select a construction site, but also authorized them to send someone "to Ohio or elsewhere" to study plans and buildings for asylums that would allow Missouri to erect the most suitable facility. To carry out this evaluation, the commissioners chose Dr. William J. McElheney, who traveled during August to Ohio, Indiana, and Maryland. Although not a part of the legislative instructions, the commissioners also asked McElheney to study the methods of treatment utilized in those asylums.

His report to the commissioners, dated September 2, 1847, provided a very detailed analysis of the type of building that should be built, including a discussion of how it should be heated and ventilated. McElheney had first traveled to Indiana to examine a new state asylum currently under construction. He then had journeyed to the Ohio Lunatic Asylum in Columbus and, from there, to Maryland where he examined the state's asylum as well as a private asylum, both in Baltimore. Rather than return to Missouri from Baltimore, McElheney had returned to Indiana for several more days of conversation with architects and excursions throughout the new facility. His conclusion was that Missouri should model its hospital on the new building at Indianapolis. There was, however, one major drawback—such a building would cost approximately $60,000, double what the legislature in Jefferson City had approved.[20]

At his September 2 meeting with legislators, McElheney learned that not even $30,000 was available. Governor John Edwards, citing the failure of the president of the Senate to sign the joint legislative resolution that gave him the right to use state monies for construction, refused to authorize any expenditures. It was not until March 1849 that the Fulton newspaper could report that a plan for construction had finally been adopted and that sealed bids would be received on or before April 16.[21] Solomon Jenkins of St. Charles, the low bidder, signed a contract shortly thereafter to build the facility for $47,450.[22] But then, in December 1850, Missouri's new governor,

---

20. "To the Commissioners of the Lunatic Asylum of Missouri," *Senate Journal Appendix*, 15th G.A. (1848/1849), 109–14. Before construction, Missouri officials also sought the advice of Dr. Thomas Kirkbride of the Philadelphia Hospital for the Insane. Kirkbride eventually published a guide to hospital construction that recommended an institution that was both awe-inspiring and comfortable. See Kirkbride, *On the Construction, Organization, and General Arrangement of Hospitals for the Insane* (Philadelphia: Lippincott, 1880). For a fuller discussion of Kirkbride's construction philosophy, see Tomes, *Generous Confidence*.

21. "An Act Amendatory of an Act for the Creation of a Lunatic Asylum," *Missouri Telegraph*, March 16, 1849, 1.

22. Report of the Commissioners of the Lunatic Asylum, January 4, 1851, *Senate Journal Appendix*, 16th G.A. (1850/1851), 134–37.

This 1857 engraving shows the early vision of architect Solomon Jenkins for the asylum (Missouri State Archives).

Austin King, informed the legislators that their predecessors had only appropriated sufficient money to cover construction; they would need another appropriation to furnish it.²³

When one reads between the lines of the General Assembly's few surviving records on this subject, there obviously was opposition to appropriating money in addition to the original $30,000 request. M. C. Hawkins, the chairman of the committee on the lunatic asylum during the 1848–1849 session, felt compelled to emphasize to his brethren both humanitarian and practical reasons for increasing funding. Reminding his colleagues that "civilization" and a "sense of justice" required legislative action, he also indicated that the state's regional reputation would suffer if no asylum was built. Furthermore, building an institution would allow the state for "a trifling cost" of only $10–$60 per patient, to cure the troubled insane in Missouri and return them to their families. Currently, he noted, Missouri taxpayers supported incarceration of the insane in county jails and elsewhere, but there, not only was a cure unlikely, but also the insane would become more, not less, disturbed. By establishing an asylum that could cure the patients, Missouri's legislature would then actually be saving their constituents money in the long term.²⁴

The bulk of Hawkins's appeal, however, relied on the fact of poor treat-

---

23. *Senate Journal*, 16th G.A. (1850/1851), 30.
24. Report of the Committee on the Lunatic Asylum, no date, *House Journal Appendix*, 15th G.A. (1848/1849), 195–99.

ment of Missouri's insane. Breaking from the earlier reports, he used Missouri examples, not the cases of patients in other states or in Europe. Some Missouri counties, he lamented, "let out" the insane, turning their care over to the lowest bidder. This system fostered conditions that could only intensify one's insanity. Such patients were often "divested of all comfort in the cold of winter, without fire, frequently without necessary clothing, unprotected and almost unprovided for . . . and treated in every respect as if no spark of recollection ever crossed their minds." The desire of such counties to spend their money in the most economical manner caused them, he argued, to utilize coercion and to provide only that which would keep the patient at the cheapest rate, "in the same way as would be provided for a wild animal." Even the kindest of jailers had no clue about how to best treat the insane. Insanity, in Hawkins's view, was produced by a physical cause and was thus treatable by knowledgeable persons in a hospital setting. Such care was simply not possible in the county jail or in the lowest-bidder system. In those settings a patient who became disruptive might well be tied to a chair and have cold water poured over him until "it runs down over its body shivering with cold, until the animal heat is exhausted, and the poor sufferer ceases to complain."[25]

In January 1849, Commissioners McElheney, Horner, and Hughes, using the words of national advocate Dorothea Dix, also urged the legislature to provide sufficient funding for the asylum:

> In the words of Miss Dix: "these unfortunate beings have claims, those claims which bitter misery and adversity creates, and which it is our solemn obligation as citizens and legislators to cancel. . . . Examine with patient care the condition of this suffering, dependent multitude, which are gathered to your alms houses, and your prisons, and scattered under adverse circumstances in indigent families; weigh the iron chains and shackles and balls and ring bolts and manacles; breathe the foul atmosphere of those cells and dens, which too surely poisons the springs of life; examine the furniture of those dreary abodes; some for a bed have the luxury of a truss of straw; and some have the cheaper couch which the hard plank supplies. Examine their apparel. The air of heaven is their only vesture. The revolting exposure of men; the infinitely more revolting and shocking exposure of women; with combinations of miseries and horrors that will not bear recital."

The commissioners concluded that it could not be denied that her description, although not based on Missouri's experience, was "a true picture of the situation of those unfortunate and miserable creatures in our state."[26]

25. Ibid.
26. Report of the Commissioners to Locate [a] Lunatic Asylum, January 3, 1849, *Senate Journal Appendix*, 15th G.A. (1848/1849), 108. Dix was visiting in St. Louis in December 1846 when the asylum bill was initially proposed in the General Assembly.

The appeals of men like Hawkins, McElheney, Horner, and Hughes carried the day. One senator expressed his overwhelming agreement in early 1851: "the result is of too high a moral value to be estimated by any pecuniary standard." When Jenkins, the contractor, reported in January 1851 that total costs had reached $50,000, he had to submit a very detailed analysis of all the expenditures to the legislature and in subsequent correspondence explain what still needed to be done. Whatever the legislators thought of Jenkins's argument—that, compared to New Jersey, whose expenditures to just build its asylum and not even furnish it were $150,000, Missouri had been well served by his modest construction costs—they did allow him to draw $25,000 more from the state treasury to continue construction.[27]

27. Senator Preston Reed, Chairman, Joint Committee Appointed to Visit the Asylum for the Insane, *Senate Journal Appendix*, 16th G.A. (1850/1851), 211; the plans, specifications and architectural drawings for the facility are found in Fulton Lunatic Asylum Specifications and Blueprints, 1849–1851, MSA.

2
Overcoming Obstacles
The First Decade, 1850–1860

Transferred to the state in August 1851, the new building was equipped to house 100 patients and to feed up to 140 patients and staff members. The unexpected higher construction costs, however, meant that the kitchens, the storage areas, the fencing around the building and its six acres of land, and the landscaping of those six acres were not completed. The enclosure plan was scrapped altogether. Funding did authorize an initial acquisition of six horses and twenty cows, together with other stock, as well as farming tools. The Senate committee on the asylum also urged the legislature to consider adding verandas for the patients who could not exercise outside the wards during bad weather. It additionally requested an accommodation "of the most substantial character" to handle the "furiously insane." Finally, it urged that landscaping of the surrounding acreage was essential: "A pleasing landscape in constant view, [would] exert a friendly influence on the health of the mind—an influence [that should] not be disregarded in our provisions for the restoration of the insane." To fail to make these additional improvements, the senators argued, would risk "the pride and honor of the state" and ignore "the interests of humanity." It would not be the material possessions of the state—its mines and its fertile fields—that would become the "jewels" of the state; instead, they declared, the state's greatest treasure would be its commitment to "the relief of suffering and sorrowing humanity."[1]

While the building was being completed, the legislature, in late February 1851, appointed seven men to serve on a board of managers: four to serve

---

1. William S. Allen, Chair, Report of the Standing Committee on the State Lunatic Asylum, February 11, 1851, *House Journal*, Appendix, 16th G.A. (1850/1851), 227–28.

The town of Fulton developed as the asylum and its jobs became a reality. This view shows the downtown, including the Courthouse, looking west along Fifth Street (Kingdom of Callaway Historical Society).

for two years and three to serve for four years. They were to be appointed by the Senate, but when that body was not in session, they could be appointed by the governor to serve until the Senate reconvened in regular session to affirm or reject the governor's selections. They were given the right to control and direct the operations of the asylum, including the right to select the superintendent, treasurer, steward, and matron. At their discretion, and apparently for any reason, they could fire any employee except the superintendent, who could be dismissed only for incompetence, willful neglect, refusal to exercise his duties, or actions that rendered him unfit for the office. The managers were also required to recommend to the governor, secretary of state, attorney general, and auditor the annual salaries to be paid to the asylum's four top officials. At least two of the managers were required to visit the asylum each month; a majority of them had to visit each quarter; and all of them had to visit together once each year. No doubt because of these visit stipulations, the legislature required that four of the seven managers live within a thirty-mile radius of Fulton.[2]

2. "An Act to Provide for the Organization and Government of the State Lunatic Asylum," *Laws of the State of Missouri*, 1851, 219–25.

Six members of the original board—John Leeper, Thomas Harris, and Charles Hardin of Callaway County, James Minor of Cole County, John Snelson of Howard County, and George Sibley of St. Charles County—chose, within weeks of their appointment, Dr. Turner R. H. Smith as the new superintendent.[3] By law, the superintendent had to be "a physician of knowledge, skill and ability in his profession, and if such a person can be obtained, of experience in the management and treatment of the insane."[4] While Smith, a well-respected physician in Columbia, Missouri, did not meet the last criterion, that was not unusual in antebellum America. Treatment of the insane was in its infancy in the United States. Between 1813 and 1867, no medical school in this country taught a course on the treatment of mental disease. And, until 1883, only one book had been published in the United States on the subject—authored by the father of American psychiatry, Dr. Benjamin Rush, in 1812.[5] Men like Smith, who turned their professional focus to the insane, learned from apprenticeships in institutions or by their own "hands-on" experiences.

Born in Kentucky, the thirty-one-year-old Smith had studied under Dr. W. H. Richardson at the Medical College of Transylvania University in Lexington, Kentucky. Upon graduation in 1840, he moved to Columbia, Missouri, and less than a year later married Mary Hardin, daughter of a prominent family in the community and sister of future governor Charles H. Hardin.[6] Since appointments to state jobs often hinged on patronage, his social, economic, and political ties, coupled with his medical credentials, made him an attractive selection.

Since by law the superintendent had to live in the asylum, since the building was not yet habitable at the time of his April appointment, and since he had to wrap up his affairs in Columbia, Smith's duties were not scheduled to begin until August. In his role as superintendent, he would oversee the daily operations of the institution. He would supervise the hiring and dismissal of all employees, including attendants, laborers, and servants, except for the treasurer, steward, and matron. He would, most importantly, supervise the medical, moral and physical treatment of each patient. Finally, working with the Board of Managers, he would also report periodically to the state legislature and to the counties that housed their citizens at the asylum.[7]

3. Report of the Board of Managers, no date, *Senate Journal Appendix*, 17th G.A. (1852), 157.
4. "An Act to Provide for the Organization and Government of the State Lunatic Asylum," *Laws of the State of Missouri*, 1851, 221.
5. Deutsch, *Mentally Ill in America*, 282.
6. *History of Callaway County, Missouri* (St. Louis: National Historical Company, 1884), 716–19.
7. Nineteenth-century asylum superintendent-physicians, like Smith, were expected not only to medically treat patients but also to oversee the everyday details of asylum management, including heating, lighting, and water. See Grob, *Mad among Us*, 73.

Neither Smith nor his board members felt knowledgeable enough to organize the new hospital without assistance. As a result, in May, the board sent Smith to Philadelphia to attend the annual convention of lunatic asylum superintendents and to visit, both before and after the meetings, asylums in that region of the country. Annual meetings of superintendents had only recently begun. In October 1844, the superintendents of thirteen asylums had decided to meet annually in Philadelphia and to create a formal organization—the Association of Medical Superintendents of American Institutions for the Insane (AMSAII), which eventually was renamed the American Psychiatric Association. They also agreed in that year to begin publication of a journal, entitled the *American Journal of Insanity*, which in 1921 was also renamed, becoming the *American Journal of Psychiatry*. Theirs was the first national society of physicians in the United States. As Smith informed residents of Fulton, he would be "acquainting himself fully with every thing that pertains to such institutions," drawing upon the experience and knowledge of his fellow superintendents across the nation.[8]

Under Smith served a steward and a matron. The steward became the purchasing agent for the institution and was the one who normally would hire and dismiss subordinate personnel. He was also in charge of the operations at the asylum, including the heating plant, farm operations, and grounds maintenance. The matron was in charge of all the "domestic concerns" of the institution. She oversaw the upkeep of the inside of the asylum as well as the treatment of the female patients. She served as the nutritionist for the institution, reported on the activities of all attendants, and was given responsibility for all operations in the kitchen, laundry, and sewing areas.[9] Smith was also authorized to hire an assistant physician, who would join him each morning in his visits in the wards, who would visit each patient individually every evening, and who would be responsible for the administration of all medicines and for the exercise and amusement of the patients. Although authorized, no assistant physician would join the staff until the arrival of Dr. William Lincoln in 1853.

Before hiring any subordinate personnel in 1851, the Board of Managers created a detailed organizational plan, including job descriptions for each employee. Included in the document were not only the duties of personnel, but also a list of rules applicable to them. The following guidelines reveal an institutional leadership intimately concerned with its employees' appearance, actions, and attitudes.

8. "Lunatic Asylum," *Missouri Telegraph*, May 2, 1851, 2. For a discussion of one of the original thirteen founders of the AMSAII, see Tomes, *Generous Confidence*.

9. For a detailed description of the duties and responsibilities of the steward and matron, see "By-Laws for the Organization, Government and Direction of the State Lunatic Asylum," *Senate Journal Appendix*, 17th G.A. (1852), 170–72.

Their dress shall be always neat and clean. . . . The men shall not wear hats in the house, nor go in their shirtsleeves. None shall indulge in loud talking or laughing, nor use profane or vulgar language; nor play at any game with one another, or with patients. . . .

No attendant or assistant, while connected with the asylum, shall, at any time, at home or abroad, make use of distilled spirits or intoxicating liquor of any kind; nor use tobacco, or smoke a cigar, or procure them for any patient. . . .

Any attendant or assistant receiving any present or gratuity from any patient or the friend of a patient in the asylum, or from any visitor, or selling to or buying anything from a patient, or making any perquisite, of any kind whatever, may be instantly dismissed.

The attendants and assistants shall never leave the asylum without the permission from the superintendent, or a resident officer.

No male attendant, without permission, shall ever enter a female department.

The indispensable duty of the attendants and assistants: Halls and apartments are to be washed ordinarily twice in each week, and Swept every morning, and the dining rooms swept after each meal, and Every portion of the premises as much oftener as the most rigid neatness may require. The water-closets, urinals, spittoons, etc., are to be scrupulously attended to. . . . Chamber vessels are always to be covered when removed, and thoroughly cleaned immediately after use. Any noisome odor is evidence of neglect.

The attendants shall treat the patients with uniform attention and respect. . . . Under all circumstances, be tender and affectionate, speak in a mild, persuasive tone of voice; never address a patient coarsely, by a nickname, nor by a Christian, nor by a surname without the addition of Mr., Mrs., or Miss. They should never forget the motto: "All things whatsoever ye would that men should do to you, do ye even to them." Those who do not at heart adopt this sentiment are unfit to take charge of the insane, and those who violate this principle are not wanted here.[10]

Much of the organizational rhetoric emphasized this humane treatment of the patient, coupled with an almost military set of rules and procedures. For example, every morning at eight in the summer and at nine in the winter, the wards would be inspected. Prior to that inspection, the attendants and assistants had to insure that each patient under their care was "thoroughly washed" and had a neat appearance with clean clothes, shoes, and boots. Each bed had to be made, and each room swept.[11]

---

10. Ibid., 169–82.
11. *Senate Journal Appendix,* 17th G.A. (1852), 173–75. Szasz, in *Cruel Compassion,* characterizes such rules as "coercive-paternalistic domination" under the guise of humane rhetoric and of being one's brother's keeper.

Attendants and assistants were to work closely with the physicians in observing the patients. They were to count all forks and knives after each meal to insure that a patient had not acquired a weapon with which to hurt himself or herself or other patients or employees. They were to notice if their charges were not eating or if they changed their habits or attitudes. Any major changes were to be reported to the physicians quickly. They were also to administer any oral medicines prescribed by the physicians.

The rules and regulations for attendants and assistants could be quite detailed, as this example of what to do with persons with smelly feet reveals. "Patients who have offensive feet are to change their socks daily. Those taken off to be rinsed in hot water and put in the drying closet for the succeeding day. If under this management, the feet still smell, they must be washed daily in cold water. There is no excuse for foul odor from this cause in the building." Other stipulations warned employees not to try to take shortcuts in the care of the patient. If a patient wet the bed, not only were the clothes, sheets, and pillow cases changed as needed, but they were also reminded that "no attempt is ever to be made to dry the bed without first removing the wet straw or whatever material may be used in filling the tick."[12]

Writing in 1812, Dr. Benjamin Rush, had argued that "terror acts powerfully on the body through the medium of the mind, and should be employed in the cure of madness."[13] By 1851, however, that approach had been rejected by those at the Fulton facility. Its cardinal rule became: "Violent hands shall never be laid on a patient, under any provocation. A blow shall never be returned, nor any other insult." While employees may face abusive language, personal insult or attack, they must neither "recriminate, scold, threaten, or dictate in the language of authority." Furthermore, employees were cautioned to never ridicule, mock, or imitate patients but, instead, to treat them kindly and, in all dealings with them, remain truthful: "Deceptions must always be avoided, and special care is to be taken that promises are not to be made unless they can be complied with in every particular."[14]

While Superintendent Smith and his employees prepared for the reception of the insane, county governments were alerted that as soon as the facility was completed, they could begin sending their patients to Fulton.

12. *Senate Journal Appendix*, 17th G.A. (1852), 178.

13. Quoted in Deutsch, *Mentally Ill in America*, 80. Rush's multivolume study was entitled *Medical Inquiries and Observations upon Diseases of the Mind* (Philadelphia: Kimber and Richardson, 1812).

14. "By-Laws . . . State Lunatic Asylum," *Senate Journal Appendix*, 17th G.A. (1852), 174–75, 177. It is unclear whether Smith was familiar with the articles published by English asylum superintendent John Connolly, written between 1830 and 1856. Nevertheless, his approach to the handling and treatment of the insane shares many similarities with Connolly's.

There would be two types of patients: those sent to the asylum by a court order, and those placed in the asylum by other means. The process for committing persons into public facilities, whether at the state or local level, had been established by the state legislature in 1835 and remained virtually unchanged at midcentury. Any private citizen or officer of the court could, in writing, petition the court to evaluate an individual's sanity. Upon receipt of that petition, the court would order the person to be evaluated to appear before the court, together, as appropriate, with relevant witnesses to support both the petitioner's arguments as well as those of the person being evaluated. This whole process would occur before a jury, which would make the final determination on whether the individual was or was not insane. If the person was determined to be sane, then the person petitioning the court initially, unless it was an officer of the court, had to pay for all costs of the process, a penalty clearly intended to deter frivolous, unfounded petitions.[15]

While this process appeared to protect an allegedly insane person from arbitrary diagnosis or institutionalization, it contained a significant flaw, as revealed in the case of Mary Waggoner. In May 1846, a Jacob Waggoner petitioned the Callaway court to determine Mary's sanity. Upon receiving his petition, the court immediately convened a twelve-man jury to hear his evidence. There is no indication in the court records that Mary was present to offer counterevidence, that she had a legal representative present, or that she was even notified of the hearing or given time to prepare counterarguments. The jury found Jacob's explanation convincing, concluded that Mary was insane, and recommended that the court appoint a legal guardian who must post a seven-hundred-dollar bond.[16]

Legal guardians were not always required to post a bond. An earlier case reveals that the jury or the court could have waived the posting of a bond if it was convinced the guardian would soundly manage an insane person's affairs without such a monetary guarantee.[17] A declaration of insanity by a jury meant that the court-appointed legal guardian would then legally be able to commit the person to care. If a person declared insane was indigent, then the county was responsible for covering the costs associated with his or her care.

Patients in the second category, the nonindigent, committed by their own decision or that of family members or guardians, would not be accepted at the Fulton institution unless the insane poor sent by all counties did not fill the beds at the asylum. Furthermore, no private admission would be accepted without a signed certificate from two physicians attesting to the per-

15. "An Act Relative to Insane Persons," *Revised Statues of the State of Missouri, 1835*, 327.
16. Callaway County Court Records, 1844–1847, 482, Callaway County Archives, Office of the County Clerk, Fulton, Missouri.
17. Ibid., 296.

son's insanity, without receipt of the costs for the first month's housing and care, and without an individual bond pledging that the person so bonded would pay all charges incurred by the private patient.[18]

The county governments were responsible for paying for the transportation of all county patients admitted to the asylum, except for private admissions. Each county was also required to pay the asylum quarterly and in advance for the housing and care of each of its residents transferred to the Fulton facility. In 1851, that meant $1.50 each week for each patient. Private admissions were charged between $2.00 and $10.00 each week, depending on the expenses each patient incurred and the degree of trouble the patient caused.[19] Whether a public or private admission, the hospital would not receive a patient whose condition, in the opinion of the doctors at the hospital, could not possibly be improved by the care offered in Fulton. The superintendent also had the right to discharge any patient once he determined that the patient's condition could not be improved. Despite this apparent rigidity, a number of patients admitted in the middle of the century often remained at the institution for their entire lives and were not sent back to the county jails or poorhouses or to families and friends.

Smith instituted another policy requiring that the counties sending a patient, or the families and friends of that person, prepare a detailed written history of the case. He also strongly encouraged someone acquainted with the patient for some length of time to travel to Fulton and provide him with a detailed description of the patient's history and development of the insanity.[20]

Just as the superintendent had clear dress and cleanliness standards for his staff, he also provided the same for patients arriving at the institution. He required that each newly admitted patient be "free from vermin, or any contagious or infectious disease." Each was to have, upon arrival, two new shirts, one pair of new shoes or boots, undergarments, socks or stockings, and one new warm coat or outer garment. The asylum also urged that "better apparel" be sent for religious services or for walking or riding, thereby helping each patient to preserve his or her self-respect. No jewelry was permissible.[21]

With staff instructed on how to behave and how to perform their duties, and with rules in place for the handling of patient admission and care, the State Insane Asylum at Fulton advertised that its doors would open on December 1, 1851. But as that date drew near and as the board and superin-

18. "By-Laws . . . State Lunatic Asylum," *Senate Journal Appendix*, 17th G.A. (1852), 181.
19. Ibid., 182.
20. Ibid.
21. Ibid., 169.

tendent realized that repeated construction delays meant that the patient wings would not be ready for occupancy, they reversed course. They released a new announcement that, due to an improperly installed heating system that was being redesigned and constructed, patients should not yet be sent to Fulton, since they could not be housed comfortably during the winter. Despite that decision, the asylum did admit several patients between December and March, although not until late spring was it ready to provide patients the facilities and care deemed essential to their treatment. The first two patients admitted that December were Thomas G. of Jackson County and H. F. H. of Callaway County.[22]

Perhaps Smith reasoned that care, although not perfect at the asylum over the winter of 1851–1852, was better than what some patients might receive elsewhere. To describe the abysmal condition of Missouri's mentally ill, he borrowed a description initially applied to residents in another state. But, as he informed the state legislature, it was "equally applicable" to this state as well:

> They are confined in cellars, and out-houses or log-pens suffering the extremity of cold in winter, and exposed to a burning sun in summer, with accompanying trappings of iron balls, collars, manacles, fetters, and chains; and it must be added, the heavy blow to quicken obedience, and the stinging lash to enforce silence; pelted with sticks and stones, as an amusement by unthinking boys; a scanty meal tossed in through a narrow aperture, as to a wild beast, their dens, for that is the only appropriate term I can apply to them, cleaned out of the accumulated filth at distant intervals.[23]

Despite Smith's bleak portrayal of the life of the insane outside the institution, public perception of his asylum in 1851 and 1852 was mixed. Some counties, individual families and friends or guardians were eager to transfer a patient to the care of the institution. It was not uncommon for them to be transported in carriages and wagons wrapped securely in ropes and chains, which Smith almost inevitably ordered immediately removed. For other Missourians, however, the asylum was a place to be feared; where loved ones who needed care would, no doubt, be chained to walls in dungeonlike areas and where they would be "cared for" by sadistic attendants who would administer the severest of punishments. While Smith lamented the latter perception, he admitted that only the passage of time, coupled with the grow-

---

22. "Preliminary Data, Historical Sketch of State Hospital No. 1, Fulton, Missouri," manuscript, 1936, 10 (FSHA).
23. Quoted in Report of Superintendent, November 29, 1852, *Senate Journal Appendix*, 17th G.A. (1852), 196.

ing knowledge of how Missouri was actually treating the insane in Fulton, would shatter it.[24]

Despite the existence of such a negative perception, by November 1852, Smith reported to the legislature that his institution had admitted seventy patients since the preceding December and had discharged eight. Of those admitted, thirty-six had been men and thirty-four had been women; fifty-two had been sent by counties and eighteen by friends or families. One-third had come from St. Louis County alone. As to the cause for their insanity, Smith was less certain. Written reports and oral interviews with friends and relatives proved so inaccurate and indefinite that he concluded, even in the best-case scenario, their correctness "is barely within the bounds of probability." One of the critical problems, he lamented, was that the asylum community in the United States and its physicians had created no reliable, precisely defined terminology used in diagnosis of the insane's condition. Words used by a St. Louis physician, for example, might not mean the same thing to a physician who read his report at the asylum in Fulton. Without "the most rigid precision" in the use of words in describing a patient's condition, the hospital could not hope to develop an accurate case history of a patient or determine with precision why the insanity emerged. Nevertheless, the entry records for those first seventy patients indicate the "probable cause" of their disease.[25] Those causes, together with the number of patients identified with them, included:

> Miasmatic fevers 15
> Indigestion 4
> Religious anxiety 5
> Loss of property 3
> Disappointed love 5
> Unkind treatment of relatives 2
> Intense study 1
> Scurvy 1
> Jaundice 1
> Epilepsy 7
> Blows on the head 2
> Puerperal 2
> Domestic trouble 1
> Concussion from explosion of steamboat 1
> Jealousy 1
> Unknown 19

---

24. Ibid., 189. Both Szasz (in *Cruel Compassion*) and Tomes (in *Generous Confidence*) agree that changing family relationships and functions convinced many elders, not just those in the United States, to transfer their insane to, or in other cases dump them upon, asylums.

25. Ibid., 187, 191.

Reflecting upon the causes of insanity, Smith speculated that the experiences of patients in their youth predisposed them to mental illness. Those things often cited by physicians as the cause of insanity—whether jealousy, disappointment in love, masturbation, domestic trouble, religious excitement, or whatever—were experienced by many people who never became insane. What then predisposed one to react to these factors in such a way that brings on insanity? Smith believed the root causes were found in the neglect and misdirection of early education. "How often have teachers, by overtaxing the minds of sprightly children and disregarding the proper education of the physical system, been instrumental in producing these mournful instances of premature decay? And how often have parents in their anxiety to clothe the brows of their children with the early laurels for the triumph of learning . . . had all their fondest hopes destroyed. . . . These actions predispose people to mental disease."[26]

By the fall of 1852, Smith could not say with certainty how many of the patients admitted to the asylum, whatever the stated cause, would recover. Since a successful treatment would take at minimum between four to six months and since many of the patients had not been in the asylum that long, he could not match the 90 percent curable rate touted in the late 1840s during appropriation hearings. Perhaps Smith realized that those optimistic curable numbers, initially used so widely in both Europe and the United States, had by the 1850s, within the asylum communities at least, become viewed as more and more unrealistic. He did hedge in his report to the legislature, noting that between 80 and 90 percent of those patients treated within the first three months of the onset of the insanity could be cured. (By 1854, he would change it to 70 to 90 percent.) But he also cautioned the legislature that Fulton's rates would likely remain low for some time to come because "the lamentable truth is that nearly all our admissions have been cases of long duration." If the asylum received a patient who had been insane for two or more years, he reported, the chances of a cure fell to less than 20 percent. Although Smith did not know it at the time, Charles T., whom he admitted in 1852, would be discharged four times, only to return and eventually die at the institution fifty-nine years after his first admission, still uncured.[27]

Two other realities at the Fulton facility would also probably mean its cur-

---

26. Report of Superintendent, November 27, 1854, *Senate Journal Appendix*, 18th G.A. (1854/1855), 60–61. Grob, in *Mad among Us*, asserts that many U.S. superintendents shared Smith's view of early education.

27. Report of Superintendent, November 29, 1852, ibid., 17th G.A. (1852), 189; Report of Superintendent, November 27, 1854, ibid., 18th G.A. (1854/1855), 56–57; and "Preliminary Data," 10.

able rate would remain low. Smith believed that even when he had "cured" a patient, it was essential to retain that patient at the institution for another two or three months of observation. However, too often, families and friends refused to accept the extended stay, wanting their loved ones back home. With too early a removal of patients, the superintendent observed, there was a highly increased possibility that the patient could relapse into insanity. Furthermore, the facilities at Fulton, although less than two years old, were inadequate and hindered recovery.

No doubt many legislators shuddered at that observation. They had already significantly exceeded the initial appropriations budget for the facility. While by the fall of 1852, the legislature had spent almost $75,000 at the asylum, Smith warned that it was not enough. There was no room to separate types of patients from one another. Instead they were expected to reside in the wards together. Such an architectural design did not allow for the proper classification and housing of those with the same types of symptoms. Although Smith had in his first year ordered carpenters to strengthen the rooms on the fourth, and highest, floor of the building by creating door frames of oak and not pine and by installing wooden shutters and locks on the inside of each window, this was not a suitable arrangement for the housing of the "furiously insane." Those furious and noisy patients' screams could be heard throughout the entire facility, a condition not conducive to the successful treatment of other patients. "In order to achieve the proper classification of patients, and the preservation of good order, quietness, and peace in our household, two additional buildings or wings for the most excited—one for males and one for females—are absolutely essential and indispensable," Smith argued. Nor would that construction alone suffice. He also urged construction of a parlor or day room for the patients, where they could sit and mingle during the day, much as families would do. In addition, he advocated construction of an "associated dormitory," a large room to house suicidal patients built next to an attendant's room. Such close proximity was essential in supervising what he saw as his most troublesome patients and the ones who needed the closest attention. Equally lamentable was the absence of any chapel for religious exercises. Also, in Smith's opinion, it was equally necessary to erect a neat but substantial nine- to ten-foot fence around the main building and forty acres of land. Inside that fence, the grounds would be carefully landscaped and groomed. Perhaps because earlier requests for landscaping and fencing had been rejected, Smith went into some detail on why this last request was so essential.[28]

---

28. The following discussion of the needs of the asylum is based on Smith's Report of Superintendent, November 29, 1852, *Senate Journal Appendix*, 17th G.A. (1852), 192–200; and the Report of Board of Managers, no date, *House Journal Appendix*, ibid., 155–63.

> The history of all insane institutions . . . has abundantly proven that their grounds should always be made highly ornamental and attractive. If there be any thing in nature calculated to furnish pure and inexhaustible occupation and delight to the most excited patient; divert the melancholic from his morbid fancies; and cause the convalescent to rejoice, it is grounds, whose features are rendered all pleasing and cheerful by the art of landscape gardening. With a majority of the patients in every lunatic asylum, the influences produced by handsomely embellished grounds, and a great variety of ornamental arrangements, constitute by far the most valuable means of successful treatment.[29]

Even with such landscaping, the absence of a fence would make it impossible to allow patients out of doors to enjoy the landscaping.

This was already a formidable list of needs, but Smith added one final major request. The asylum was too small to handle the anticipated numbers of insane patients in Missouri. The legislature should, therefore, double the normal bed capacity of the institution from 100 to 200 patients by building two new wings, one for men and one for women.

Having outlined the asylum's major needs, he then went on to indicate other essential, but not particularly costly, needs, including a medical library, surgical instruments, a mechanic's workshop and tools, and some farm improvements. The total cost of the superintendent's requests, which was supported by the Board of Managers, was the tremendous sum of $80,000.

By 1854, the legislature had agreed to add one new 60' × 40' wing of four stories to the south of the main building. It was to be connected to the main building by a 40' × 76' four-story pavilion, running east to west, which would consist of dining rooms, parlors, associated dormitories for the suicidal, and clothes rooms. Legislators also appropriated funds to build a 250-seat chapel and a two-story building that would connect the boiler plant with the main building. But once again they rejected fencing and landscaping.[30]

In late 1854, the Board of Managers complained that the absence of such fencing enabled some patients to escape the grounds during the past year. It reported, however, that Smith had come up with his own solution. He had ordered the steward to plant sixteen thousand Osage orange trees around a forty-acre tract surrounding the main buildings. That would, the board hoped, provide a natural enclosure "more attractive to the eye and more suitable than any wall or fence." Indeed, Smith argued at the time that trees would be better than a plank or brick fence. Those fences "would exert a

---

29. Ibid., 194–95. Operating a fenceless asylum was most unusual in America in the middle nineteenth century.

30. Report Board of Managers, November 27, 1854, *Senate Journal Appendix*, 18th G.A. (1854/1855), 39–40.

very unhappy influence upon our patients in consequence of the prison-like features that would, in a striking manner, be imparted to the institution."[31] At minimal cost, Smith and his laborers most likely created the fence by putting crushed Osage orange fruits into barrels, adding water, and letting them turn into a slurry. After that, they probably plowed a furrow where they wanted the trees and poured the slurry (with seeds) into the furrow. However, it probably took some years before they had an effective fence.

There was one bright spot in the financial picture. Between November 1851 and November 1852, the asylum's farm operations had produced 1,000 bushels of corn, 1,000 bushels of oats, 225 bushels of potatoes, 18 tons of hay, and 187 bushels of other vegetables, including onions, beets, turnips, beans, cucumbers, parsnips, and tomatoes. It also produced 4,108 pounds of pork. All this, of course, reduced the costs of the institution. As more farmland came under cultivation and as the farm operations increased, so, too, did the institution's ability to provide much of its own food needs. In 1853 and 1854, for example, pork production had jumped to 12,000 pounds. The quantity of production generally increased but so did the variety of vegetables planted. In addition to the vegetables produced in 1852, the steward added corn, peas, carrots, squash, lettuce, and watermelon.[32]

As new wings were added, the staff of the institution grew. At the end of 1852, the sixty-two patients were cared for by four male and three female attendants. There was also an apothecary, a painter, a seamstress, a carpenter, an engineer/mechanic, a gardener, a fireman (for the boiler), two washerwomen, an assistant washerwoman, a cook and an assistant cook, two house servants, and two laborers. Seven of the employees—the cook and his assistant, the assistant washerwoman, and the two house servants and two laborers—were "colored." The house servants and the assistant cook were the lowest-paid employees, earning five to six dollars per month, while the engineer/mechanic was the highest-paid nonadministrative employee at fifty dollars per month.[33]

Smith was constantly seeking the best ways to treat his patients. It is clear that he was familiar with treatments being exercised in eastern hospitals and that he was reading the reports and journal of the Association of Medical Superintendents. By 1852 and 1853, he was aware that the purgatives and emetics so widely used in the early part of the century were no longer gen-

---

31. Report Board of Managers, November 27, 1854, *Senate Journal Appendix*, 18th G.A. (1854/1855), 38–40, 68–69.
32. Report of Superintendent, November 29, 1852, ibid., 17th G.A. (1852), 203; Report of Superintendent, November 27, 1854, ibid., 18th G.A. (1854/1855), 79.
33. Report of Superintendent, November 29, 1852, ibid., 17th G.A. (1852), 204.

erally considered a desirable method of treatment. However, he was highly skeptical of the decision of many of his fellow superintendents in the 1850s to rely heavily on drugs such as opium to treat their patients. In Smith's opinion, the practice in other institutions of using heavy doses of narcotics almost to the exclusion of other remedies posed a "great danger" to the patients. Perhaps, he thought, after a careful case-by-case analysis, he would use narcotics to treat certain patients at Fulton, but he rejected what he perceived to be the almost blanket use of drugs on all patients at some other institutions in the United States.[34]

Smith, as well as the Board of Managers, continued to believe that the best strategy was to treat the patients with respect, placing them in a caring environment where the use of force and insult were absolutely prohibited, varying their routine so that body and mind were actively engaged, and surrounding them with pleasant facilities, both inside and out, as well as with books, newspapers, music, and other amusements. They also believed that the use of patients, insofar as they were willing, to work on the farm, in the hospital's workshops, or in the production of clothes and other asylum necessities, contributed to their cure. A blanket treatment policy—one method to use on all—was rejected in favor of tailoring treatment to the individual case.

"No position is more responsible and important in the moral treatment of the insane," Smith argued, "than that of attendants."[35] A physician at an asylum would see a patient only once or twice a day, but attendants were constantly in their presence. It was the attendant who soothed troubled patients, who helped them put on their clothes, who helped bathe them, who engaged them in conversation, and who kept them neat throughout the day. To perform their tasks well and to be the eyes and ears of the physician throughout the day, the attendants could not be selected based solely on their strength and ability to subdue patients. That would be perhaps the least important role they were to perform. Rather, in selecting attendants, Smith looked for those who had a good education, who had an unblemished moral character, who demonstrated kind and benevolent feelings, who seemed quick and perceptive, and who had infinite patience and were therefore unlikely to become angry and insulting.

Given his emphasis on caring, on patience, and on allowing the insane as much freedom as possible, consistent with their own safety and the safety of those around them, it is not surprising that Smith believed that no restraining apparatus should be used to secure the vast majority of patients in the

---

34. Ibid., 200. To compare Smith's attitudes with those of a fellow superintendent in Pennsylvania, see Tomes, *Generous Confidence*, 196–97.

35. Ibid., 201.

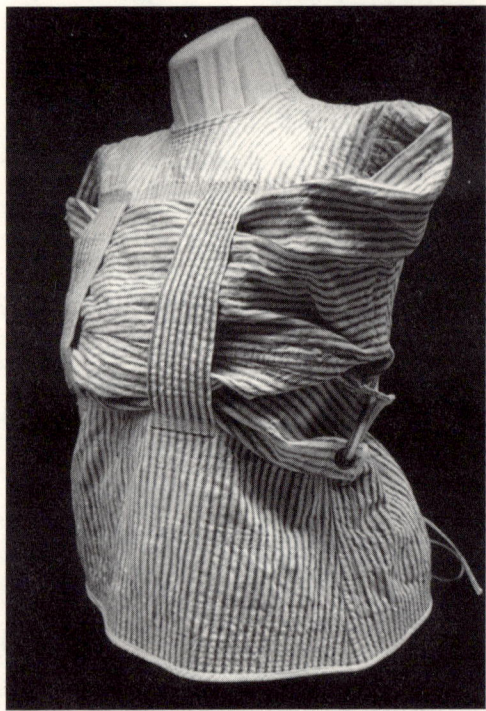

This ruffled straitjacket, prepared for an exhibition by the Missouri State Archives, is a rare feminine version of the well-known restraining garment. Worn with a long skirt, these straitjackets allowed their wearers to appear to be dressed normally (Missouri State Archives).

Fulton facility. Even if such devices absolutely had to be used to restrain a patient who would otherwise harm himself or herself or others, they were to be used only for "the shortest possible period." Use of restraints should clearly be the exception, not the rule. Smith's approach was closer to those advocated in Britain by the middle of the century than to those adopted in many U.S. institutions, although that was changing. In 1844, American superintendents had gone on record at their national meeting as opposing the British movement to abandon straitjackets, muffs, handcuffs, covered beds, and other restraints that restricted a patient's movements and were difficult to remove; but by 1855, a majority, like Smith, had concluded that the British approach seemed to produce better results.[36]

By the middle of the 1850s, Smith lamented that the numbers of patients seeking admission outnumbered the number of beds available, even though he began to place two in a room initially designed for one. As a result, by the end of 1854 he felt compelled to use the power granted to him by the legislature in 1851, discharging some of those patients who were unlikely to be cured so that he could admit those cases where the onset of insanity had

36. Deutsch, *Mentally Ill in America*, 215–28.

occurred within the last twelve months. Nevertheless, in 1854 alone, the asylum turned away seventy applicants.[37]

Death of asylum patients was a regular occurrence, just as death was a regular occurrence outside the institution. The first death occurred in late 1851 or early 1852: a woman whose insanity had already lasted twelve years and who was, upon admission, "almost a living skeleton," unable to walk.[38] Between November 1852 and November 1854, thirty-eight other patients died. The accidental death, probably in January or February 1854, of Theodore McGready, a boy admitted in April 1853, was, at least indirectly, due to flaws in initial construction.[39] Contractors in 1851 had improperly placed the hot-air flues that were to keep the building warm in winter. While that was supposedly "fixed" before the hospital received patients in 1852, those repairs proved to be unsatisfactory. During the coldest weather, patients could not safely or comfortably remain in their rooms. Attendants had to escort them, a few at a time, to the center of the main building where "stove rooms" would keep them warm. On such nights, it was the custom to transfer those patients suffering most from the cold to the stove rooms first. McGready was apparently in such pain that he was the first patient the attendants took to a stove room. Stretched thin in such circumstances, no attendant remained with the boy. As they returned to other rooms to lead other patients to warmth, they heard McGready's screams as he burned to death. Given the circumstances, Smith concluded that no attendant had been negligent and that since the boy had been in the stove room many times and had never approached the stove close enough to risk igniting his clothes, the staff had acted logically.

Whether McGready's family members chose to have him buried in the asylum cemetery or whether they paid for his body to be shipped home is unknown. The earliest legible tombstone in the graveyard located just east of the main buildings reads, "Born in Campbell Co., Va., Nov 4, 1804; Died Dec 14, 1854." Still surprisingly isolated from the main buildings and from Fulton itself, the stones, often eroded, cracked, or damaged, mark the final resting place of hundreds of men and women whose stories, experiences, and names have been lost. By 1861, 119 patients had died at the asylum, although not all were buried on its grounds.[40] Most of those deaths were attributed to fevers, epilepsy, mania, and other physical and mental maladies. Only four, according to hospital records, had died by unnatural causes. Two had died in accidents: McGready of accidental burning, and another pa-

37. Report Board of Managers, November 27, 1854, *Senate Journal Appendix*, 18th G.A. (1854/1855), 41.
38. Report of Superintendent, November 29, 1852, ibid., 17th G.A. (1852), 190.
39. Report of Superintendent, November 27, 1854, ibid., 18th G.A. (1854/1855), 59.
40. Report of Superintendent, no date, *House Journal Appendix*, 21st G.A. (1860/1861), 547.

The asylum graveyard, photographed in 2002 (Lael photo).

tient of accidental choking. One patient had used his sheet to commit suicide. One had been murdered, kicked and stomped by a fellow patient.

In the latter half of the 1850s, the asylum continued to expand with a new wing and pavilion added to the north of the central building and two additions for the most violent patients. By 1859, with those additions nearing completion, the hospital could house 350 patients. Looking back at the 1850s, Smith and his board could have felt justifiably proud that the institution had not only survived, but also thrived. And, as they looked toward the coming decade, they had every reason to assume that the funding needed for future projects was likely to be less onerous than in the decade just passed, thanks to the state legislature's decision to impose an asylum tax on property to fund the institution's operations.

While the state could certainly pat itself on the back for its progress, by 1859–1860 Smith reminded legislators that there remained major needs. The asylum needed extensive landscaping, two infirmaries, one for men and one for women, a steam laundry, gas lighting to replace the oil lamps, and a bowling alley and billiard tables for the recreation of the patients. It also needed to replace an aging and inadequate sewer system and to build a new reservoir. To provide more individualized treatment to patients, the asylum also needed to hire more personnel. While that list was impressive, the appropriations to cover such renovation or new construction were likely to be small in comparison to the financial demands of the previous ten years. There was no reason to assume that a legislature that had rather generously funded request after request, even given the budget concerns of the state in these politically turbulent antebellum years, would not likely meet these new, lesser needs.

The legislature continued to fund these requests, even when faced with unexpected financial "surprises." Within less than five years of the arrival of the first patient, the legislature was forced to refloor the entire institution, since Jenkins, the contractor, had originally installed white pine floors and not yellow pine. The white pine floors had proven too soft to handle the wear. The legislature continued to fund additions even when a July 1857 windstorm removed a 60′ × 25′ section of slate roofing—requiring of course another significant, but unanticipated, expense. It had also continued to fund construction even when, almost immediately, it learned that it would have to finance a redesign of the original heating system. And even after that redesign and annual tinkering failed to solve the problem, it had to remove the old heating system and install a new one, although the institution had not yet celebrated its tenth birthday.

At the end of 1859, reflecting over the past decade and looking forward to the next, Smith and his board might be excused for perhaps leaning back with a great sigh of contentment and relishing the victories. Smith, himself, for the first time since he and his family moved into the asylum, might even look forward to the coming winter. The new boiler authorized by the legislature provided Smith and his patients warmth in their rooms in the winter of 1859 for the first time in the hospital's history. A heating system that actually worked, coupled with two newly constructed wings for patients seemed, no doubt, a sign of good things to come.

3
Disaster and Rebirth, 1861–1872

For residents of Fulton, the future looked rosy, and they must have been pleased as they looked back over a decade of significant progress. Callaway County, organized in late 1820 with a population of less than two thousand, had decided to erect its county seat in what was to become Fulton. Acquiring fifty acres of land from George Nichols, the county created a plat for the new community, formally filed in January 1827. The original design located the town between First and Sixth streets and Bluff and Nichols streets. By 1828, the county had constructed a two-story brick courthouse, which served until 1856, when it was replaced with a newer structure.

By the winter of 1851–1852, when the asylum opened its doors to patients, Fulton was thriving, with a Masonic lodge, ten mercantile houses, two drugstores, three hotels, three saddlery shops, two cabinet shops, two wagon factories, one bakery, one barbershop, one sawmill, two livery stables, one furniture store, and five grocery stores. Many other businesses flourished as well to serve the community of seven hundred and their agricultural neighbors.

Its selection as the site of the insane asylum may well have convinced aspiring entrepreneurs to test the waters. Fulton's *Missouri Telegraph* carried many notices within the next few years of newly opened shops. Among these new businesses were Letcher and Wilson, a tailor shop; R. Prosser and Co., a carriage- and wagon-building shop; John McClanahan, a cabinet maker; the Missouri Hotel, which housed both transients and permanent boarders; and a new general store opened by D. M., J. H., and W. B. Tucker. To provide educational opportunities, in February 1849, James Love and Mrs.

This early 1884 image shows the asylum as it was first built (Missouri State Archives).

L. A. Love opened two twenty-week academies, one for men and one for women.

In April 1851, Reverend W. W. Robertson and Mrs. N. Dauber opened another educational institution, the Fulton Female Academy, that envisioned a three-year program of study. Nor did Robertson and other Fultonians stop there. In early 1851, the Fulton Presbyterian Church, Robertson's church, agreed to support the creation of Fulton College for men. Acquiring land from Harry Bailey due west across town from the State Insane Asylum, it began classes in October for the fifty or so young men who enrolled. Robertson and state senator Preston Reed of Fulton wanted the Presbyterian Synod of Missouri, not just the local congregation, to support Fulton College. By their efforts, the synod convened in Fulton in 1852 as it debated whether it wished to build a church-backed institution in Missouri and where such a school should be located. Fulton, Richmond, Boonville, and St. Charles all had supporters who wished such an institution to be built in their communities. But as they had done with the insane asylum, Fultonians pledged more support and money for the project than any competitor, so they won the contest. Fultonians pledged $15,391, clear ownership to eighteen acres together with the buildings of Fulton College, and a scholarship fund of $20,000. The synod representatives agreed to support an institution in Fulton and to take bids for a new, 90′ × 60′ academic building. It also agreed to rename the institution Westminster College.[1]

Nor did Fulton's good fortune end there. On March 21, 1851, the lead story in the *Telegraph* celebrated the General Assembly's decision to establish a "Deaf and Dumb" asylum in Fulton, to be located on forty acres of the land initially given by the community for the insane asylum.[2] That institution would be open to individuals between ten and thirty, who until now had often traveled out of state to find a suitable institution to assist them. Although between 1851 and 1853 the Deaf and Dumb Asylum was housed in a farmhouse, it would begin construction of its own permanent buildings in the latter year.

The town's recent prosperity prompted several leaders in Fulton and Callaway County to flirt with the idea that they should support the construction of a plank road between Glasgow and St. Louis that would run through both Columbia and Fulton. While that particular plan died fairly quickly, the community's enthusiasm about the future was not diminished.

Despite the optimism about the local economy and the success of the community in securing, within the span of three years, three significant institutions—the Insane Asylum, the Deaf and Dumb Asylum, and Westminster College—the future of communities like Fulton throughout the nation lay in other hands. For decades, the debate over slavery, states' rights, and federal power had intensified. By 1854, dissatisfied with existing political choices and angered by the passage of the Kansas-Nebraska Act permitting the possibility of expansion of slavery into the territories, men throughout the North and Upper Midwest joined to create a new party—the Republican Party. It was a party that firmly opposed the expansion of slavery and, in relation to such things as internal improvements, favored an increase in federal authority. Equally important, it was a party that rejected the need for Southern supporters. While James Buchanan's election as president in 1856 pleased the South, his exceedingly narrow victory did not. The South had long since lost majority control in the U.S. House of Representatives. With the admission of California in 1850, it had also lost control of the U.S. Senate, if each senator voted on the issue of slavery according to the status in his state. Abraham Lincoln's election in 1860 therefore signaled not only the loss of the presidency in early 1861 when he would be inaugu-

---

1. For a history of Westminster College, see William Parrish, *Westminster College: An Informal History, 1851–1999* (Fulton: Westminster College, 2000).

2. "An Act to Establish an Asylum for the Deaf and Dumb," *Missouri Telegraph*, 1. For a history of the Deaf and Dumb Asylum, see Richard Reed, *Historic MSD: The Story of the Missouri School for the Deaf* (Fulton: Richard Reed, 2000).

rated, but also the eventual loss of the federal judiciary, as Lincoln and a Republican congress would likely select Republicans to federal judgeships.

Abraham Lincoln's electoral victory in 1860 prompted South Carolinians to convene a specially elected convention to debate leaving the Union. Five days before Christmas, voting 169 to 0, delegates approved secession. By February 1, 1861, Mississippi, Florida, Alabama, Georgia, Louisiana, and Texas had also seceded. By June 8, Virginia, Arkansas, North Carolina, and Tennessee had followed.

In April, President Jefferson Davis of the newly formed Confederate States of America also ordered Confederate General P. G. T. Beauregard to seize the federal garrison at Fort Sumter, thus eliminating the Union presence in one of the Confederacy's most important ports. Following orders, Beauregard opened fire on Fort Sumter on April 12. Learning of that attack, President Lincoln on April 15 called for 75,000 men to join the 13,000 soldiers of the regular army, to suppress the rebellion.

Four slave states remained. Kentucky initially declared its neutrality, while Delaware remained in the Union. Whether Maryland would have formally seceded is not clear. Given its strategic importance to Washington, D.C., Lincoln on April 27 suspended habeas corpus rights in that state and authorized his commanders to arrest and detain any who may threaten the Union, including those members of the Maryland legislature likely to vote for secession. Maryland, then, would remain in the Union.

That left Missouri. In the 1860 presidential election, it had supported Stephen A. Douglas, a Democrat, and John Bell, a former Whig, almost equally. Lincoln had run fourth, securing only a little over 17,000 Missouri votes. At the state level, Missouri elected Claiborne Jackson, a pro-slavery Democrat, as its new governor. Inaugurated in January 1861, Governor Jackson, soon joined by the state legislature, called for a Missouri convention to determine the state's future political course. Convening in late February, newly elected convention delegates rejected secession and urged both North and South to avoid conflict. When, however, in mid-April Lincoln asked Governor Jackson to provide four thousand men to enlarge the Union army, Jackson refused. Rather, he asked for the help of the Confederate government to seize the Union arsenal at St. Louis.

Following a clash between pro- and anti-Union forces in St. Louis, Jackson, in May, secured passage in the legislature of a measure that allowed for the enrollment of all able-bodied men in Missouri to protect the state. To pay for this mobilization, the legislature allocated the funds heretofore reserved to the state schools and institutions, as well as authorized the issuance of bonds and the borrowing of money. The new Missouri militia, named the Missouri State Guard, was commanded by Sterling Price, who had served as a colonel in the Mexican War and as state governor from 1853 to

1857. By June, Jackson and many legislators had fled Jefferson City to Boonville, as a Union force moved toward the capital. The State Guard and Union forces skirmished for the first time at Boonville shortly thereafter.

Within two months of Union occupation of Jefferson City, Missouri had two governors—Jackson, who favored secession, and Hamilton Gamble, a Republican chosen by dubious constitutional means as the new governor when Jackson had fled the capital. As more and more Missourians now chose sides, more military battles and skirmishes followed. Jackson joined with those legislators of the Twenty-first General Assembly who had fled with him to formally proclaim secession on November 3. Gamble and his supporters reaffirmed Missouri's commitment to remain in the Union.

Choosing sides divided neighbors, friends, families, and churches. Contributing to destabilization were not only the clashes of Union and Confederate armies, but also the emergence in Missouri of guerrilla war. To survive in these increasingly disturbed times, individuals, businesses, and institutions in the state had to adapt quickly. One Fulton resident pointed out in April 1862 just how hard the "adaptation" to increased strife had been:

> Eighteen months ago, Fulton was one of the most thrifty and enterprising inland towns in the State. We had one of the most prosperous colleges in the West, with over one hundred and fifty students in attendance. Now this institution is nearly or quite broken up. There are in attendance at present about twenty-five students with a skeleton of a faculty. At that time, we had two female seminaries, both filled with pupils. Now, there is only one, and that with a very few pupils. Then, our Deaf and Dumb Asylum was full of students; then our Insane Asylum was crowded with patients. Now, these benevolent and charitable institutions are closed, or rather used as quarters for troops, the inmates—unfortunate and helpless as they are—have been thrown out—driven from a home where they were cared for, and have to seek what protection and care they can from the cold charities of strangers. These institutions caused to be spent annually in our midst, about two hundred thousand dollars. This sum was circulated among all classes of our citizens—the merchant, the farmer, the mechanic. . . . Now we are deprived of this. Then there was not a vacant house in Fulton; now, one-fourth of the residences in town are without tenants. Then, we were at peace and a happy people; now, what are we?[3]

Even had the political unrest not done so, the General Assembly's decision in May 1861 to divert its financial support of state institutions to the State Guard doomed the State Lunatic Asylum. As monies raised from the asylum tax—which should have paid for the two new wings and funded

---

3. "The Question Brought Home," *Missouri Telegraph*, April 25, 1862, 1.

the care and upkeep of the 258 patients at the asylum—went elsewhere, the Board of Managers faced a crisis. Appealing to counties on May 20, the board explained that, due to the absence of funds, it had become necessary to require counties to pay in advance for the board of each of their patients at Fulton. If they refused or were unable to do so, the counties were required to remove those patients from the asylum and house them in whatever manner the county courts thought best.[4] While many counties did forward sufficient money to cover three months' board, others, in as much disarray as the state government, were unwilling or unable to do so.

When the Missouri state auditor told the board that no additional monies would soon be forthcoming from the state, and when it became clear the county monies would not be sufficient to keep the institution open, the board members, on June 24, announced that no new patients would be admitted. They also reluctantly informed all county governments and all guardians and families of private patients that they must retrieve those they had placed at the asylum. By August 23, few of the patients had been removed, so the board ordered the superintendent to send the patients home, which he had mostly accomplished by the end of September. On September 28, the board also authorized the superintendent to sell "such property as could not be profitably kept," including livestock, coal, and wagons.[5]

As part of his preparations for shutting down the asylum, Superintendent Smith ordered various hospital supplies to be shifted into locked rooms in the central building for safekeeping. That action was for naught. Late in the evening of September 26, approximately seventy-five to one hundred State Guard supporters demanded the keys to the storerooms. When Smith refused, he and his family were confined to their rooms while the doors to the supply rooms were broken down and a large supply of blankets, sheets, and clothes were stolen. The superintendent later reported that he asked why he was being confined during the theft. The spokesman for the raid "very candidly replied there were prominent men of the county who might be passing about that I would likely know, and I might be called upon to make a statement at some future time, and of course, these prominent gentlemen might thus have a stigma placed upon their character." On the other hand, the pro-Southern local newspaper very carefully insinuated that the robbers were Union, not Confederate, sympathizers. "We are wholly ignorant as to who took the property. There are different rumors about the matter, in none of which we place any confidence. Our readers know that we are under parole not to charge any Federals with anything wrong, unless we can prove its

---

4. Report of the Late Managers of the Missouri Lunatic Asylum, February 21, 1863, *House Journal*, Appendix, 23rd G.A. (1864/1865), 270.
5. Ibid., 271.

truth—and then not do it—therefore, be it known, that we do not upon our own responsibility, nor the responsibility of any one else, charge the Feds with having taken the said blankets, comforts, etc."[6]

The livestock and wagons not seized in the raid were sold as advertised two days later. The board, however, shaken by the theft, decided to schedule additional sales to remove furniture and other items that might well later be illegally removed. Those sales were held on October 7, 8, 9, and 18. Before those sales, however, a second theft occurred at the asylum on September 30, again probably by Southern sympathizers.

Without patients and without furnishings, the asylum did not need attendants, physicians, or support laborers. All were dismissed. Smith retired to the county. He placed one of the attendants, Milton J. Hall, in charge as caretaker of the grounds. When the asylum reopened two years later, in September 1863, the Board of Managers commended Hall's care and attention that, in their view, had left the asylum "in a far better state of preservation than we could have reasonably expected."[7]

The lack of adequate funds, coupled with the unstable political condition prevailing in central Missouri in those early war years, made prolonged closure of the institution necessary. Although the departure of many pro-Southern politicians from Jefferson City in 1861 meant the capital was in Union hands, many residents in Callaway County and in Fulton remained sympathetic to the South. Writing in October 1861, Brigadier General Chester Harding Jr., who led 650 men, with artillery support, north from the capital to break up a "considerable force of rebels encamped about 8 miles north of Fulton," estimated that "there are not 200 Union men in the county of Callaway. That whole region is disloyal."[8] Harding frustratedly reported that he could not seize Southern supporters or their property lest other pro-Southern Fultonians take their vengeance out on the Union loyalists.

He may well have been correct, if the local newspaper was representative of local feelings. During the first months of the war it revealed a clear pro-South sympathy. One letter in the late summer of 1861 appealed to every "Southern Rights" woman in the county to aid "those gallant sons of Callaway" who were fighting for their rights and independence. At the same

---

6. Smith to H. J. Fisher, Chairman, Committee State Lunatic Asylum, February 2, 1863, *House Journal Appendix*, 22nd G.A. (1862/1863), 267; "State Lunatic Asylum," *Missouri Telegraph*, October 4, 1861, 4.

7. Report Board of Managers, November 30, 1863, *Senate Journal Appendix*, 22nd G.A. (1862/1863), 87.

8. "Report of Brig. Gen. Chester Harding, Jr.," October 31, 1861, U.S. War Department, *The War of the Rebellion: A Compilation of the Official Records of the Union and Confederate Armies* (Washington, D.C.: GPO, 1881), series 1, III, 254.

time, the author implored, "let our souls be lifted in humble prayer to Almighty God, who alone can save us from the dark lowering clouds of tyranny, the threatening voice of political despotism, and the surging waves of Northern licentiousness that threaten to devastate the fair land of the South."[9]

Rufus Abbott, a local physician and Fulton councilman sympathetic to the Union, confirmed the friction in town. Writing to his brother in New Hampshire in late spring of 1861, he reported that "there is here a very bad state of feeling between the [pro-South and Unionist] parties." He added, "I would not be surprised at any time to see an outbreak and people at work cutting each others throats." Abbott also reported that two years of crop failures, followed by the suspension of banking in Fulton in 1861, further contributed to the heightened tension.[10]

By April 1862, perhaps because Union troops had been permanently quartered at the Callaway County courthouse, Fulton and its surrounding communities appeared peaceful. Nevertheless occasional skirmishes continued to occur in the county. In May, for example, Union soldiers and local draft resisters engaged in a firefight on Whetstone Creek north of Williamsburg. Throughout this time, federal officials were also on the lookout for Southern military recruiters who might try to lure local men into the Confederate Army. The *Telegraph* reported in late May that a military commission had just convicted Henry Willing for burning railroad bridges and for encouraging desertion from the Union army and for enlisting civilians into the South's army. He was executed for these crimes. In late July, Confederate and Union forces clashed at Moore's Mill in Callaway County. Thereafter, the peace that the local paper had proclaimed in April returned.[11]

Nevertheless, the divisions and tensions in Callaway County remained, as demonstrated by Abbott's letters:

> September 26, 1862 (while traveling from Jefferson City to Fulton): "My way was blocked by [pro-Confederate] guerrillas. We still have over 320 Dutch [German] cavalry in town whose business it is to scour the surrounding country and drive out the secesh [secessionists]...."
>
> July 27, 1863: "The Fulton troops captured two bushwackers Friday night and they have been sent to Mexico for trial.... I think that we in north Missouri have seen the worst of the Rebellion."

9. "A Southern Woman," *Missouri Telegraph*, September 6, 1861, 1.

10. Rufus Abbott to Zebadiah Abbott, May 19, 1861, Abbott Letters, Westminster College Archives, Fulton, Missouri.

11. "Military Commission," *Missouri Telegraph*, May 23, 1862, 2. For a participant's account of events surrounding the Moore's Mill battle, see Joseph Mudd's *With Porter in North Missouri* (Washington: National Publishing Company, 1909).

April 24, 1865: "It is now better here but there is no security for life or property in the country around towns. Murder & robbery are frequent and I fear will be for years."[12]

In the midst of his Fulton chronicles, Abbott reported on July 27, 1863, that he had just agreed to become the new assistant physician at the State Lunatic Asylum and expected to assume his duties by the end of August. His employment was made possible by the state legislature in March, when it approved a $10,000 appropriation allowing administrators to prepare to reopen the asylum.

Although Union troops had occupied asylum buildings at various times during the preceding two years, damage to the property did not appear to be great. In contrast, the buildings at the neighboring Deaf and Dumb Asylum had "suffered very considerably from ill usage. . . . The floors, ceilings, and walls of the principal rooms, and the seats, desks, windows and doors had received such injuries as might have been expected from a long occupation by soldiers."[13] Surveying his own campus to determine what repairs would be needed, a relieved Superintendent Smith informed the General Assembly that "the building has been, to some extent, defaced by the occupation of [Union] troops, but the damage the building has sustained is slight compared with the front grounds. These have been appropriated for cavalry horses, and hence all the young trees, shrubbery, grass, etc., have been almost entirely destroyed." A joint legislative committee agreed with his assessment of the front grounds but downplayed other damage. It simply reported that "the lower rooms of the center buildings were somewhat defaced by the soldiers who occupied them. . . . All else belonging to the institution seemed to have been preserved in good condition." Although in a subsequent report Smith attributed to Union troops some damage done to the smokehouse, he admitted that it was already "in a very dilapidated condition" before the arrival of soldiers. Further deemphasizing Union damage, he noted that while soldiers defaced some of the walls, those same walls had not been repainted since first constructed in 1850.[14]

While damage caused by Union forces seemed relatively minor in terms of cost, Smith and the board warned the legislature that significant appro-

---

12. Rufus Abbott to Zebadiah Abbott, Abbott Letters. By "Dutch," he was referring to Union cavalry, often made up of newer German immigrants, nearly all of whom supported the Union and abolition of slavery.

13. Report of the Joint Committee to Visit the State Asylums at Fulton, no date, *House Journal Appendix*, 22nd G.A. (1863/1864), 31.

14. Smith to H. J. Fisher, Chairman, Committee State Lunatic Asylum, February 2, 1863, *House Journal Appendix*, 22nd G.A. (1863/1864), 268; Report of the Joint Committee, no date, ibid., 30; Special Report of Superintendent, November 30, 1863, *Senate Journal Appendix*, 22nd G.A. (1863/1864), 48.

priations would be needed. Before the closing in 1861, the asylum carried a debt of $20,000, which in 1863 remained unpaid. Furthermore, while the expansion of the hospital's bed capacity to handle 350 patients in 1860–1861 had been completed, the expansion of the rest of the infrastructure to handle those patients had not. In addition, the normal wear and tear expected after a decade of use, coupled with two years standing empty and unheated, required significant repair and replacement. Last, the institution would have to replace the personnel released in 1861 and to replace those furnishings and supplies sold or stolen during the war.[15]

When Superintendent Smith sent notices to counties that the institution would reopen for patients on September 7, 1863, limited resources forced him to cap admissions at one hundred. Receiving additional funds from the legislature to treat the patients, Smith had hired Abbott as the assistant physician, Abbott's wife as the matron, and the wartime caretaker, Hall, as steward. Mrs. Abbott and Hall had then proceeded to hire additional staff. Smith and Hall oversaw the complete repair, refurbishing, and repainting of the central building and the two oldest wings, together with the expansion and repair of the reservoir. They watched with pride the installation of new machinery in the laundry that would allow them to employ only two washerwomen instead of the former eight to ten. And they oversaw the construction of a new fence around one hundred acres of farmland, which would enable them to graze the institution's cattle and sheep and create an "additional beauty and symmetry that imparts a pleasant moral effect upon patients."[16] The only major project not completed before reopening was the construction of a new smokehouse.

Unhappy that he could admit only 100 patients in a facility designed for 350, and concerned that the General Assembly might want to cut corners, Smith's 1865 appeal to the legislature tackled the financial issue head-on. The decision of the General Assembly in 1863 to charge county governments $2.50 per week for each patient rather than the prewar $1.50 wasn't working—the cost of operations could not be met with that fee. Between 1863 and 1865, Smith reported, the costs for supplies such as bacon and flour had doubled—some had even quadrupled. The prewar debt of $20,000 remained unpaid. The institution still had no funds to increase occupancy to 350. And finally, the current patient population needed more recreational, mental, and physical opportunities, including bowling alleys, billiard tables, libraries in each ward, and a gymnasium.[17]

There were three solutions to the current financial problem. The state

---

15. Report of Board of Managers, no date, and Report of Superintendent, no date, *House Journal Appendix*, 23rd G.A. (1864/1865), 52–70.

16. Report of Superintendent, no date, *House Journal Appendix*, 23rd G.A. (1864/1865), 56, 64.

17. Ibid., 57–70.

could raise the county payments to between four and five dollars per week; it could reinstitute the state asylum property tax that had expired during the war; or it could cut supplies and personnel costs at the institution. Smith explained that the last option would be a disaster:

> We might curtail our expenses to the lowest possible amount to keep life in our patients—reduce the number of attendants, so that all their time would be consumed in half cleaning the wards, and none left to devote to the well being of the insane, their exercise, recreation and amusement, and as a consequence of all this, introduce the various means of restrain[t] and barbarous restrictions that have long since been abandoned as revolting to humanity and a disgrace to any civilized community. I say, we might do all this in our efforts to diminish expenses, but when done, what would be the result? The unfortunate committed to our charge would cease to enjoy the advantages of all the various means and appliances for meliorating their condition, that have resulted from the profound study of the sane and insane mind, and the combined experience and observation of the most gifted and philanthropic spirits—this noble charity would lose all its elevating and distinguishing characteristics as a curative institution—no longer be regarded a proud monument of justice and mercy, but converted, truly, into a poor house, a prison house, a receptacle for rendering the hopeful hopeless, the curable incurable.[18]

In the view of the superintendent and his board, the notion of raising the fee assessed to counties was undesirable because the counties were often slow, unwilling, or unable to pay. Smith and his board recommended to the General Assembly the reimposition of the state insane property tax.

Rather than accept that recommendation, the state, in December, made a special appropriation of $20,000 to remove the prewar debts and would, as it deemed necessary, continue to make regular appropriations for the asylum. By that time, Smith had resigned as superintendent, citing ill health, and had moved near St. Louis. Regaining his health, in 1872 he became the chief physician and superintendent of the St. Louis County Insane Asylum.

Assuming the duties of superintendent in Fulton on March 1, 1865, was former assistant physician Rufus Abbott. He retained his wife as matron and employed his son as druggist. Neither Abbott nor his wife felt that the demands of office were particularly great. "My duties," he wrote his brother, "are no more laborious than when assistant and the pay much better." "My wife," he added, "thinks that she has not more to do than while we were keeping house." Abbott's view of operations over the next twelve months was quite optimistic: "Every thing is going prosperously at the asylum," he

---

18. Ibid., 66–67.

noted upon return from a trip East, "and the crazy folks seemed very glad to see me."[19]

Courtesy of the new state appropriations, the Lunatic Asylum's population grew to 266 by November 1866 and to an overcrowded 368 two years later. One factor in that growth was the admission of "colored" patients, beginning in the fall of 1865. Superintendent Abbott had initially refused, uncertain that he could legally admit such patients. Once the state's attorney general had issued an opinion that admission was perfectly legal, that fall, Abbott admitted five men and three women. They were, he reported, housed in a way that would "prevent association with other patients."[20]

Lest a future attorney general read the law differently, by early December, a bill was introduced into the Missouri Senate that would guarantee the admission of blacks into the Lunatic Asylum, guided "by the same regulations as those admitting white patients—no distinction to be made on account of color." When that bill was presented on the floor of the Senate in March, it was tabled when a committee pointed out that neither the Missouri constitution nor the laws initially establishing the asylum imposed any racial criteria on patients seeking admission. While the absence of a specific legislative guarantee did not prompt a change of admission policy at Fulton, the newly arrived superintendent Charles H. Hughes recommended in the fall of 1868 that the legislature consider building a separate structure for the "colored" because of what he believed to be a greater tendency toward racism among the insane.[21]

A year and a half earlier, the Missouri House, concerned about the fate of both "colored" and white patients not housed at the Fulton asylum, considered granting each county the right to appoint three commissioners who could legally "break open inner and outer doors" of any non-state building housing insane persons. Legislators also considered whether those commissioners should be required each month to visit "all lunatic, insane or other asylums, or houses of refuge or any and all places where persons of unsound mind or destitute persons are confined," thereafter reporting to the counties on the name, age, sex, length of confinement, cause of confinement, and condition of the patient. The proposed bill also allowed the commissioners to determine whether a patient was unjustly and illegally being held against his or her will. When in doubt, the commissioners were to inform

---

19. Rufus Abbott to Zebadiah Abbott, April 24, 1865, and May 27, 1866, Abbott Letters.

20. Report of Superintendent, November 30, 1868, *House and Senate Journals Appendix*, 25th G.A. (1869), 6; and Report of Superintendent, November 29, 1870, ibid., 26th G.A. (1871), 8; Report of Superintendent, November 26, 1866, *House Journal Appendix*, 24th G.A. (1867), 444.

21. "An Act to Provide for the Admission of Colored Patients to the State Lunatic Asylum," Capitol Fire Documents, reel S-419, folder 12599, MSA. Report of Superintendent, November 30, 1868, *House and Senate Journals Appendix*, 25th G.A. (1869), 15–16.

county officials and were to conduct an investigation.[22] Such a broad grant of authority to commissioners, however, proved too unpalatable to legislators. The bill died in committee.

Nevertheless, for the first time in the state's history, the legislature had, on paper at least, finally extended mental health treatment to all its citizens, regardless of race, and was at least debating legislation that would protect those patients in the care of counties, cities, private citizens, and businesses.

As the wartime decade ended, Superintendent Hughes could happily report that the hospital was running efficiently and no longer operating above capacity. The opening of the St. Louis County Insane Asylum in April 1869, he noted, had temporarily relieved the Fulton asylum's population dilemma. Administrators there had quickly accepted 131 Fulton patients, which helped fill its 250-person capacity. Hughes also applauded the concern expressed by legislators for the welfare of patients who might be incarcerated against their will in non-state institutions. However, he suggested that the General Assembly modify the admissions policy for private patients into the Fulton asylum. Under his plan, it would take more than just having two doctors sign a certificate to authorize admission. Those doctors would now have to appear before a judge and make their case for admission formally. Patients would not be admitted unless an affidavit by those doctors, duly witnessed by the judge and carrying his judicial seal, was presented to the asylum administrators. Committed to the dictum that "no person shall be deprived of life, liberty or property without due process of law," Hughes explained that this procedure would help insure that no one would be unjustly deprived of his or her personal liberty. He quickly added that it was not as if there were people at the Fulton asylum who had been placed there wrongly. But he stressed: "People are jealous of the personal liberty of the citizens, sane or insane, and our laws should respect that jealously."[23]

T. R. H. Smith's resignation as superintendent in March 1865 provided an opportunity for his successors, including Hughes, to consider alternative views of treatment. As his valedictory message to the legislature in 1865 cautioning against choosing the cost-cutting option had revealed, he had consistently seen the asylum as a curative, and not as a caretaker, institution. He had consistently argued that its staff needed to be trained so that they could work with the physicians in assisting each patient, whenever possible, to return to society whole. And he had consistently denounced the too-ready use of restraints and the wholesale use of drugs as a medical treatment.

---

22. "An Act Concerning Lunatic and Other Asylums," Capitol Fire Documents, reel S-422, folder 12759, MSA.

23. Report of Superintendent, November 29, 1870, *House and Senate Journals Appendix*, 26th G.A. (1871), 8, 36–37.

In his first report, Rufus Abbott, Smith's replacement, informed Missouri legislators: "In the general management of the institution, I have not departed from the system of treatment practiced here from the organization of the asylum." Smith's departure, then, appeared not to have changed the mission and vision of the facility. While details of how Abbott treated the patients under his care are no longer available, his successor, Charles H. Hughes, implied that the methods of care had changed. "The distinguishing feature in the present management of the insane, as compared with that of the past," he wrote the legislature, "consists in the substitution, wherever practical, of persuasion for coercion, and always kindness for violence."[24] In reality, Hughes's initial rhetoric about treatment mirrored that of both Smith and Abbott. Nevertheless, reading Hughes's later discussion of the treatments in use at Fulton in the late 1860s and the early 1870s, it becomes clear that coercion and restraint, as well as a growing reliance on drugs, were an important part of the therapeutic mix at the institution.

While acknowledging that personal observation was the best method of handling patients rather than mechanical restraints, and that "insanity [was] not a diabolical possession—an evil spirit—to be frightened away by flagellation or the inspiration of terror," Hughes admitted that "the insane are still restrained, but restricted with a view to cure, and not with the sole object of preventing violence or mischief." He found the use of a darkened room, of shower baths, or of other such techniques to inflict punishment or to inspire terror in the patient unsuitable. However, if overcrowding prevented attendants from performing their ideal functions, or if the violence or destructiveness of a patient required him to be calmed or restrained, then the asylum might use a strait-waist, a leather wristlet, a lock seat, or a crib bedstead. Hughes argued that those who think patients are thrown into cells, chained to walls, or whipped were clinging to obsolete images of the "madhouse." He explained that the strait-waist, for example, was simply an ordinary jacket with the ends of the sleeves closed, fitted onto "indifferent and careless" patients who might, during cold weather, rip off their clothes otherwise. Similarly, the lock seat and the crib bedstead—the former, an ordinary seat that locks patients into a sitting position, and the latter, a regular bed with sides and cover added to secure suicidal patients—did not torture patients. The leather wristlet, leather mittens, and leather muffs simply confined a patient's hands so that they may not do damage. All of these types of restraints, Hughes noted, were quite humane. Indeed, he reported, the ability of male attendants to control the men meant that few mechanical re-

---

24. Report of Superintendent, November 26, 1866, *House Journal Appendix*, 24th G.A. (1867), 441; Report of Superintendent, November 29, 1870, *House and Senate Journals Appendix*, 26th G.A. (1871), 17.

straints were used in the male wards at all. However, he added, the "timidity of our female attendants" required such restraints to be used much more liberally in the female wards.[25]

To prevent abuse with restraining devices, Hughes insisted that no attendant use such a device without the explicit order of the superintendent or one of his resident officers. Indeed, given his own preferences, Hughes would not normally use any of these devices. If control was really needed, his most desirable approach was to rely on anesthetics and narcotics. "The whole class of narcotics comes to our aid, and opium is the *sine qua non*. I would part with any other remedy before I would give up opium."[26]

Hughes also identified other techniques he believed could assist patients in their recovery. He used laxatives to purge the system, various tonics to restore strength and quiet, and various drugs to induce sleep: "If, through the temporary administration of alcoholic beverages, the patient can be induced to remember his misery no more, we consider the treatment justifiable." Hughes also pointed out that creating "uneasiness and pain" in the patient by the use of scarification, setons (thread or tape drawn through the skin to allow draining), blisters, and emetics "rouse[d] the system" and diverted patients' attention from their delusions. Bathing patients was also therapeutic. The warm bath calmed the nervous system while the cold bath "prove[d] highly beneficial in the debility of exhausting mania."[27]

These medical practices alone, Hughes admitted, would not cure a patient. Recovery at Fulton would only improve if the legislature appropriated sufficient money to renovate a facility in steady physical decline, to landscape surrounding grounds to provide patients an exercise area where long walks amid grass, trees, and bushes on sunny days would be possible, and to make available amusements and opportunities for recreation, whether in the form of circuses, gymnasiums, bowling alleys, chess, cards, lectures, theater, or music.

Like his predecessors, Hughes firmly believed that work was also therapeutic for his patients. However, unlike his predecessors, he favored a more active approach to get patients to "volunteer" their skills. "I would make labor, in a certain sense, compulsory. I would lead the patient out to work by a system of rewards and special privileges for any manual labor he might

---

25. Report of Superintendent, November 29, 1870, *House and Senate Journals Appendix*, 26th G.A. (1871), 22–23. Hughes's views on restraint were similar to those followed at the Pennsylvania Hospital for the Insane. See Tomes, *Generous Confidence*, 197.

26. Report of Superintendent, November 30, 1868, ibid., 25th G.A. (1869), 27.

27. Ibid.; and Report of Superintendent, November 29, 1870, ibid., 26th G.A. (1870), 29–30. Hughes's attitudes toward the use of laxatives, purgatives, and blisters were again mirrored by policies at Pennsylvania's Hospital for the Insane.

perform, and deprive him of those rewards in case of refusal."[28] What would be most desirable, in Hughes's view, would be to combine work with something the patient saw as pleasurable. Failing that, patients should still work. Most patients under his care worked in their respective wards. Most men also worked in some capacity on the farm, in the dairy, or in the garden, while most women worked in the laundry, the kitchen, or the sewing room.

Patient labor under Hughes, however, rarely reduced the need for hired labor. Using both patients and hired workers, the asylum produced significant quantities of farm and finished goods. In 1869 and 1870, for example, it produced over a thousand dresses, 625 drawers (underwear), 712 towels, 794 sheets, and thousands of other items, including bonnets, shirts, gowns, aprons, bed ticks, pillow slips, pants, and bedspreads. In those same two years, the farm operations generated 15,000 pounds of pork, 33,954 gallons of milk, and 6,000 pounds of beef, plus thousands of bushels of corn, potatoes, grapes, onions, strawberries, beans, squash, pickles, peas, peaches, carrots, apples, and other fruits and vegetables.[29]

Despite such local output, it still cost almost $100,000 each year to operate the asylum. Hughes pointed out that the costs would have been higher, except that, because of low state appropriations, he employed only one attendant for every twelve patients, when the desired ratio was one for every seven or eight. Such cost efficiency, however, was more expensive in the long term, he reasoned, since patient recoveries were less likely with such a ratio.[30]

Whether because of the attendant ratio or because patients continued to come to the asylum after years of insanity, or because of other factors, between November 30, 1868, and November 28, 1870, only 13.7 percent of Fulton's patients were discharged as "recovered," and only 10.4 percent were discharged as "improved." But, despite the prewar rhetoric about the possibility of achieving a 70 to 90 percent cure rate, the prewar recovered and improved categories were not so remarkably different: the 1852–1854 cure rate was 23.2 percent "recovered" and 3.8 percent "much improved"; the 1854–1856 rate was 20 percent recovered and 2 percent much improved; the 1856–1858 rate was 17.5 percent recovered and 4.7 percent

---

28. Ibid., 25. Gerald Grob reports that the incentive-reward system was widely used in nineteenth-century asylums (*Mad among Us*, 68).

29. Carrie McNair, Matron, "Biennial Statement of Articles Made in the Sewing Room for the Years 1869 and 1870," November 1870, *House and Senate Journals Appendix*, 26th G.A. (1871), 60; and J. E. Campbell, Steward, "Steward's Estimate of the Products of the Farm, Garden, and Dairy for 1869 and 1870," November 1870, ibid., 58.

30. Report of Superintendent, November 29, 1870, ibid., 51.

much improved; and the 1858–1860 rate was 13 percent recovered and 3.3 percent much improved.[31]

By 1871, those low recovery rates occurred even though Superintendent Hughes believed that knowledge of the causes of insanity had measurably progressed. Citing studies from other state institutions as well as his own experience, he identified two groups of causes of insanity: direct causes and indirect causes. In the direct category he listed physical injuries to the brain caused by a fall or a blow. Also, it was believed that any irritation of the spine or any part of the nervous system, such as a toothache, a rusty nail in the foot, or neuralgia, might cause insanity. Poisons such as tobacco, alcohol, and other stimulants, when habitually used, could cause insanity. Additionally, "retained bile, urea, carbon, etc., and many salts, are poisons to the blood and brain and must be regularly carried out of the system, or they will react upon and derange it. Diseases, therefore, of the physical organs, the lungs, bowels, kidneys, liver and spleen, which carry off these poisonous elements, may cause insanity."[32]

Joining the direct causes Hughes cited were experiences and surroundings that impaired one's physical health, including improper diet, excessive joy or anger, sudden fright, unrequited love, unsatisfied avarice, fear, sorrow, and vicious indulgences and dissipations. Intemperance, especially, had a "fatally destructive power." An individual who concentrated his mind too long without diversion on a particular problem or issue also could induce insanity.[33]

Among the "indirect" causes was one over which the patient had no control—heredity: "Hereditary transmission of constitutional defects in the parents, such as insanity, rickets, epilepsy and intemperance," Hughes explained, "are very common causes of insanity. No truth is clearer than that the physical defects and diseases of parents, resulting from unbridled lusts and passions, are visited upon, and intensified in their children, even to the third and fourth generations."[34]

Whether Hughes's analysis of the causes of insanity were shared by mid-Missourians is not clear, but he seemed unusually sensitive to their perceptions of his institution. He warned legislators that they should not listen to

31. 1868–1870: Report of Superintendent, November 29, 1870, ibid., 8. 1852–1854: Report of Superintendent, November 27, 1854, *Senate Journal Appendix*, 18th G.A. (1854/1855), 50. 1854–1856: Report of Superintendent, no date, *House Journal Appendix*, 19th G.A. (1856/1857), 60. 1856–1858: Report of Superintendent, no date, *Senate Journal Appendix*, 20th G.A. (1858/1859), 332. 1858–1860: Report of Superintendent, no date, *House Journal Appendix*, 21st G.A. (1860/1861), 545.

32. Report of Superintendent, November 29, 1870, *House and Senate Journals Appendix*, 26th G.A. (1871), 24–25.

33. Ibid., 25.

34. Ibid.

the stories of escaped or unrecovered patients: "Their testimony is often unfavorable. They do not feel kindly towards those who have restrained them, or urged medicines upon them, or prevented them from injuring themselves or others." Nor should one listen to the views of otherwise fair-minded people who, because of the unfounded stories of former patients, claim mistreatment and cruelty. Nor should one listen to visitors whose infrequent inspections often lead to "erroneous impressions" and who may irrationally jump to conclusions about foul play on the part of relatives or courts in committing someone to the asylum.[35]

Twice between 1871 and 1873, institution leaders, including Hughes, had to convince critics that care for the insane was in fact humane at the Fulton facility. The more famous case involved the alleged mistreatment of Sterling Price Jr. in 1871, leading to his death. In November of that year, one of Price's relatives, Mr. R. B. Price of Columbia, demanded that the Board of Managers launch an investigation. The board agreed and pledged to reveal its findings by February 1872. In the interim, Price requested a legislative investigation as well. While neither investigation was open to the public, the legislative hearings did permit the attendance of members of the local press. Not surprisingly, the testimony taken during the hearings ended up in the *Fulton Telegraph*, where the editor, John Williams, and Superintendent Hughes soon engaged in a battle of interpretation of that testimony. Hughes and his staff were ultimately cleared of any wrongdoing. The final report by the Board of Managers concluded that "not one of the charges has any foundation in fact. We further find it proven to our satisfaction that the patients in the asylum are uniformly treated with kindness and with great care both by the Superintendent and by his assistants and attendants; and that the institution is generally well conducted, and especially so in respect to the care and kindness bestowed upon the patients."[36]

Almost exactly one year later, in November 1873, the board received another demand for an investigation; this time it was the alleged mistreatment of William Weber. The charges of neglect, cruelty, and mistreatment included assertions that the staff allowed Weber's toes to be frozen during the winter and that they allowed his head and beard to remain full of vermin. While the board did acknowledge that Weber's toes were frostbitten, they concluded that the staff had made every effort to keep the patient warm but that, upon their departure on an especially cold night, he had discarded his six blankets and suffered the consequences. While the testimony did confirm

---

35. Ibid., 52.
36. See *Fulton Telegraph* between February 23 and March 8, 1872; Journal State Lunatic Asylum: Board of Managers Minutes (December 28, 1866–July 7, 1874), February 28, 1872, 135 (FSHA).

that some vermin did live in his beard and hair, they were insufficient to justify any blame or censure of the superintendent or staff.[37]

Following these two investigations, the consensus of Missouri officials was that the asylum personnel were providing the best care possible with the resources available from the counties and the state. For the hospital administrators, that welcome conclusion capped a decade of successes that saw the institution slowly recover from devastating Civil War setbacks. Nevertheless, despite those successes, a battle that had begun in 1869 between Superintendent Hughes and his board signaled trouble ahead.

37. Journal State Lunatic Asylum, January 7–8, 1873, 191–93.

4
Administration Gridlock and Recovery, 1869–1897

While hospital staff and administrators had been cleared of any wrongdoing or neglect in the Price and Weber investigations, visitors to the asylum did blame them for the sewage odor that often pervaded the halls of the wards as well as the administrative areas. By the early 1870s, the original twenty- to twenty-two-inch sewer lines were overwhelmed with waste. Water closets overflowed, sewer gases seemed ever-present, and the smell from the main basements was fetid. They had become reservoirs of sewage and drainage waters over the years; when the basements were eventually cleared in 1874, they contained mire two feet deep.

The Board of Managers had formally acknowledged those problems on December 1, 1868. But a tug-of-war between Superintendent Hughes and the Board of Managers forced patients and employees alike for an additional five years to cope with this "ventilation problem." Their ongoing dispute eventually led to a formal legislative investigation of the financial management of the institution and to the removal of several board members by the governor and their subsequent reinstatement following a court order.

In the waning days of 1868, no one, however, foresaw the personal and political battle that was to so complicate day-to-day asylum operations, including decisions about sewage and ventilation. At its December 1 meeting, the Board of Managers had voted to renew Hughes's contract, first approved on February 28, 1867. The only debate was whether the contract should be renewed for five or ten years. Those favoring a five-year contract, to run from January 1, 1869, to December 31, 1873, won.[1]

1. Journal State Lunatic Asylum: Board of Managers Minutes (December 28, 1866–July 7, 1874), December 1, 1868, 29 (FSHA).

Exactly what prompted the estrangement between Hughes and the board is unclear, although there is no doubt that within two months of his contract renewal, the board began to micromanage the institution. On March 30, 1869, the board established a subcommittee—composed of members from Callaway County: William Thomas, Hiram Cornell, and a Mr. Newsom—to oversee all acquisitions, except for liquor and medicine. At the same time, it created a second subcommittee, composed of the three board members who were themselves physicians—James Martien, Wesley Humphrey, and Chas. Stevens—to oversee all liquor and medicine acquisitions. The subcommittees supplanted the normal purchase process overseen, in the first instance, by the steward, with the superintendent's approval, and in the second instance, by the superintendent. The board also stipulated that its Callaway subcommittee would have supervisory control of the employees of the institution, a power heretofore exercised by the superintendent. Just as it undercut the superintendent's purchasing and supervisory authority and circumscribed his ability to determine what liquors and medicines should be purchased for patients, so too did it further undercut the superintendent's and steward's authority to manage farm operations. At the same meeting, the board granted the Callaway subcommittee the power "to employ a competent hand by the month subject to their control and removal at anytime to take charge of and work the farm and garden of the asylum."[2]

At the end of June, the board, by a four-to-three vote, agreed to end its supervisory control of employees, "having accomplished the purpose for which it was made."[3] At the same meeting, members reported that the former steward had been terminated and a new steward would be sought. Clearly the board was concerned about the financial expenditures of the institution. On April 1 it had required the steward to purchase items from the lowest bidder. The close vote, however, indicated that a minority of the board still believed that supervisory authority ought to be retained by the board's subcommittee rather than returning it to the superintendent and his staff.

For almost a year, the new system appeared to be working. But in April 1870, following the failure of the Missouri General Assembly to approve the funding request submitted by the superintendent and the board, the board adopted a resolution urging upon the superintendent and steward "the imperative necessity of strict economy and most untiring efforts on their part

---

2. The preceding discussion of the relationship between Superintendent Hughes and the Board of Managers was based on Journal State Lunatic Asylum: Board of Managers Minutes (December 28, 1866–July 7, 1874), entries between 1868 and 1871 (FSHA); see pages 35–36 for the board's instructions to the subcommittee.

3. Ibid., June 22, 1869, 45. In favor were Chas. Stevens, John P. Clark, Wesley Humphrey, and Hiram Cornell; in opposition were James Martien, "Newsom" (whose first name remains unknown), and William Thomas.

to husband the small means at our command in the purchase only of such articles of consumption as necessity demands compatible with the good of the inmates."[4] Hughes did not perceive this as a collegial request, but one that implied criticism of his handling of the financial operations of the asylum—which, given subsequent events, it probably was.

Hughes had not been idle during this period. He proposed to the Missouri Senate a new bill to prevent conflict-of-interest issues from emerging in construction-purchase decisions made by members of the Board of Managers. The legislature, he argued, should enact a law that stipulated that "no Manager shall be interested in any building or other contract, or in the purchase or sale of any building material or article of supply for the use of the asylum, or be eligible to any office of the asylum during his term of office as manager of said asylum or within one year thereafter."[5]

Hughes subsequently cited three reasons for his proposal. First, had such a law been in place when he had first been hired in 1867, or even when he was rehired in 1868, the reputations of the managers and the superintendent would probably not have been sullied by charges raised by "respectable and trustworthy citizens of the town of Fulton." Responding to those charges, the General Assembly had recently dispatched a special investigative committee to determine whether "the General management of the Lunatic Asylum under its present management is working serious and dangerous results both to the state and to the inmates of the institution, [whether] the funds of the institution are being squandered foolishly, [and whether] there are gross swindles and corruptions on the part of some of the present managers." Although the committee found no substance to the complaints, Hughes argued that the episode had "cast public suspicion upon the reputations of us all."[6]

Second, Hughes argued that only four states in the Union in 1870, including Missouri, had failed to enact legislation similar to what he proposed to help insure that rumors of self-gain did not attach themselves to members of the board.[7]

Third, while the General Assembly focused on the current administration and board members, Hughes observed that residents of Fulton had believed at least since 1867 that some previous members of the Board of Managers had used their positions for personal profit, an assertion that, Hughes noted, at least two of the current managers had confirmed to him in private conversations.[8]

4. Ibid., April 14, 1870, 62.
5. Ibid., May 31, 1870, 70.
6. Ibid., June 17, 1870, 86–88.
7. Ibid.
8. Ibid.

Hughes insisted that his proposal did not reflect negatively upon any current board member's character, honesty, or integrity, and it also did not imply that any of them had committed any unlawful act or tried to use their position for personal gain in the granting of supplies contracts. However, the members of the board were offended. The strained relationship between Hughes and the board degenerated further.

On May 31, 1870, the board passed eight resolutions that "hereby ordered and required" the superintendent to respond in detail and in writing to the board, providing:

> 1. a detailed statement and explanation of the number of days he had been absent from the asylum during his entire term of office;
> 2. a detailed statement and explanation of how and why he had restricted the duties of First Assistant Physician Hamilton Shidy to the male wards only;
> 3. a listing of all body or family servants he had employed since his employment at the asylum, together with an accounting of how much and in what manner they were paid;
> 4. a full accounting of all expenditures relating to the repair of the farm house;
> 5. a full accounting of all expenditures relating to the purchase of all supplies and building materials he had made during his term of office;
> 6. a full accounting of all expenditures relating to construction of a drainage system for the north wing of the asylum;
> 7. a copy of all correspondence, both official and personal, "having reference to asylum matters, its board of managers, or individual members of said board"; and
> 8. a full response relating to his proposed bill to the Missouri Senate, particularly any evidence he had that any member of the current board had used his position for personal profit at the expense of the asylum or whose actions of any type would make him unfit to continue in his managerial position.

The board contended in the eight resolutions that Hughes's proposed bill to the Senate "is a reflection upon the character, honesty and integrity of the Board of Managers, or individual members thereof, and is calculated to create the impression that corrupt, improper, and unlawful acts have been committed and carried on by the said Board, or individual members thereof." Hughes had until June 8 to reply.[9]

When the board convened on June 8, it lacked a quorum, so it rescheduled its meeting to the seventeenth. At that meeting, Superintendent Hughes read his responses to the board. Brief excerpts of his responses to

---

9. Ibid., 68–72.

Administration Gridlock and Recovery

selected issues during his presentation reveal the deepening animosity between him and the board.

> ISSUE 1: "I derive my authority to absent myself from the asylum whenever its interests may be subserved thereby, from the law of the State which makes the Superintendent the chief executive office of the asylum and assigns him the care and control of everything connected therewith, subject ONLY [his emphasis] to the rules, regulations and laws of the asylum, there being nothing in any rule, regulation or by-law of the asylum prohibiting the Superintendent from leaving the asylum, whenever in his judgment, it may be necessary. . . . The law requires the managers as well as the Superintendent to conform to the law."
>
> ISSUE 2: "[As to Dr. Shidy,] I have a right by your authority to assign him to any duty connected with the medical department. Dr. Shidy is in duty bound to attend to the patients . . . as I may choose to require without the assignment of any reasons, on my part, to the Board. . . ."
>
> ISSUE 3: "You have nothing to do with the number of my body or family servants. . . . This is a private matter over which you have no control. . . ."
>
> ISSUE 5: [Refuting the implication that he had improperly taken control of building purchases from the Steward:] "The duty of purchasing building material in improvements and special purposes has not been and is not imposed upon the Steward. . . . The duty would, and does devolve upon me by authority of law as the Chief Executive Officer. . . . I answer that I have never relieved the Steward of any of his lawful duties. . . ."
>
> ISSUE 7: "I keep no copies of personal or private letters written by myself, and if I did, I would not produce them. This board has not the authority to compel me, or the right to ask me to make known with what members of the General Assembly, I may sustain, or may have sustained confidential personal relations."
>
> ISSUE 8: "The bill is not a reflection upon any body's character, honesty, or integrity, and is not calculated to, and did not create the impression that corrupt and unlawful acts have been committed or carried on by the Board of Managers or individual members thereof. [However,] Captain Hiram Cornell, one of the present managers has been a paid employee of the asylum, acting by your order in the capacity of Superintendent of Improvements. It is not within my province to pass upon the fitness, or unfitness of employees of the Board, but I answer, since you demand an answer, that in my opinion, a careful examination of the asylum records of expenditures made by and under the direction of Capt. Cornell, and of labor performed by and under his direction and supervision, would satisfy your honorable body that he has (to say the least) been an unprofitable servant."

Hughes then cited several examples where Cornell's supervision of construction projects was shoddy and unacceptable, even though he charged between 10–25 percent of total project costs for overseeing those projects, "rather more I think than a skillful architect and Supt would have asked for his services."

Having concluded his responses, Hughes then reflected upon the board's preemptory demands:

> Permit me to say that I regard these resolutions as ridiculous and frivolous, and drafted on the part of one or more of your members in a malignant, hasty, and ungenerous spirit, and upon the supposition that your Superintendent has no rights which you are bound to respect. They evidence an unwarrantable and unpardonable disregard of the law and the recorded acts and precedents of the Board. . . .
>
> These resolutions are hardly such as should emanate from a body of wise, honorable, and prudent men, such as you are presumed to be, seeking only after truth from an official servant. They savor of hate and passion. You have not calmly reasoned together. . . . You cannot divide the duties assigned by law to the Supt with any other officer or person, nor can you lawfully assume them yourselves. . . . The law is against you and you are against yourselves in your acts. . . . I am worthy of honorable treatment. The law accords it to me and so should the consciences of those of you who wish to be regarded as men.
>
> Convince me that I am unworthy to longer continue as your Superintendent and I will resign . . . but until you do that, I must remain where you have placed me, for the rest of my term of office, or until you shall be strong enough in numbers, and in the law, to remove me.[10]

And so the war between Superintendent Hughes and the board deepened. Nevertheless, by December 1870, following its preliminary examination of Hughes's management, a divided board, by a 4-2-1 vote, concluded that there was insufficient evidence to justify his removal. In February, the governor intervened, removing Managers Dr. James Martien, Hiram Cornell, and William Thomas, and appointing in their place A. C. Stewart, Nathan L. Rice, and William H. Bailey to complete their unexpired terms. Cornell and Thomas immediately filed suit against the governor in the Circuit Court of Callaway County, arguing that he lacked the power to remove them from office before the regular end of their term in March 1873. However, until a court ruled otherwise, the governor's appointments were legal members of the board. Dr. Hughes, probably to confirm his apparent victory, submitted his resignation to the reconstituted board. The response was immediate: The board unanimously requested that Hughes withdraw his

10. Ibid., 75–93.

resignation and remain as superintendent. He agreed. The board, however, accepted, indeed expedited, the resignation of First Assistant Physician Shidy and accepted Dr. Hughes's nominee for the position. It appeared, therefore, that Hughes, with the assistance of the governor, had prevailed.[11]

The battle for control of the asylum, however, resumed in February and April 1872. Concerned about the financial management of the institution and probably aware of the charges and countercharges made by Hughes and some members of the board, the General Assembly ordered a special investigation into all financial expenditures during 1871. Weeks later, the Circuit Court of Callaway ruled that the governor of Missouri had acted illegally in removing Cornell and Thomas and that they must be reinstated to the board, while the governor's appointees must be removed. On May 29, Superintendent Hughes submitted his resignation; this time the board, with Cornell and Thomas as reinstated members, accepted it, effective immediately.[12]

The members of the joint legislative committee who investigated the financial operations of the institution for the year 1871 were so disgusted with every one of the administrators at the asylum, including the superintendent, assistant physicians, steward, matron, and Board of Managers, that they recommended to the General Assembly that it pass a bill "ousting and removing the superintendent and resident officers of the asylum and also the entire Board of Managers from office and [launch] the entire reorganization of the institution." The financial records of the institution were distinctly unsatisfactory, preventing the committee from determining how legislative appropriations had been spent. The fault was clearly systemic, not the failure of just one or two individuals. While the General Assembly refused to authorize a clean sweep of personnel, it did order the current Board of Managers to conduct a detailed evaluation of legislative appropriations for 1871, together with a detailed accounting of how those funds were expended. Concluding its evaluation in November 1872, the board was forced to admit to the legislature that the asylum had overspent the legislative appropriation of $57,000 in 1871 by $12,425.88. However, the board insisted that "said expenditures were absolutely necessary."[13] Until it received the

11. The December 1870 vote was split thus: Yes: Humphrey, Clark, Thomas, John Gamble; No: Edwin Parker, Cornell; Not voting: Martien. Journal State Lunatic Asylum, March 30–31, 1871, 110–112A.

12. The board recorded the court's ruling. See ibid., 109–10. Dr. Martien did not join in the suit against the governor. For Hughes's resignation, see the entry for May 29, 1872, 144. In the initial vote, the following voted to accept Hughes's resignation: [unknown first name] Donelan, Humphrey, Thomas, T. B. Harris, and Clark; voting not to accept were Walter Lenoir and Cornell. A second vote was unanimous.

13. The committee report and recommendations were inserted into the Journal State Lunatic Asylum, 158–60. For the board admission, see the entry of November 25, 1872, 167–68.

next legislative appropriations, the board reported that it would issue warrants to creditors—promises to pay as soon as monies had been received. In the interim, it would pay an interest rate on the warrants equal to 10 percent per year.

Under pressure, the Board of Managers decided to modify its bylaws. While the superintendent would continue to determine the kind, quality, and quantity of needed supplies and would continue to supervise the steward in their acquisition, the steward no longer could secure supplies in any given week costing over $150 except by issuing a contract and except with the express authorization by two members of the Board of Managers.

Nor could those contracts be issued quickly or quietly. No contract could be issued until a public notification—"advertised for three weeks in the weekly papers in Fulton"—had described the kind, quality, and quantity of supplies required. While these changed bylaws did not stipulate that contracts must be awarded to the lowest bidder, or that the bids had to be sealed and opened at one time, those indeed had become the practices of the asylum by the summer of 1873.[14] Because the minutes of the Board of Managers for the remainder of the century have been lost or destroyed, it is not clear whether subsequent boards followed these 1873 purchasing practices.

Having narrowly avoided the firing of all hospital leaders, including themselves, members of the board were highly motivated to hire a new superintendent who had an unblemished reputation and one with a proven record of working well with the Missouri General Assembly. As a result, the board, at its November 25 meeting, gave only cursory consideration to all but one of the applicants for superintendent. The candidate its members really wanted was former superintendent Dr. T. R. H. Smith.

The battle between Superintendent Hughes and the Board of Managers, together with the subsequent intervention of both the governor and the General Assembly in asylum operations, was a clear reminder that to be successful a superintendent had to be not only a good administrator and a good physician, but also a leader sensitive to political realities. Smith had already established a record at Fulton of possessing all three of these essential traits. Therefore, to help convince him to resign his position as superintendent of the St. Louis asylum, and to return to Fulton where he could refurbish the asylum's tarnished public and political image, they offered him a five-year contract and a salary of $3,000, $500 more than they had originally intended to offer. He accepted.

Smith returned to an institution that was under extensive renovation due to a special appropriation of over $46,000. New boilers were being installed,

---

14. Journal State Lunatic Asylum, February 28, 1872, 133–34. For examples of the bidding process, see entries of May 27, 1873, and July 1, 1873, 238–46.

walls and floors were being refurbished, the reservoir was being enlarged, and the laundry and ventilation systems were being upgraded. Nevertheless, he faced an institution that was, in the view of the Board of Managers, "in a crippled condition, with a large debt hanging over it."[15] County governments were simply not making their payments as required by law, but they were still sending their patients to Fulton. Furthermore, when the asylum sued for recovery in the courts, the State Supreme Court eventually ruled that the asylum lacked the power to coerce payments.

Overcrowding had been a clear problem for administrators in the first three-quarters of 1872, but by late fall, the opening of State Lunatic Asylum No. 2 at St. Joseph had eased the pressure. As soon as was feasible, Fulton transferred twenty-two patients to that new facility. Even so, Fulton still held 315 patients. Smith, as he had before the war, continued to believe that if patients were brought to the asylum within three months of the onset of insanity, 80 percent of them could be cured. But once insanity had lasted over a year, curable rates rarely exceeded 20 percent. Unfortunately, the majority of Fulton's patients fell in the latter category. Of the 338 patients housed there in November 1874, Smith believed that 86 percent were unlikely to be cured.[16]

In his first year back at the Fulton asylum, Smith discovered the worst case of self-inflicted injury he had seen in his long career. The patient, who committed suicide, also revealed the difficulty in determining when patients were cured. Just days before she was to be released, the patient took a pair of old, rusty scissors, with both points broken off, inside a water closet. "She caught the flesh of the abdomen between the fingers of one hand and continued cutting with the other till she penetrated the cavity. She then cut in a line downwards five or six inches, drew out the small intestines and severed piece after piece, till the whole nearly filled an ordinary wash basin. She lived between eleven and twelve hours."[17] Smith reassured the legislature that her death could not have been anticipated nor prevented. Despite the best of care and diligence, he lamented, suicides would likely be a reality in this as in all other such institutions throughout the nation.

There was another problem, however, which Smith insisted could be corrected. In 1873, the national gathering of superintendents of insane asylums in Baltimore approved a resolution condemning the practice adopted by so many state legislatures, including Missouri's, of incarcerating the criminally insane in a regular hospital for the insane.[18] The criminally insane,

15. Report of Board of Managers, no date, *House and Senate Journals*, Appendix, 28th G.A. (1875), 13.
16. Ibid.
17. Ibid., 39.
18. The resolution is quoted in ibid., 46.

they reasoned, should be held neither in penitentiaries as regular criminals nor in insane hospitals alongside noncriminal patients. Rather, the superintendents urged, each state should construct a special hospital for the criminally insane. At no time should the criminally insane be treated in the wards of a regular hospital for the insane, or even in a separate building on the grounds of that hospital. Smith enthusiastically embraced this national recommendation and urged the Missouri General Assembly, as he had in 1858, to reverse its prewar decision to mix the criminal insane with the noncriminal and house them instead elsewhere.

To this recommendation, Smith added three others critical to the future strength of the Fulton institution: The state must reinstitute the prewar asylum property tax, must improve the physical appearance of the institution and its grounds, and must build two infirmaries, one for men and one for women.

Despite Smith's appeals, and those of Superintendent Hughes two years earlier, the General Assembly did not reverse its policy on the criminally insane until 1881, when it appropriated $15,000 to build a hospital for those patients. That facility, built to the southeast of the main building and under the supervision of the superintendent and the Board of Managers, received its first fourteen patients in June 1882. Its construction meant the addition of another physician, thereafter known as the "Third Assistant," whose duty it was to oversee the patients in the new wing.[19]

The legislature did not reestablish an asylum tax nor allow the hospital to increase the county rate per week above the $2.50 authorized in the last years of the Civil War. Smith and his board had argued that requiring counties to pay for the institutionalization of their poor frequently meant that counties delayed doing so until absolutely necessary, thereby preventing the mentally ill from reaching the asylum within the first three months of the onset of their illness. If the asylum received a patient who had been mentally ill for longer than three months, they believed that the possibility for cure dropped precipitously. They also argued that the poor at Fulton were often stigmatized by the paying patients, thereby harming their recovery process. Finally, they argued that a permanent asylum tax would allow for sounder planning and management.[20] None of these arguments, however, proved effective in convincing the legislature to establish either an asylum

---

19. Report of Board of Managers, January 1, 1883, *House and Senate Journals Appendix*, 32nd G.A. (1883), 10–12; and Report of Superintendent, no date, ibid., 29–30.

20. Report of Superintendent, no date, ibid., 29th G.A. (1877), 19–50; and Report of Board of Managers, no date, ibid., 7–16. See also Smith to Governor Silas Woodson, December 11, 1873, Governor Silas Woodson Papers, box 21, folder 9, MSA. The financial crisis facing the Fulton asylum in the decades following the Civil War was not unusual. South Carolina's lunatic asylum suffered similar problems. See McCandless, *Moonlight, Magnolias, and Madness*, 222–34.

tax or higher county rates. Their appeal did, however, lead to one victory—the legislature adopted a measure that effectively forced counties to pay their bills on time to the asylum.

Something else the superintendents had kept requesting was funding to create a more parklike setting at the hospital grounds. Why should the governor and the General Assembly support the creation of a more aesthetic environment at Fulton? "The first impression of patients in approaching an asylum," Smith reasoned, "are generally the most lasting and should therefore be of the most pleasant character. If everything should indicate a supreme desire on our part to contribute to their enjoyment and happiness, we secure, at once, their confidence and affection, which become a source of influence and power that constitute an essential element in the most successful treatment."[21] But the legislature remained unconvinced.

Similarly, the General Assembly was not swayed by Smith's logic on the need for two infirmaries, one for each wing, or Hughes's alternative in 1870 for one infirmary with two wards, one for women and one for men. They had urged the legislature to act so as to provide seriously ill patients an airy, quiet, and well-ventilated room, separate from the regular noise and confusion of the wards. Such separate facilities would also allow the institution to segregate those with contagious diseases. Not until the early twentieth century would the legislature finally agree to fund the infirmaries.

Finally, the General Assembly ignored Smith's complaints year after year that the asylum was becoming overcrowded. By 1881, because of a fire at the St. Joseph facility, the Fulton hospital housed 507 patients, although it had been renovated to handle only 350. Even though patients were placed two to a room and the parlors were converted into rooms, patients still had to sleep in the corridors. But even without the special overcrowding in 1881, Fulton's facility was bursting at the seams. In a lengthy letter to Governor Silas Woodson in December 1873, Smith complained that "so great has been the demand for admissions, during the last two months, we have been compelled to discharge some of our most unpromising cases of long standing to make room, as the law requires, for those of recent date (less than 12 months duration)."[22] He assured the governor, however, that those discharged were the "most quiet and harmless" patients. While lamenting the necessity for this practice, Smith reminded the governor that it was more humane to accept patients who had a chance of being cured rather than those beyond hope of a cure.

By the early 1880s, he urged the General Assembly to make suitable provision for all the insane of Missouri. There was, he warned, a dangerous

---

21. Smith to Woodson, December 11, 1873, Woodson Papers.
22. Ibid.

Despite the tremendous debate over the best way to treat the mentally ill, the campus was a popular place to visit. Here, bicycle riders pass the Museum Hall, designed by M. F. Bell, circa 1880 (Kingdom of Callaway Historical Society).

trend among the causes of insanity. The nine leading causes, in descending order, among the patients admitted to Fulton, were heredity, menstrual irregularities, masturbation, puerperal (diseases associated with childbirth and its immediate aftermath), domestic troubles, grief, religious anxiety, intemperance, and malaria. The increase of masturbation admissions in the late 1870s and early 1880s, however, particularly bothered Smith: "I very much fear this pernicious habit, with all its withering influence upon mind and body, prevails among the young of both sexes to an alarming extent. . . . The expenditure and exhaustion of nerve power, resulting from the frequent repetition of this habit, and the constant excitation to which the brain is thus exposed, slowly and permanently damage the delicate nerve cells, the supreme centers of life, and so wreck the unfortunate subjects, physically and mentally, as renders them among the saddest of the hopeless."[23] By 1887, masturbation was listed as the second most important cause of insanity at Fulton, preceded only by heredity.

The superintendent's growing preoccupation with masturbation was

23. Report of Superintendent, no date, *House and Senate Journals Appendix*, 29th G.A. (1875/1876), 31–32.

shared by many asylum physicians across the nation. In 1766 Swiss physician S. A. A. D. Tissot's study, *Onanism: A Study of the Illnesses Caused by Masturbation*, had raised the alarm. Benjamin Rush echoed those concerns by the early nineteenth century in the United States. Medical casebooks and professional journals throughout the nineteenth century also repeatedly warned that masturbation contributed to the development of mental illness.[24]

Having served as superintendent at the Fulton asylum off and on during its first thirty-four years, Smith died "in harness" on December 21, 1885, the masturbation issue unresolved. His successes, however, far outnumbered his failures. Perhaps most importantly, in his second thirteen years of service, he had taken a hospital with significant debt and had made it debt-free while continuing to emphasize the asylum as a compassionate, curative institution. Despite repeated efforts, however, he had not managed to convince the General Assembly to authorize a much-needed renovation and expansion of the entire facility. That victory would belong to his successor, W. R. Rodes, who, working with architect M. F. Bell, would oversee a significant expansion and renovation in the late 1880s that allowed the patient population to rise significantly—to approximately 540–550 by 1889.[25] By literally raising the roof several feet, Bell's renovation not only dramatically altered the external architectural profile of the facility, but also opened more spacious wards on the fourth floor for patients.

Despite the dramatic change in external appearances, no such transformation occurred in the rate of patient recovery. Dr. Rodes and his staff saw their recovery rates decline to 13.2 percent of those admitted between 1886 and 1888.[26] Gone was the prewar optimism that touted high cure rates. Replacing it was a view shared by many physicians treating the insane that recovery was not likely for the vast majority of those admitted to the asylums. New York's legislature had formally acknowledged that reality as early as 1869 when it opened Willard State Hospital for patients whom no one thought would ever be cured or released.

Why had asylums failed to achieve the optimistic cure rates frequently touted when they were established? Neither medical personnel of the late nineteenth century nor modern historians can provide a definitive answer. In 1877, asylum superintendent and author Pliny Earle, one of the original thirteen founders of the American Institutions for the Insane over three decades earlier, asserted that the moral treatment philosophy—removing the ill to asylums located in idyllic settings, providing a systematic regimen

---

24. Grob, *Mad among Us*, 60; and Gamwell and Tomes, *Madness in America*, 111.
25. Report of Superintendent, no date, *House and Senate Journals Appendix*, 36th G.A. (1891), 8.
26. Report of Superintendent, no date, ibid., 35th G.A. (1889), 8.

including opportunities to work, and providing incentives to patients to behave properly—had never been successful, despite repeated assertions to the contrary. In his judgment, many asylum superintendents had inflated cure figures to deflect criticism, to secure financial assistance, and to solidify public support. Given Fulton's reported low recovery rates, perhaps this criticism should not apply to its administrators in those decades following the Civil War.

Earle's attack on the effectiveness of moral treatment sparked a heated debate among asylum administrators. Led by Thomas Kirkbride, a fellow-founder of the AMSAII, moral treatment supporters rejected Earle's criticisms. Nevertheless, in 1880 moral treatment critics established the National Association for the Protection of the Insane and the Prevention of Insanity. Its very title reflected two important assaults upon the asylum's image—that the asylum insane needed someone from outside the institution to protect them, and that prevention was a better goal than institutionalization that sought cures that were unlikely to be found. Although this organization survived only a few years, a much more influential and successful organization replaced it in 1909, the National Committee for Mental Hygiene.

The modern psychiatrist Thomas Szasz also argues, although for different reasons, that moral treatment had always been a failure. In his judgment the combination of charity with coercion and regimentation could only lead to patients' resentment of the asylum, their growing sense of dependence and not independence, and their determination to resist the loss of identity, leading to even further rounds of coercion, regulation, resentment, and resistance.[27]

The steady rise of the numbers of chronically ill, coupled with depressingly low recovery rates, led to such growing criticism that the best and brightest physicians shunned the asylum. Additional influential factors impacting one's career choice, in addition to the surging patient population rates and the growing wave of internal and external criticism, included facilities constantly short of money and in physical decline, the too-frequent absence of creative medical opportunities, and a dull medical routine compounded by too few physicians serving too many patients.

Many historians now concede that, for these reasons, by the late 1880s and after, more and more insane asylums simply made custodianship of patients—not cure—their focus. Indeed, Edward Shorter, in his *History of Psychiatry*, concludes, "by 1900, psychiatry had reached a dead end. Its practitioners were concentrated for the most part in asylums, and asylums had become mainly warehouses in which any hope of therapy was illusory. Psychiatrists themselves had a rather poor reputation among their medical col-

---

27. Szasz, *Cruel Compassion*, xii.

leagues as the dull and the second rate."[28] Somewhat ironically, it was at the same time that nurses and physicians saw more opportunities for formal training in treatment of the insane. The first permanent training school for nurses of the insane, for example, opened in 1882 in Massachusetts.

Whether most asylum officials were "second-rate" by the late nineteenth century, or whether, as historian Gerald Grob asserts, administrators and physicians too frequently saw asylum employment as a sinecure requiring little imagination and imposing few demands or burdens, most historians agree that rhetoric about curing patients seemed to decline precipitously in the late nineteenth century.[29] Asylums more frequently were viewed as custodial warehouses where growing numbers of the incurable gathered. Drug use became increasingly popular—not as a means to cure but as a means to provide momentary relief or to simply keep the patients quiet and under control. To meet drug demand in the last decades of the century, entrepreneurs launched new companies or, as in the case of Bayer in 1888, simply opened a pharmaceutical division. In addition to the growing dependence on drugs was an increasing reliance upon restraints as a way to control patients, to enforce discipline and order, and to serve as a substitute for therapy.

However unpromising the possibility of curing a patient appeared to be, the number of patients needing treatment seemed to grow ever larger. By the early 1890s, Fulton was adding new wards, an icehouse, and a larger chapel and was converting its old gymnasium into two wards capable of housing fifty patients. This still was not sufficient. In 1893, Superintendent R. S. Wilson also urged the construction of new fire escapes, several airing pavilions for open-air exercise and sunbaths, and workshops that would allow patients to produce mattresses, brooms, rugs, and shoes. By 1895, he urged the creation of a hospital on campus to serve the 563 patients and, perhaps, the 106 employees. He also requested funding for a morgue and pathological laboratory that would allow the asylum's physicians to conduct autopsies and microscopic examinations in order to advance knowledge in the pathology and morbid history of mental diseases.[30]

Wilson's request for workshops reflected his belief that using patients as laborers at the institution was not only good therapy but also allowed the asylum to reduce its annual expenses. In that respect, he mirrored the thinking of his predecessors. However, in one crucial regard, he rejected a principle that had guided T. R. H. Smith throughout his years as superintendent: Wilson no longer considered his attendants critical partners in the care of patients. Therefore, attendants no longer needed careful or lengthy in-

28. Shorter, *History of Psychiatry*, 65.
29. Ibid., 65; Grob, *State and the Mentally Ill*, 199.
30. Report of Superintendent, no date, *House and Senate Journals Appendix*, 37th G.A. (1893); Report of Superintendent, no date, ibid., 38th G.A. (1895).

The chapel was an early addition to the asylum campus. This photo was taken in 1903 (Missouri State Archives).

struction in the care of those patients. At the same time, Wilson and his fellow Missouri physicians of the state's insane asylums had intensified their efforts to share ideas and work together to determine the best way of handling patients. Indeed, their first joint meetings, together with members of their boards of managers, began in the mid-1890s at the suggestion of Dr. Gustav Ettmueller, one of Fulton's Board of Managers. Whether these changes were actually beneficial or whether the criteria for defining recovery had changed, by 1897 newly appointed Superintendent J. L. Warden reported a 42 percent recovery rate of those admitted during the last two years at Fulton, by far the highest in the hospital's history.[31] If those figures were accurate and could be maintained, then perhaps the late-nineteenth-century pessimists who envisioned asylums as caretaker institutions were wrong after all.

31. Report of Superintendent, no date, ibid., 38th G.A. (1895), 27; Report of Superintendent, November 30, 1896, ibid., 39th G.A. (1897), 16.

5

"To the Victors Belong the Spoils"
Asylum Patronage, 1872-1923

The Board of Managers' victory over Superintendent Hughes in 1872 occurred despite the governor's support of the superintendent. Its members realized that their victory had been a narrow one, due to judicial intervention rather than to the board's own power. As a result, the political skills of T. R. H. Smith became an important factor in his rehiring in the winter of 1872-1873. But while his skills enabled him to ease the anger of state legislators toward hospital leaders, he failed to convince the General Assembly to make appropriations he deemed vital to the institution's well-being. As the experiences of both Hughes and Smith clearly demonstrated, the governor and the General Assembly, either by the power of political appointment or by their control of the purse strings, could determine the fate of the institution.

Politics, therefore, remained paramount in the operation of the asylum despite the Hughes affair. Asylum job applicants petitioned the governor, boards petitioned and complained to the governor, and constituents placed before the governor the names of friends and colleagues who should, in their judgment, be hired or appointed. At the Fulton asylum, as at any other state institution, there were always numerous opportunities to exercise patronage. Members of the asylum's board were nominated by the governor and confirmed by the Senate. Governors could nominate members without consulting anyone, and normally they could use the process to satisfy influential individuals or constituencies. The board would then select the superintendent, physicians, and, normally, the steward and matron. Those individuals would then choose other employees. The Board of Managers, working with the superintendent and the steward, also authorized the purchase of services

Asylum nurses, circa 1914 (Kingdom of Callaway Historical Society).

and supplies for the institution, which presented perfect opportunities to reward political friends and penalize those out of favor or those who held the wrong political views.[1]

While the Hughes case demonstrated that there were times when members of the Board of Managers and the governor clashed over the appointment of members of the board because of their stand on controversial issues, at other times, confrontation occurred for more practical reasons. In January 1871, for example, in the midst of the struggle at Fulton, the Board of Managers' secretary wrote to Governor B. Gratz Brown complaining of his recommendation that Dr. S. H. Melcher of St. Louis be added to the board. His complaint, however, hinged on the practical operation of the board and on the sense of local ownership of its members, rather than on Melcher's particular qualifications:

> I respectfully beg leave to call your attention to the following facts.
>
> 1st. It is important for the proper conduct and management of the institution to have at least a quorum of the Board at Fulton, or at such convenient distance from the institution as to make it practicable to convene a quorum at short notice, in cases of emergency.
>
> 2nd. The members of the present Board are distributed as follows: Two at Mexico. One at Saint Charles, two at Saint Louis, two at Fulton . . . and one four miles from Fulton.
>
> 3rd. Members of the Board receive no compensation for their services as Managers. It is unreasonable to ask or expect those living at a

---

1. To see how politics and patronage impacted another late-nineteenth-century state asylum, see McCandless, *Moonlight, Magnolias, and Madness*, 235–48.

distance to visit the institution and attend the business meetings of the Board, as often as is desirable and necessary.

4th. The traveling expenses of the distant members of the Board must be defrayed out of the asylum funds. Economy to the state therefore suggests the propriety of appointing managers who reside convenient to the institution.

5th. Saint Louis County has an insane asylum of its own. Citizens of that county cannot be expected to take a deep interest in the State Asylum. One of the Saint Louis members of the Board made but one visit to the institution during the past year, and the other Saint Louis member, at the annual meeting in November, declared it to be his intention to make but one visit during the present year.

6th. The Statutes prescribe that "two of the managers shall together visit the asylum monthly; a majority of them together quarterly; and all of them together make one visit during the year." In consequence of the non attendance of distant members these monthly visits are either neglected or devolve upon the few members located near the institution.

7th. I am not aware that any of the Board have been consulted with regard to the appointment of Dr. Melcher. I think I am safe in saying that a majority of them prefer the appointment of someone located near the institution.

8th. The citizens of Fulton, and the County of Callaway, take a deep interest in the institutions located there. It appears but reasonable and proper that they should have time and opportunity afforded them to lay before your excellency their views and wishes with regard to this appointment. I am of the opinion that they desire you to retain Mr. [E. R.] Parker [as a continuing Board member]—whither this be so or not, they regard their own citizens quite as capable, and trustworthy, as are the citizens of Saint Louis.

9th. Mr. Parker was appointed by your predecessor during the recess of the Senate. . . . Of course his name has not been before the Senate for confirmation. Mr. Parker, heretofore, has some four or five years experience as one of the Board of Managers. He resides in Fulton—has plenty of leisure—is a man of means, strict integrity, and excellent business qualifications. The interests of the State could not be placed in safer hands.

The object of this communication is to induce you to withdraw the name of Dr. Melcher.[2]

This particular appeal to the governor failed; Melcher joined the board.

In August 1872, Hiram Cornell, a candidate for the position of steward at the asylum, objected to the governor's apparent intervention in the se-

---

2. Hiram Cornell to Governor B. Gratz Brown, January 25, 1871, Governor B. Gratz Brown Papers, box 1, folder 29, MSA.

lection process, normally left to the superintendent and the Board of Managers. He wrote the governor,

> I became a candidate for the position, and received the support of Dr. [W. B.] Lenoir [a member of the board], and expected also to have received the vote of Mr. [Thomas] Harris [another board member]; but it appears something was said to Mr. Harris by your Excellency, at the time you appointed Dr. Lenoir, that he, (Harris), understood to mean that in case of the appointment of Dr. Lenoir, it must be upon condition that in no case was he (Harris) to support me for Steward or any other position in the asylum.
>
> I am unwilling to believe you intended to place any restrictions upon Mr. Harris or anyone else, as a condition to this appointment; but if you did so intend, I claim it to be unfair and unjust towards me; and without any provocation or reasonable cause; and I do therefore now respectfully and earnestly request your Excellency to reconsider.[3]

Seventeen years later, similar efforts to influence gubernatorial appointments at the Fulton facility were still much in evidence. In January 1889, as Governor David Francis considered filling several vacancies at Fulton, including members of the Board of Managers, he received both solicited and unsolicited advice. One Fultonian wrote, "As per your request I send you a list of representative men of this county." But having submitted a list of seven candidates, he added: "The opinion is quite prevalent here, and in Boone Co., that the Callaway County Savings Bank will control the appointment of these boards. They have been doing so for the past twenty years, and I know to my certain knowledge, that they are making a desperate effort to do so now."[4] An owner of the Auxvasse Roller Flour and Saw Mills, a former steward at the institution, offered, unsolicited, the names of two nominees, writing, "I take the liberty of suggesting the names of two men who are competent, efficient and satisfactory to the people. . . . Sound in politics; original Francis men. Successful business men both. Honorable and honest." But he, too, then turned to the undue influence of Fulton banks. "It is the sense of the best Democrats in Callaway County that these appointments should be absolved from the Banks of Fulton. They fight each other and wrangle over the affairs of the institution frequently to the disgust of good people."[5] M. Fred Bell, architect for the renovations at the institution in the 1880s, also submitted his own list of nominees for the board positions, explaining that "we [in Fulton] naturally feel a deep anxiety in the future of

---

3. Hiram Cornell to Governor B. Gratz Brown, August 21, 1872, ibid.
4. W. A. Tiehmon to Governor David Francis, January 18, 1889, Governor David Francis Papers, box 46, folder 5, MSA.
5. E. Swon to Governor David Francis, January 29, 1889, ibid.

In 1904, the tower on the Callaway County courthouse was visible from the cattle barns on the asylum campus (Kingdom of Callaway Historical Society).

these asylums. . . . [We] earnestly desire the selection of men who will best care for the unfortunates, men of high moral and social standing."[6]

Of the names submitted by these individuals, the governor chose only one—a non-bank nominee, C. W. Jamison. Politics could be equally important in the selection of physicians. One letter to Governor Francis that same January not only emphasized the ability of a candidate as a doctor but also noted that he was "a lifelong Democrat."[7]

These sorts of patronage letters were normal. Indeed, except for the Hughes episode, gubernatorial intervention into the affairs at the Fulton asylum during its first forty-five years generally focused on the routine appointment of personnel, following the end of normal terms of employment. It was unusual for a governor, as occurred in the Hughes crisis, to fire current board members before the expiration of their term and replace them with his own personnel. By the early twentieth century, however, the removal of three board members by a governor would seem much less momentous. By 1902, for example, governors had done what the General Assembly investigative committee had wanted—but failed—to do in 1872: remove, on

---

6. Bell to Lon V. Stephens, May 8, 1889; Stephens to Governor David Francis, May 11, 1889, ibid. Bell wrote Stephens, asking him to help influence the governor. Stephens then wrote the governor, enclosing Bell's letter.

7. F. C. Oabe, Auditor, St. Louis and Hannibal Railway, to Governor David Francis, January 25, 1889, ibid.

two separate occasions, all the physicians, including the superintendents as well as some members of the Board of Managers at the Fulton asylum.

These gubernatorial actions came amid an era of vigorous debate as to the usefulness of the asylum as well as to the methods of treating or trying to cure those with mental illnesses, whether in or out of those institutions. The *Journal of Nervous and Mental Diseases*, established by neurologists in 1874, had quickly begun to question the effectiveness of asylums in treating mental illness. Paralleling this discussion of institutionalization, many physicians also began to question whether insanity was primarily caused by "moral" causes (emotions, passions, affections, and so on) or by "physical" causes (diseases, injuries, brain malfunctions, and the like). Emil Kraepelin, a German physician and author of an internationally respected text on mental illness, declared in his 1893 edition that while he had heretofore supported biological psychiatry, with its emphasis on anatomy and pathology and the use of brain postmortems to understand mental illness, he had begun to shift his emphasis to the clinical study of the living, "based on bedside observation of patients over time." By 1899, Kraepelin had also recategorized psychiatric illnesses, indicating which problems he thought were likely to be cured and which were likely to be chronic.[8]

Fulton physicians were caught up in this rethinking and reclassifying and in the debate over an asylum's treatment of the mentally ill. By 1899, for example, the superintendent's annual report to the General Assembly had abandoned its old categories of the alleged causes of insanity in favor of a new classification, broken down into "Moral Causes" and "Physical Causes."[9]

Unlike the financial controversies and personal animosities among asylum personnel of the 1870s or the normal debate over the qualifications and political loyalty of nominees for asylum positions, gubernatorial intervention into the affairs of the Fulton institution between 1897 and 1907 revolved around these debates on the nature of therapies provided to asylum patients.

While asylum supporters and physicians who sought to improve the care of the mentally ill, whether in the eighteenth or nineteenth centuries, could agree that the asylum held greater promise than the jail cell, cellar, or attic in treating mental illness, they did not always agree on the best method of treatment that should be adopted in those institutions. Those differences of opinion hinged, in part, on how one defined mental illness and what one believed to be its causes. Was mental illness biological, based significantly on heredity or brain malfunction; or was it psychosocial, based significantly on

8. Shorter, *History of Psychiatry*, 106.
9. Report of Superintendent, no date, *House and Senate Journals*, Appendix, 40th G.A. (1899).

one's environment, morality, or personal passions? Also influencing the treatment of patients was the prevailing optimism or pessimism on how many patients were likely to be cured. In Missouri in the 1840s and 1850s, asylum proponents had emphasized a potential cure rate of 90 percent. However, during the decades following the end of the Civil War, Fulton superintendents were reporting annual cure rates of under 14 percent.

Complicating the debate over appropriate treatments, whether in 1840, 1851, or 1899, were three critical factors. As early as 1851, Superintendent Smith had alerted the General Assembly of the first: The ability to cure a patient rested in part on whether that patient arrived at the asylum soon after the first signs of mental illness had appeared, or years afterward. If the bulk of an institution's patients were in the first category, then the rate of cure would likely be high; if they were in the second, the rate of cure would likely be low. Depending upon which patient population was most prevalent, the institution would focus on becoming a curative institution or a caretaker institution.

The second factor, equally important, was the ratio of staff to patients. Even if the bulk of patients arrived within the first year of illness, without adequate staff the institution could still be forced to focus on caretaking rather than cure. Many physicians in the nineteenth century, including superintendents like Smith, argued that a close doctor-patient relationship, as well as a close staff-patient relationship, was essential in effecting a cure for (or improvement in) mental illness. Even if an institution began with a good ratio of patients to physicians and staff, to remain effective it had to constantly increase its staff as the patient population grew. Meanwhile, there was no national or international consensus on the ideal ratio of staff to patients.

The third factor affecting treatment was closely related to the second: adequate funding for the institution. Without sufficient support from families or counties or a state's legislature, no state facility could provide the best service, whether its focus was on curing or caretaking. Throughout the nineteenth century in Missouri, superintendents complained that the General Assembly's appropriations, even when coupled with the counties' payments for indigent patients, were often insufficient to meet the needs of a steadily growing patient population.

Nor was there a magic formula for calculating patient population growth. A superintendent at Fulton, serving as both chief administrator and as chief physician, rarely had time to reflect on the factors influencing the demographics of insanity. Instead of studying how and why patient populations could increase, he was more often focusing on much more practical matters—hiring, budgets, and meeting the needs of current patients. Even historians of asylums and mental illness vigorously disagreed at the end of the twentieth century on those factors that led to the rapid expansion of patients in asylums across the United States one hundred years earlier. Routine population growth, they argued, did not alone account for the increased numbers of mentally ill. Did the numbers jump because the attitudes of families of the mentally ill had changed? Did they no longer see asylums as impersonal, brutal institutions? Did they no longer feel a strong obligation to care for family members themselves, no matter how time-consuming or onerous that task may be? Did the transition from a rural, agricultural society to an urban, industrial society affect attitudes toward familial support for the mentally ill? Did county or state governments have new incentives, financial or otherwise, for placing more of their inhabitants in an asylum? Were institutions now simply a convenient place to send those who deviated from the social norms of a community, using the concept of mental illness as merely a ruse? Or, as the result of a growing awareness and knowledge of mental illness, were doctors and families able to more easily recognize the signs of mental illness, and were they more convinced that sending persons to the institutions could result in a cure? Or had there been a real rise in the number of mentally ill—either as a result of biological or environmental factors?

Whatever the cause, the increase in the number of mentally ill in Missouri being sent to the asylum far exceeded the normal population growth of the state. The Fulton facility, renamed State Hospital No. 1 as other state asylums opened at St. Joseph, Nevada, and Farmington between 1876 and 1903, saw its population increase from 552 in 1886, to 905 in 1900, to 1,061 in 1914, to 1,648 in 1930. A report to the General Assembly in 1931 explained that while the population of Missouri had increased 6.38 percent between the 1920 and the 1930 census, the population of the mentally ill in the four state asylums had jumped by 37 percent.[10]

Based on available records, it does not appear that Missouri systematically used the asylum to house social deviants, nor did Missouri counties have any special incentive between 1851 and 1931 to send additional patients to the state asylums. Whether in 1851 or in 1931, counties had to pay for the housing of all their indigent patients. Had the General Assembly imposed a special asylum tax on all its inhabitants, and dropped its charges to each county—a proposal urged by Superintendent Smith in the 1850s and 1870s—counties could have shipped indigent mentally ill to the asylums at no cost to themselves. But that funding mechanism was not adopted and counties had to pay for every indigent patient transported to the four asy-

10. Report of Board of Managers, State Eleemosynary Institutions, no date, *House and Senate Journals Appendix*, 56th G.A. (1931), 13.

lums. That system was indeed a break for frugal county governments. Rather than pay the state for care, the county saved money when it resisted asking the courts to classify residents as insane or mentally ill.

Family attitudes in Missouri toward the asylum and toward its own personal caretaking role of mentally ill members had certainly changed during those first eighty years of operation. Between 1886 and 1888, 29.5 percent of those admitted into the asylum were placed there by family or friends who assumed all financial support. Between 1909 and 1910, that percentage had climbed to 38.4 percent, while between 1919 and 1920, the last years these statistics were kept, the number had reached 40.1 percent.[11]

Added to these three older, much-debated factors influencing treatment in Fulton at the turn of the century was a newer vigorous debate between the allopathic and homeopathic schools of medicine. It was this debate that in 1897 and 1902 led to the most glaring exercise of patronage at Fulton by Missouri governors.

The election of Lon V. Stephens as governor of Missouri in 1896 foreshadowed a five-year struggle for control of the asylum at Fulton. Within months of election, Stephens had decided to shift the medical control at Fulton from the allopathic school of treatment to the homeopathic school. To effect this change, he selected Dr. James T. Coombs, the brother-in-law of his private secretary and a graduate from the Chicago Homeopathic College in 1890, as the physician to fill the currently open position of superintendent of the Fulton asylum. Two members of the Board of Managers at Fulton, Dr. D. H. Young, who himself wanted to be named superintendent, and Dr. M. O. Biggs, responded in March 1897 with letters of protest to physicians of Missouri and to the *Fulton Daily Sun*.[12] They denounced homeopaths as rejecting the science of medicine, demonstrated, in the physicians' view, by the homeopaths' refusal to use vaccinations and anesthetics. No homeopath, they asserted, had ever received appointment to an army, navy, or government hospital. And for good reason, according to allopathic theory: They were a threat to the health and safety of their patients.

Not only did these allopathic physicians take their case to the public, they also took it to the Missouri Senate, where they requested an appropriations amendment denying public funds to any homeopath placed at Fulton, or,

---

11. Based on data contained in Reports of Superintendents for 1886–1888, 1909–1910, and 1919–1920, contained respectively in *House and Senate Journals Appendix*, 35th G.A. (1889), 46th G.A. (1911), and 55th G.A. (1921).

12. For a fuller discussion of the struggle, see Donald H. Ewalt Jr., "Patients, Politics and Physicians: The Struggle for Control of State Lunatic Asylum No. 1, Fulton, Missouri," *Missouri Historical Review* 77, no. 2: 170–88. See also *Fulton Daily Sun*, *Fulton Weekly Gazette*, and *Fulton Telegraph*, March to May 1897.

for that matter, at any of the other asylums. While the Senate passed such an amendment, it failed passage in the House and was not included in the final bill that emerged from the conference committee.

Angered by Young and Biggs's public assault and the appeal to the General Assembly, Governor Stephens requested their immediate resignation from the Fulton Board of Managers. When they refused, he declared their positions vacant and filled them with two homeopath supporters. The reconstituted board then proceeded to name Dr. Coombs as superintendent. Upon assumption of his duties, Coombs then replaced the allopath physicians at the asylum with homeopaths. Although he would resign three years later, Fulton remained under control of the homeopaths.

The homeopathic physicians at Fulton clearly rejected the heavy reliance on drugs that had often characterized the allopathic approach at Fulton since the tenure of Superintendent Hughes in the 1870s. In his 1901 report to the General Assembly, Superintendent W. L. Ray, who had replaced Coombs, proudly proclaimed that "the use of morphine, chloral hydrate, paralydehyde, etc., is now unknown at this institution. . . . The constant use of purgatives and laxatives in large quantities has [also] been abandoned." The homeopaths had not only abolished the position of druggist, but also reemphasized the importance of patients engaging in work and entertainment. Their goal was to keep the patients calm without the use of hypnotics, and to provide them "surrounding[s] to soothe and restore the shattered nervous system and to induce natural sleep which alone is 'nature's sweet restorer.'"[13] Engaging the patients in dance, music, art, and reading, employing them on the farm or in the laundry or in any number of other institutionally available jobs, and providing them liberty of movement commensurate with their safety, the physicians believed, was a superior treatment to that provided by their allopathic, often drug-reliant predecessors.

Having lost in 1897, allopaths did not abandon the battle. Their efforts to return the Fulton asylum to their hands succeeded in March 1902 when Governor Alexander Dockery, himself a physician, used his power of patronage to oust Superintendent Ray and the homeopaths and to once again place the allopaths in control.[14]

Despite such public and controversial examples of political patronage intermixed with professional medical disagreements, not until 1921 did the Missouri General Assembly move to reduce the impact of patronage in the higher levels of management of the asylums. In the spring of that year, it passed the Eleemosynary Act, creating a single Board of Managers for six eleemosynary institutions: State Hospital No. 1 (Fulton); State Hospital No.

---

13. Report of Superintendent, no date, *House and Senate Journals Appendix*, 41st G.A. (1901), 19.
14. Report of Board of Managers, no date, ibid., 42nd G.A. (1903), 5.

2 (St. Joseph); State Hospital No. 3 (Nevada); State Hospital No. 4 (Farmington); the Colony for Feeble-Minded (Marshall); and the State Sanatorium (Mt. Vernon). Establishing such a centralized regulatory board, considered so undesirable a half century earlier, drew heavily upon the experiences of the Progressive Era at both the state and federal levels. Local control to regulate and to protect citizens appeared to have failed not just in the care of the mentally ill but in other areas as well, whether in providing the best education, in ensuring that drugs and foods sold to consumers were safe, or in preventing abuses by unscrupulous, greedy corporations.

On June 19, a new bipartisan board, appointed by the governor, replaced the six individual boards of managers that had overseen each of their respective institutions since their creation. In its first report to the General Assembly in 1923, the board reported that its members had gone beyond the intent of the act to create a bipartisan atmosphere. "Every act," it reported, "has been non-partisan rather than bipartisan or partisan."[15] While the new system reduced patronage at the board, superintendent, and physician levels, it did not alter the patronage system that guided the hiring of all other asylum employees.

Rather than overseeing six separate budgets and six sets of purchases for its member institutions, the new board, as required by law, prepared a unified budget covering the expenditures of all the institutions. It would also facilitate central purchasing of supplies for the state hospitals. This idea of central purchasing had first been tested between 1913 and 1914 when the stewards of six state hospitals, including the four treating the insane, began unified purchases of coal and beans. By 1915, joint contracts for $200,000 in coal and $4,250 in beans had been issued. The fuller implementation of this unified-purchases experiment would also effect, or so it was hoped, significant economies of scale.[16]

The new unified board's president, H. D. Evans, would now be a full-time state employee, responsible for supervising the business management of the institutions. Working with each steward, the president and steward together now became the purchasing agents. The new law also stipulated that, except in order to meet emergency situations, no purchase could be made except by competitive bid. One important advantage of this new purchasing system, in addition to reducing political favoritism in issuing purchasing contracts, was that it allowed superintendents to focus more time on the medical, rather than the budgetary side of asylum management.

The new law also helped formalize the cooperation and sharing of knowl-

---

15. Report of Board of Managers, State Eleemosynary Institutions, January 1, 1923, ibid., 52nd G.A. (1923), 10.
16. Report of Board of Charities and Corrections, no date, ibid., 48th G.A. (1915), 36–37.

edge of superintendents and assistant physicians at the various institutions. It created the new position of health supervisor, who would automatically become an ex-officio member of the board. This individual would consult with all superintendents and assistant physicians regularly and was also required to visit each facility at least once every two months. Additionally, this person would prescribe the qualifications necessary for a candidate to be hired as a superintendent. Together with each superintendent, the health supervisor appointed all assistant physicians. The supervisor also had the power to recommend to the board the removal of any superintendent or assistant physician. By controlling the job qualifications for superintendents and assistant physicians, the office could also upgrade the quality of the medical staff at the various institutions. By serving as a central clearinghouse for information on treatment and by sharing the medical successes and failures at each institution, the supervisor's office could insure that the entire statewide system utilized the best, most appropriate, scientific methods.

With two years of experience behind it, the board members reported in 1923 that their and the health supervisor's efforts to upgrade medical standards had been successful, and that "the old-time political doctor has practically disappeared from these institutions." The board also reported success in moving the institutions toward the standardization of forms and records and ending "the peculiarities and idiosyncrasies of the respective managing officers."[17] The era of decentralization of Missouri mental asylums, where each asylum set its own administrative and medical standards, had formally ended. The new hope was that, operating under the guidelines of the 1921 Eleemosynary Act, many of the financial irregularities, the competition over legislative appropriations, and the impact of politics on asylum management so evident in the last three decades of the nineteenth century and the first decade of the twentieth could be significantly diminished. Yet although, as the board noted in 1923, successes had occurred as a result of the reforms of 1921, the patronage system that had chosen those "old-time political doctors" had not been completely overthrown. That would not occur for another two decades.

---

17. Report of Board of Managers, State Eleemosynary Institutions, January 1, 1923, ibid., 52nd G.A. (1923), 10–11.

6

Search for a Cure

Treatments in Transition, 1905–1940

Just as treatments at Fulton varied at the turn of the century depending on whether the physicians were of the homeopathic or allopathic schools, treatments also reflected the many approaches being debated in Europe and the United States in the late nineteenth century and opening decades of the twentieth.

Some approaches practiced at the Fulton asylum at the turn of the century were not new. Superintendents continued to emphasize the importance of an outdoor experience as "one of the most important factors in the treatment and cure of the insane." By planting trees, shrubs, and flowers, constructing a lake and several fountains, erecting airing pavilions for activities and sunbaths, and by paving long stretches of sidewalks for exercise, hospital officials strove to create a pleasing, soothing environment for their patients. As Superintendent J. W. Smith informed legislators in 1905, "hundreds spend hours on the lawns, seated on rustic seats beneath the shade trees" or "walking with the attendant about the grounds."[1]

They also continued to emphasize, whenever possible and agreeable with a patient, the importance of manual labor, with jobs assigned according to a patient's ability. Superintendent R. S. Wilson reminded the legislature in 1893 that the erection of shops at Fulton to make mattresses, mats, brooms, brushes, rugs, and shoes, just as the use of male patients in farm operations and female patients in the sewing rooms, improved the patients' physical and mental condition, gave them a sense of pride and satisfaction, and made

---

1. Report of Superintendent, no date, *House and Senate Journals*, Appendix, 41st G.A. (1901), 16; Report of Superintendent, no date, ibid., 43rd G.A. (1905), 11.

them "less trouble to care for." That view continued to be reflected in superintendent and steward reports well into the twentieth century. Officials repeatedly emphasized to the legislature not only the benefits to the patient of this work system, but also the financial benefits to the institution. In the 1928–1929 report, the Board of Managers of the State Eleemosynary Institutions submitted to the legislature comparative charts on how much each institution contributed to its own financial well-being. That report listed in detail income from vegetable production, poultry, hog and beef operations, orchards, sewing rooms, mattress factories, shoe shops, and so forth. Such reports were made every two years to the General Assembly. While the legislature only received annual or biennial statistics, these production figures were so important that Fulton administrators kept a detailed monthly breakdown, for example, of all garments manufactured at the institution between May 1937 and December 1970.[2] Similar records were retained for other areas of output.

While administrators at all the state's mental hospitals remained committed to manual labor for as many patients as possible, that philosophy underwent a major change in 1922, reflecting the growing emphasis on treatments tailored to the individual needs of each patient. That year, each of the state hospitals opened a department of occupational therapy. Superintendent Biggs at Fulton described occupational therapy as "any activity, mental or physical, definitely prescribed and guided for the distinct purpose of contributing to, and hastening recovery from disease or injury." While occupational therapy could involve working on the farm, in a sewing room, or in other asylum shops—jobs available to patients prior to the implementation of occupational therapy—it could also include schoolwork. The distinction between this program and its predecessor work program was the tailoring of the mental or physical experience to the medical needs of the patient and the supervision of the patients by a trained occupational therapist. As Biggs explained, however, the underlying philosophy of the two programs remained the same: "Satan finds mischief for hands and minds too long idle. . . . The man or woman that does nothing is likely to go to the devil. . . . If the convalescent does not quickly use the faculties which have been put out of commission, he is in danger of the scrap heap." The Eleemosynary Board of Managers described its benefits more formally: "No single remedy . . . does as much to promote the happiness, well-being and improvement of the insane as employment applied in a rational way. It matters not whether the employment is on the farm or garden, in the factory or class room, the essential factor is the adoption of employment for the cor-

---

2. Report of Superintendent, no date, ibid., 37th G.A. (1893), 23–24; Garments Ledger, May 1937–December 1970 (FSHA).

For the female patients, work in the sewing room provided occupation and also helped the hospital meet its costs. This photo was taken around 1910 (Fulton State Hospital).

rection of the individual patient's mode of thought and action."[3] The new focus of the work program proved so beneficial that in 1927 Superintendent Biggs requested additional funding from the legislature to allow his institution to meet the needs of all the patients who could benefit from this individualized approach.

Although attendants were no longer treated as partners with the physicians in the treatment of mental illness, they still were seen as crucial to the patient's comfort. By 1906, a new manual explicitly outlined the duties of attendants:

> [attendants] must dance with patients
> must never mal-treat patients; doing so will lead to discharge
> must notice the habits and conduct of patients and promptly inform the Physician of all circumstances requiring attention
> must induce the patients to take their medicine . . . but never to resort to force except in the presence or under the direction of a Physician

3. Report of Superintendent, no date; ibid., 61; Report of Board of Managers, State Eleemosynary Institutions, January 1, 1923, ibid., 13.

must never imitate, ridicule or mock the patients

must always avoid deception of patients

must at meal time always be present to carve, distribute the food, and see that every patient has a proper supply

must count knives and forks before and after meals

must frequently search patients to insure that they do not secrete any instruments of iron or steel

must look especially to the clothing and bedding of the patients, and see that all are clean and of the proper kind and quality

must see that the beds are always free from bugs, and the bed rooms free from bad odor

must see that bathing is properly done.

That manual also imposed other obligations upon attendants. Unless ill or on duty in the wards, attendants had to attend religious services in the chapel. If they resided at the institution, they had to be in bed by 9:30 p.m. Under no circumstance could employees visit employees of the other sex in their rooms, even when they were off-duty. If, through their neglect, a patient escaped, then the attendant was responsible for either all or part of the expenses incurred in returning the escapee to the hospital. Finally, when on duty and when a physician came through their ward, they were to stand and follow the physician throughout his ward rounds.[4]

By 1910, as physicians increasingly acknowledged that there was no stereotypical medical cure for insanity and that treatments needed to be formulated on a case-by-case basis, the role of the attendants became even more important. In that year, Missouri established its first regular training school for attendants, who by now were renamed "nurses." By 1913, Elsie Binder, the newly hired resident director for nurse training, had established a training school at the Fulton asylum but with far less ambitious goals than those anticipated at the school established in 1910 at State Hospital No. 3 at Nevada. Candidates for the Nevada school had to be between the ages of nineteen and thirty, had to be of good moral character, and had to be in good health. During the anticipated two and one-half years of training, they would be classified as "pupil nurse" while they acquired a practical and theoretical understanding of mental illness and nursing as well as an understanding of the importance of general behavior, neatness, willingness to work, and the kindly treatment of patients. An effort to have this school serve all the state mental hospitals had failed, causing Fulton to strike out on its own. At the second annual meeting of the Conference of Officers of State Eleemosynary and Penal Institutions of Missouri on January 10, 1912, Dr. George Williams, Superintendent at Fulton, outlined his own plans that culminated in the hiring of Mrs. Binder the next year.

4. State Hospital No. 1, *By-Laws and Service Manual* (Fulton: Press of the Gazette, 1906).

Williams favored a regular plan of instruction, perhaps over a six-month period, rather than sessions offered sporadically; favored mandatory sessions rather than voluntary; and favored requiring nurses to take these classes during nonwork hours: "It is our duty," he argued, "to weed out the careless and ignorant attendants and to kill off the hospital tramp." Any nurse who could not pass the exams should be discharged. Following discussion with fellow superintendents, Williams agreed that perhaps nurses should attend such classes as a part of their work schedule rather than their leisure time.[5]

Two years later, Superintendent M. O. Biggs, Fulton's new leader, reported on his experiment in placing female nurses on some men's wards. "I find that this has proved not only practical, but in many particulars has been very satisfactory. I find that our patients are more obedient and show the greatest respect to the women who have them in charge, and in no instance has any bodily harm been attempted, or any trouble of any kind developed, under this system."[6] Those women, however, made on average two to five dollars less per month than their male counterparts. It is unclear when the Fulton asylum abandoned its revolutionary policy adopted by the Board of Managers in 1872 that required that female attendants "be entitled to, and shall receive precisely the same rate of wages as male attendants, or nurses, are allowed and paid for the same services."[7] This "equalization of pay" proposal had covered not only nurses, but also any female employed at the asylum. Nevertheless, this equalization concept was no longer in effect by the second decade of the twentieth century. By 1919, Biggs complained that neither wage—those for men or women—was sufficient for the hospital to hire and to retain competent nurses.

Nor had pay improved four years later when the newly formed State Board of Eleemosynary Institutions warned the General Assembly that hiring and retaining attendants was "one of the most serious of all problems that confront the management of our institutions." How would the board correct this problem? Missouri had to pay better wages, reduce the twelve- to fourteen-hour workday, and modify its policy of having attendants sleep on the same ward they worked. "Employees who spend fourteen hours amidst insane patients are worn out physically and nervously, long before

---

5. Selected minutes of this conference are found in Report of Board of Charities and Corrections, no date, *House and Senate Journals Appendix*, 47th G.A. (1913), 103–8. Williams's comments are found on 105–6. Efforts in Missouri to launch training for asylum nurses lagged well behind those on the East Coast. Worcester State Hospital in Massachusetts, for example, had launched a similar drive almost two decades earlier.

6. Report of Superintendent, no date, ibid., 48th G.A. (1915), 17.

7. The Board of Managers adopted a similar resolution on June 22, 1869, but repealed it on August 31 of that same year. For the 1872 policy, see Journal State Lunatic Asylum: Board of Managers Minutes (December 28, 1866–July 7, 1874), November 27, 1872, 178–79 (FSHA).

the expiration of their term of duty, they lose their patience and release their self control and do things which they would not do under other conditions."[8] Failure of the state to correct these problems, it warned, would mean that quality employees would continue to move into similar jobs outside Missouri that offered higher salaries, shorter working hours, and better living arrangements. By the early 1930s, overcrowding at the Fulton facility further exacerbated the staff retention problem. Continued inadequate county payments per patient and insufficient legislative appropriations insured that this issue would not be resolved quickly or easily. Even though the role and importance of attendants and nurses had dramatically changed since the late nineteenth century, the state was not yet ready to raise wages dramatically or establish for all asylums the type of lengthy, but expensive, program for nurse training established at the Nevada asylum in 1910.

Meanwhile, reflecting the trend of replacing the politically appointed physicians with those whose training was in the treatment of mental illness, by 1895 Fulton increasingly emphasized continuing education and consultation for its physicians whether in the conduct of autopsies, in the diagnosis of insanity, or in the selection of treatment. By 1913, the Missouri Board of Charities and Corrections recommended to the General Assembly the adoption of a training program whereby young physicians in psychiatry could be trained and nurtured, guaranteeing them a system of advancement that hinged on merit. Other suggestions in that era included holding regular staff meetings at each institution as well as annual meetings of physicians from all of the state's mental institutions and borrowing a model initiated in eastern hospitals where each asylum would establish a consulting staff of outside specialists who could advise and interact with asylum personnel. With the exception of the formal training program for young physicians, by 1923 all of these suggestions had been adopted by the state's mental institutions.

The training of nurses and physicians alone was insufficient to make Fulton a modern facility. To enable attendants, for example, to contact the on-duty physician(s) quickly in the case of patient need, the Fulton asylum petitioned the legislature in 1901 for a telephone system that would connect each ward with the superintendent's office. Since no attendant could leave his or her ward unattended, an attendant would have to be relieved by another in order to seek out the physician to discuss a patient's unanticipated needs. If the physician on duty was not in his office, this process could take a considerable amount of time. Despite the acknowledged advantages of quick communication in the administration of the hospital and the care of its patients, no system was installed for four years.

8. Report of Board of Managers, State Eleemosynary Institutions, January 1, 1923, *House and Senate Journals Appendix*, 52nd G.A. (1923), 17–18.

A number of physicians in the middle of the nineteenth century argued that patients could be cured faster by removing them from their families and communities, placing them in asylums and limiting contact with family members and friends. While most superintendents at Fulton did not adhere to this philosophy and often encouraged family visits, none made any serious effort to work with family and community members when a patient was released from the institution, even after it adopted a parole system in 1905. Under that system, a paroled patient could return home for between thirty and sixty days. This option was normally available only to those patients who were not fully recovered but who, in the view of the asylum physicians, would likely benefit from a trial stay at home. Administrators were pleased with the success of this program, reporting in 1909 that 68 percent of those paroled did not need to return to the institution and were therefore discharged. In 1915, that percentage was 67 percent, and in 1921, when the term "furlough" replaced "parole," it was 58 percent.[9]

Not until 1913 did the state Board of Charities and Corrections, formally acknowledging the need to address the issue of "after-care," launch an experimental program in Kansas City to help family and friends adapt to a cured patient's reappearance in their home communities. The goal was not only to help dispel the view of the patient as "queer and unreliable" but also to help the patient readjust, including finding meaningful employment. By 1915, the board supported the hiring of one field agent for each mental institution who would be responsible for visiting each released patient and his or her family. Even though "many of these [patients] returned to the same conditions that were responsible for the original commitment," the board reasoned that the field agent, by helping the patient find employment and by counseling both the patient and the family, could help insure that the patient would not need to return to the asylum. The board launched an even more ambitious experiment twelve years later, in 1927. Working with State Hospital No. 1, it sought to prove that aftercare should include closer contact and better cooperation not just between the asylum and the released patient and his or her family but also between those individuals, local physicians, and county health and social agencies.[10]

While the asylum and aftercare focused on cure, there was growing interest in the late nineteenth and early twentieth centuries on prevention. Pennsylvania General Hospital in 1885 had established the first outpatient

---

9. Report of Superintendent, no date, ibid., 45th G.A. (1909), 9; Report of Superintendent, no date, ibid., 48th G.A. (1915), 13; Report of Superintendent, no date, ibid., 51st G.A. (1921), 10.

10. Report of Board of Charities and Corrections, no date, ibid., 47th G.A. (1913), 44; Report of Board of Charities and Corrections, no date, ibid., 48th G.A. (1915), 37–38; Report of Board Health Supervisor George Johns, no date, ibid., 54th G.A. (1927), 40.

clinic in the United States that focused on prevention. New York eventually followed, establishing forty mental health clinics to work with its state mental institutions. The National Committee for Mental Hygiene, established in 1909, focused its efforts on fostering mental health outside the asylum, not within. Throughout the nineteenth century, psychiatry had almost been synonymous with the asylum. Now that began to change, although slowly. At the annual meeting of the American Psychiatric Association in 1910, only 3.2 percent of attendees were in private practice. By 1921 that had risen to 7.3 percent.[11]

Supporters of the mental hygiene movement emphasized scientific research leading to the identification of preventive actions. They rejected the asylum's "care and custody" model. Its supporters often saw a close relationship between mental illness and education, social reform, and childhood education. One historian of mental illness has concluded, however, that physicians pursuing this alternative to the asylum were so focused on studying mental illness as an "abstraction" and so excited that they had discovered a role that enhanced their professional identity and expanded their medical knowledge, that they lost sight of the institutionalized patients: "Ironically, psychiatrists—who could have played a crucial role in creating a greater sensitivity for the welfare of the institutionalized mentally ill—chose instead to pursue other ends."[12] Those ends most particularly included a focus on scientific study and prevention in a nonasylum setting. Nevertheless, despite such criticism, these physicians no doubt saw themselves as doing something worthwhile, unlike their asylum counterparts, who seemed to have run out of ideas and approaches and who seemed too content to simply warehouse a growing number of patients without prospect of recovery.

Influenced by Pennsylvania, New York, and the mental hygiene movement, the Eleemosynary Board in January 1923 urged the creation of an outreach network in Missouri to offer preventive care. Such clinics, it argued, allowed many to entirely avoid the need for treatment in a mental hospital. While Kansas City and St. Louis established societies to focus on preventive care, nothing was done to erect a statewide network until December 1936. A meeting that month in Columbia led to the creation of the Missouri Association for Mental Hygiene, which sought to draw upon the experiences and knowledge of the two cities in creating a state program emphasizing the promotion of mental health and the prevention of mental disease. State Hospital No. 1 superintendent T. R. Frazer enthusiastically supported this new effort. By the end of 1938, the program was so success-

---

11. Shorter, *History of Psychiatry*, 161.
12. Grob, *Mental Illness and American Society*, 178.

ful that it could not adequately meet the demand for its services because of a shortage of staff and of funds.[13]

While institutional administrators, physicians, and legislators debated the desirability of outpatient care and aftercare programs in the early twentieth century, others embraced psychotherapy as a more appealing alternative to institutionalization. This was especially true in Europe, where private doctors, drawing upon the theories of Sigmund Freud and others, began to work closely with their patients to address their individual problems. In September 1909, Freud joined fellow European analysts Carl Jung and Sandor Ferenczi on a lecture tour of the United States discussing the advantages and process of psychoanalysis as a way of "escaping the asylum." Two years later, as psychoanalysis became more popular, proponents established the American Psychoanalytic Association. Reorganized in 1932 to focus on developing a set of national standards for training and conducting psychoanalysis, it helped popularize psychoanalysis as an alternative to the asylum.[14]

During this same period, the rise of the spa as a source of therapy, both in Europe and in the United States, offered another alternative to institutionalization. However, to avail oneself of either of these two options, psychoanalysis or the spa, individuals needed sufficient funds to insure that they could receive such personal attention. For the poor, these were not realistic alternatives to the asylum.

To improve the condition of those patients who had to depend upon the asylum for treatment as well as to deflect professional and public critics who claimed that they had become caretakers, asylum physicians and superintendents at the turn of the century began to experiment with a number of physical therapies, most originating initially in Europe. Drawing upon the success of hydrotherapy in European hospitals and asylums and at European spas, Superintendent George Williams at Fulton requested $3,500 in 1910 to purchase hydrotherapy equipment: "This is an age of progress," he explained, "and no hospital can hope to lay claim to being modern and properly equipped that has not installed and [placed] in use a modern hydrotherapeutic apparatus." Two years later, having acquired most of the requested equipment, a more subdued Williams noted, however, that "this method of treatment is by no means a 'panacea' or 'cure-all' remedy, and while I believe the percentage of cures claimed for it is extravagant, at the same time, however, I do believe as an adjunct to other treatments, it is very useful and our sick people are entitled to its well known efficacy as a means

---

13. Report of Board of Managers, State Eleemosynary Institutions, January 1, 1923, *House and Senate Journals Appendix*, 52nd G.A. (1923), 15–16; Report of Superintendent, no date, ibid., 60th G.A. (1939), 29–30.

14. Shorter, *History of Psychiatry*, 162–65.

of relief." For the next quarter century, the Fulton asylum extensively used hydrotherapy, expanding its facilities in 1927 and in 1936. Between 1935 and 1936, with an annual average asylum population of 1,900 (1,118 men and 782 women), the hydrotherapy department administered to women 15,320 wet sheet packs for a total of 45,680 hours, and 2,155 continuous baths for 5,820 hours. It administered to men 7,345 wet sheet packs for a total of 22,013 hours, and 3,562 continuous baths for 10,752 hours. While it administered no colonic irrigations to women, it administered 115 such treatments to male patients.[15]

Individuals receiving the wet sheet pack treatment would have their arms and legs tightly bound with a wet sheet pack so that no free motion for the legs and arms remained. Those receiving a continuous bath would be placed on a canvas hammock in a tub through which constantly ran water heated to body temperature. Once on the hammock, a second canvas sheet would cover the tub and all but the head of the patient. At Fulton, between 1935 and 1936, the wet pack treatment, on average, lasted three hours for both male and female patients. The continuous bath lasted, on average, 2.7 hours for women and 3 hours for men. Compared to Boston Psychiatric Hospital in 1935, for example, the Fulton asylum relied much less heavily on continuous baths. At the Boston Psychiatric Hospital, a continuous bath lasted on average 6.5 hours. Writing in 1955, Dr. Milton Greenblatt, a physician and author, condemned both "treatments," arguing that patients often feared and hated their application. Indeed, Greenblatt argued, some physicians and attendants administered them as punishments that masqueraded as treatments.[16]

As mental health increasingly became a specialized area of medicine, its physicians emphasized systematic research that included such procedures as the testing of drugs on patients or animals, the study of the anatomy and pathology of the nervous system by microscopic examination, and the study of the brain during autopsies. Naturally, systematic research required new equipment, new facilities, and eventually, additional medical personnel at the asylum. Although requests for a hospital at the Fulton asylum were not new, in 1895 two new items were added to the request: funding for a morgue and pathological laboratory that would allow the physicians "to advance the knowledge in this branch of medical science," and funding for a well-equipped medical library. Perhaps to nudge the General Assembly, the su-

---

15. Report of Superintendent, December 31, 1910, *House and Senate Journals Appendix*, 46th G.A. (1911), 32; Report of Superintendent, no date, ibid., 47th G.A. (1913), 19; Report of Superintendent, no date, ibid., 59th G.A. (1937), 31.

16. Milton Greenblatt, Richard York, and Esther Brown, *From Custodial to Therapeutic Patient Care in Mental Hospitals* (New York: Russell Sage Foundation, 1955), 78–80.

perintendent reported that one of his physicians had already completed a special course on microscopy and its applications in the conduct of autopsies. Even without special legislative appropriations, Superintendent J. L. Warden proudly reported in 1897 that "we have fitted up one of the neatest little morgues in the State."[17]

The lack of adequate equipment continued to plague physicians. In 1901, the superintendent warned that insufficient or outdated equipment limited his physicians' ability to diagnose or treat diseases, examine eyes, ears, noses, and throats, perform necessary chemical analyses, or conduct surgeries with the best instruments. Not until the completion of the new hospital at the Fulton asylum in 1907 did those physicians obtain modern equipment and adequate hospital and laboratory facilities for their treatment of patients and their research into mental illness. By 1923, the Eleemosynary Board had secured funding for a laboratory, to be headed by a pathologist and serologist. The lab, while located at Fulton, would handle work for all six eleemosynary institutions. Within two years, assistant physicians at all the institutions had formed a medical society that met once every two months at one of the institutions with the superintendents and, where possible, members of county medical societies and clinicians and instructors "of national reputation." Participation was not passive: "Assistant physicians [were] required to prepare and contribute to the society reports of original scientific study at suitable intervals; and also to make written reports of their observations [of the proceedings] to their respective superintendents and the Health Supervisor."[18]

Fulton's biennial reports to the General Assembly throughout the twenties and thirties provided a detailed listing of operations performed, types of laboratory analysis conducted, and numbers of autopsies undertaken. Describing the 69 autopsies performed between 1935 and 1936, the Fulton report emphasized that "post mortem examinations and studies are made on as many of our deaths as possible in an attempt to find pathologic conditions that we failed to find in life, and to confirm or correct our ante mortem diagnosis."[19] This commitment to surgical and laboratory procedures as a critical component in the care of asylum patients received an additional boost with the erection and opening of a new five-story hospital at the Fulton facility in 1938–1939.

The international debate over the desirability of asylums led to other sci-

---

17. Report of Superintendent, no date, *House and Senate Journals Appendix*, 38th G.A. (1895), 7; Report of Superintendent, November 30, 1896, ibid., 39th G.A. (1897), 11.

18. Report of Superintendent, no date, ibid., 41st G.A. (1901), 10; Report of Board of Health Supervisor George Johns, no date, ibid., 53rd G.A. (1925), 13.

19. Report of Superintendent, no date, ibid., 59th G.A. (1937), 30.

The first hospital building, photographed around 1907 (Kingdom of Callaway Historical Society).

This 1907 operating room boasted all the modern equipment (Kingdom of Callaway Historical Society).

entific approaches, which were often developed in Europe and then transferred to the United States. By 1920, for example, two European physicians, Giuseppe Epifanio and Jakob Klaesi, sought ways to transform the use of drugs as a control and custody agent into a physical therapy to cure certain forms of mental illness, especially schizophrenia. Using recently discovered barbiturates, including Luminal (phenobarbital), which was marketed by Bayer in 1912, they sought to place patients into a prolonged sleep from which they might emerge cured.[20]

A decade later, European physicians led by Manfred Sakel of Austria and Max Muller of Switzerland experimented with insulin coma therapy. Joseph Wortis, a New York psychiatrist who observed Sakel administering this therapy in Vienna in 1934, quickly introduced it to U.S. physicians. Both European and American asylum administrators thereafter "seized on insulin therapy to break out of the therapeutic impasse of custodialism."[21] Rather than relying upon barbiturates to induce a prolonged sleep, these practitioners gradually administered insulin to induce repeated comas. How fast the doses were administered and how long the patient remained in a coma—whether twenty minutes or several hours—varied from hospital to hospital. After twenty or more induced comas, doctors expected to observe signs of improvement in the patient.

In 1934, Hungarian psychiatrist Ladislas von Meduna introduced an alternative convulsive therapy. Although some thought that patient convulsions during insulin therapy were viewed as an undesirable side effect, for Meduna and his supporters they were the desired goal. For Meduna, it was the coma that was undesirable. After experimenting with different drugs, the drug of choice to induce convulsions without comas soon became Metrazol. Not until 1939, when Meduna joined the faculty at Loyola University, did the popularity of convulsive therapy begin to grow in the United States. However, as a desired therapy, it quickly lost out to a competing technique known as electroconvulsive therapy (ECT), used first by Ugo Cerletti in Italy in 1938. He argued that using electricity to shock the brain into induced convulsions could help patients to function more normally.

One final physical therapy developed in Europe in the 1930s was leucotomy, introduced by Portuguese neurologist Egas Moniz and neurosurgeon Almeida Lima. Removing or damaging the front part of the brain prevented, they determined, the development of neuroses and curbed or eliminated "frustrational behavior." Embraced in 1936 by U.S. neurologist Walter

---

20. Shorter, *History of Psychiatry*, 198–228, provides an excellent survey of this treatment as well as those discussed in the following paragraphs. See also Deutsch, *Mentally Ill in America;* and Donald Freedheim, ed., *History of Psychotherapy: A Century of Change* (Washington, D.C.: American Psychological Association, 1992).

21. Shorter, *History of Psychiatry*, 212.

Freeman and neurosurgeon James Watts, they not only touted its results but renamed the procedure lobotomy.[22]

While historically the treatments and therapies adopted at Fulton lagged considerably behind their adoption in Europe and in the eastern part of the United States, news of one of these alternatives traveled faster. In his 1939 report, Superintendent T. R. Frazer had clearly embraced insulin shock therapy, although he did not indicate knowledge of the other new approaches.

Paralleling discussion of the new therapies that emerged in the first four decades of the twentieth century was a controversial debate over a preventive measure to reduce the future number of the epileptic, feeble-minded, idiotic, imbecile, and other "mental defectives." Only once during that period did the issue of sterilization arise in the official records of the Fulton asylum. In 1915, Superintendent M. O. Biggs raised it in his report to the General Assembly: "It is agreed by all authorities that there should be no breeding from the epileptic, feeble-minded, idiotic, imbecile, or others who are mentally defective. . . . The more we know of insanity and its treatment, all the more do we come to the realization of the fact that the one main hope in dealing with it lies in 'prevention' rather than 'cure.'" If heredity was indeed one of the leading causes of insanity, what options were available? Biggs counted two: segregation and sterilization. Biggs suggested that keeping men and women who had been classified as "mental defectives" separate was not practical, which left sterilization. Although, in Biggs's opinion, "society has the moral right to interfere with the propagation of an insane race," he waffled on whether or not sterilization was truly desirable: "With our present knowledge, sterilization is still open to severe criticism and objection, and may be considered by some, if not by a majority, as premature." Nevertheless, he noted, this approach had already been adopted in Indiana and was being considered in Kansas.[23]

During the next quarter century, no other superintendent at Fulton formally raised this issue, even though the U.S. Supreme Court upheld Virginia's sterilization law in 1927. Writing the majority opinion, Justice Oliver Wendell Holmes had observed,

> We have seen more than once that the public welfare may call upon the best citizens for their lives. It would be strange if it could not call upon those who already sap the strength of the State for these lesser sacrifices, often not felt to be such by those concerned, in order to prevent our being swamped with incompetence. It is better for all the

22. Ibid.
23. Report of Superintendent, no date, *House and Senate Journals Appendix*, 60th G.A. (1939), 28; Report of Superintendent, no date, ibid., 48th G.A. (1915), 19–20.

world, if instead of waiting to execute degenerate offspring for crime, or to let them starve for their imbecility, society can prevent those who are manifestly unfit from continuing their kind. The principle that sustains compulsory vaccination is broad enough to cover cutting the Fallopian tubes. Three generations of imbeciles are enough.[24]

By 1936, twenty-five states had adopted some form of sterilization, including Missouri's neighbors—Iowa in 1911, Kansas in 1913, and Nebraska in 1915. Nancy Ordover, in a recent study of American eugenics, asserts that "at least 70,000" persons were sterilized in the United States between 1907 and 1945.[25] Missouri representative George Ballew hoped that his state would join with the others who in the 1920s were enacting sterilization legislation. His bill, introduced on January 29, 1929, called for the "sterilization of persons convicted of murder, rape, chicken stealing, automobile theft, highway robbery, bombing, mental defectives, epileptics, and persons afflicted with venereal diseases." House debate led to a significant revision on April 24 that permitted "sterilization of persons convicted of rape, incest or sodomy, habitual criminals or imbeciles, or idiots or incurable insane persons, or persons afflicted with incurable venereal diseases, or incurable epileptics," provided proper safeguards were established for these individuals. Despite this modification, on May 1, by a vote of 62 to 53, the bill failed to pass.[26]

During the next legislative session in 1931, five House members, including the chair of the Committee on Public Health and Scientific Institutions, cosponsored a much narrower bill calling for "sexual sterilization of inmates of state institutions in certain cases." Although referred to his committee, Public Health Chair William Smith failed to convince a majority of his members to recommend its approval. When the bill came up for a vote on the House floor, it was defeated by a 73–47 vote. Two years later, in January and February 1933, Representative William Weakley called for sterilization in order to protect "the state and future generations." When the Committee on Eleemosynary Institutions recommended that it not be approved, Weakley proposed an alternative that called for the "voluntary sterilization of citizens not in any institution of the state, who if not sterilized would probably procreate children with a strong tendency to physical, men-

---

24. 274 U.S. 207.
25. Nancy Ordover, *American Eugenics, Race, Queer Anatomy, and the Science of Nationalism* (Minneapolis: University of Minnesota Press, 2003), 134. For further discussion of sterilization and its logic, see Philip Reilly, *The Surgical Solution: A History of Involuntary Sterilization in the United States* (Baltimore: Johns Hopkins University Press, 1991); Marouf Arif Hasian Jr., *The Rhetoric of Eugenics in Anglo-American Thought* (Athens: University of Georgia Press, 1996); and Mark Haller, *Eugenics: Hereditarian Attitudes in American Thought* (New Brunswick: Rutgers University Press, 1963).
26. *House Journal*, 55th G.A. (1929), I, 158; and II, 1515, 1649–50.

tal or nervous disease or deficiency, and would probably become wards of the state and a menace to society." Being submitted to a different legislative committee, the Committee on Public Health, did not change the fate of the proposed legislation. Accepting the committee's negative recommendation on March 2, 1933, the legislature rejected the revised Weakley bill. Two subsequent attempts to authorize sterilization of selected inmates in state institutions, in the 1935 and the 1937 legislative sessions, also ended in failure.[27]

Thus, while acknowledging the need to reduce the future number of persons needing institutional care at the Fulton facility and elsewhere, Missouri lawmakers, unlike many of their counterparts across the nation, consistently rejected sterilization in the decades prior to World War II. Other solutions to future overcrowding would have to be found.

• • •

Just as physicians and superintendents reevaluated their treatments and therapies in light of scientific discoveries at the turn of the century, so too did they reevaluate other areas of the asylum, including the diet of patients. Responding to concerns about patient diets raised by administrators at State Hospital No. 4 at Farmington, the State Board of Charities and Corrections in 1919 employed dietitian June Findley to visit each asylum, report on the types and quantities of food served, and identify any dietary or related deficiencies that might exist at each institution.[28]

Although Findley concluded that each hospital "more than met the energy requirements" of its patients, she did recommend that each institution hire a dietitian to insure that the quantity, quality, and diversity of foods continued to remain acceptable. Fulton belatedly followed that suggestion, hiring Mrs. J. E. Fry six years later.

In 1919 at Fulton, each meal for the 1,238 patients and 168 employees was prepared in one large kitchen, located on the first floor in the main building of the hospital, where the vast majority of patients were housed. At mealtimes, patients who were able entered the dining room to sit in either a chair or on a long bench next to a table covered with a cloth tablecloth (available to those patients who were "quiet") or an oilcloth (available to those patients not quiet). For patients who were unable to serve themselves, the food was placed on each table by the attendants, whose job was to insure that each patient received sufficient food and that they ate it rather than hiding it or giving it away. Findley, however, severely criticized the use

---

27. *House Journal,* 56th G.A. (1931), I, 401; ibid., 57th G.A. (1933), I, 211, 375; ibid., 58th G.A. (1935), I, 323; and ibid., 59th G.A. (1937), I, 293.

28. The following dietary discussion is based on June Findley, "Dietary Studies of Missouri State Hospitals for the Insane," contained in Report of Board of Charities and Corrections, no date, *House and Senate Journals Appendix,* 50th G.A. (1919), 17–30.

of chipped enamelware plates and cups—a practice she found to be unsanitary and potentially dangerous, but which administrators found to be fiscally prudent since they could not afford the more desirable aluminum ware.

Findley also alerted administrators that since "the patients were more or less at the mercy of the attendants," the matron of the asylum should visit the dining room "as often as possible during meal time to see that the food was being served properly." Lest this be seen as a severe criticism of the actions of attendants she had observed, she added: "The attendants have a hard position to fill and, on the whole, were very kind to the patients and did all they could to make the surroundings as pleasant as possible and took personal interest in the welfare of their charges." She was also impressed that many patients helped their neighbors either by cutting the food on their plates or by assisting them in eating. What she failed to mention was that at the end of each meal the attendants counted the utensils to insure that none were taken by the patients.

A typical week's menu at Fulton in May 1919 included the following:

> For Breakfast: beef hash or potato stew, rolled oats or cereal, hot rolls, butter, syrup, coffee and milk;
> For Dinner: beef or mutton, beans, lettuce and radishes, corn bread, tea and milk;
> For Supper: rice custard or stewed apricots or stewed prunes, peaches, light bread, butter, syrup, coffee and milk.

As we review the diets, treatments, and therapies in the five and a half decades preceding U.S. entry into World War II, we find that the Fulton asylum had a dual focus—improving the care of the mentally ill while at the same time continuing the search for a cure. How similar were patients, and how successful were their treatments between 1886 and 1941? Data from the Fulton asylum's biennial reports of 1886–1888, 1899–1900, 1909–1910, 1919–1920, 1929–1930, and 1939–1940 provide insight into patient profiles and the alleged causes of and duration of insanity prior to admission into the asylum, as well as the length of time a patient remained at Fulton before being discharged as recovered.[29]

Although the number of admissions continued to climb—indicative of

---

29. For 1886–1888: Report of Superintendent, no date, *House and Senate Journals Appendix*, 35th G.A. (1889); for 1899–1900: Report of Superintendent, no date, ibid., 41st G.A. (1901); for 1909–1910: Report of Superintendent, December 31, 1910, ibid., 46th G.A. (1911); for 1919–1920: Report of Superintendent, no date, ibid., 51st G.A. (1921); for 1929–1930: Report of Superintendent, no date, ibid., 56th G.A. (1931); for 1939–1940: Report of Superintendent, no date, ibid., 61st G.A. (1941). The following discussion is based on data obtained from these documents.

the dramatic growth of asylums across the United States—the ratio of admitted male and female patients at the Fulton asylum remained fairly consistent during these five and a half decades. In both the 1886–1888 and 1899–1900 reporting periods, the admissions ratio was 55 percent men to 45 percent women. By 1909–1910, male admissions had climbed to 59 percent. Ten years later it had risen to 62 percent, where it basically remained between 1929–1930 and 1939–1940.

Male occupations, at least for those years for which comparable data are available, reflect the gradual shift in Missouri and elsewhere of the population from rural to urban areas, and from farm to factory, as well as the impact of World War I. Between 1886 and 1888, farmers composed 54.2 percent of male admissions while only 14.9 percent were laborers. By 1909–1910, the percentage of farmers had fallen to 28.3 percent while laborers had risen to 21.5 percent. A decade later, reflecting the impact of World War I, 20.3 percent were described as soldiers.

Female occupations, primarily focused on the home, reflect the political, social, and economic status of American women in the nineteenth and early twentieth century. According to hospital records, 90.7 percent of all women admitted between 1886 and 1888 were engaged in "domestic pursuits." By 1909–1910, 47.9 percent were housewives while 8.5 percent were domestics. By 1919–1920, the number of housewives had risen to 52.5 percent while the number of domestics had fallen to 4.1 percent.

While the percentage of patients at Fulton supported by county governments declined during these years (from 70.5 percent in 1886–1888 to 59.9 percent in 1919–1920), the county poor continued to constitute a majority of patients—exacerbating the debate, which began almost as soon as the asylum opened in 1851–1852, that county payments to the asylum were simply too small to cover the actual cost of hospitalization. The number of private patients, whose costs were borne by family and friends, steadily grew from 29.4 percent in 1886–1888 to 40.1 percent in 1919–1920. That growth could reflect a growing confidence that the asylum offered the patient a better life than had he or she remained at home, or that a patient had a better opportunity for cure there. It could reflect a change in attitudes that the inability or unwillingness to care for a family member at home reflected negatively on the family itself. Or it could reflect the successes of an expanding preventive program adopted in Missouri that sought to educate the public on mental illness and to urge them to seek care immediately upon diagnosis of the illness. Certainly the selected data between 1886 and 1910 reveal that a majority of patients had arrived at the asylum within that crucial first year of illness, the time frame most superintendents insisted was essential if a cure was likely to be effected. Between 1886 and 1888, 69.1 percent of men and 72.2 percent of women arrived at the asylum had experienced insanity for less than a year. Approximately 53 percent of men admitted between 1899 and 1900 and between 1909 and 1910 had been diagnosed within the last twelve months. For women during these same two periods, the rates hovered between 56 and 58 percent.

The data also reveal that, between 1886 and 1940, the number of people cured, as a percentage of those admitted, continued to decrease. Between 1886 and 1888, 53 percent of both men and women were discharged as cured. Male "discharged as recovered" rates fell to 38.9 percent between 1899 and 1900; to 28.3 percent between 1909 and 1910; to 25.6 percent between 1919 and 1920; to 14.2 percent between 1929 and 1930; and rising finally to 25.1 percent between 1930–1940. The rates for women "discharged as recovered" fell only slightly less precipitously—from 53 percent to 34.1 percent to 39.7 percent to 28.3 percent to 25.3 percent to 16.5 percent for the same time periods.

Such data fed the movement in both the United States and Europe that questioned the success of institutionalization and that began to emphasize other alternatives—private consultations between psychiatrists and patients and the development of more effective treatments and therapies. One positive aspect from these data was that a majority of those released between 1886 and 1888, and between 1909 and 1910—the only two periods in these sample years for which data are available—had remained at the Fulton asylum for less than a year before being declared "recovered."[30]

The nativity of admitted patients not surprisingly reveals that those born in Missouri consistently constituted the largest portion of new patients, although the percentage steadily declined from 53.7 percent in 1886–1888 to 34.8 percent in 1919–1920. Individuals born outside the United States consistently numbered under 10 percent of those admitted. Nor did "foreign-born" in these data necessarily mean that these patients remained citizens of other nations; many had indeed become naturalized U.S. citizens by the time of their admission. Based on available data, it appears that Missouri, unlike Massachusetts and California, did not disproportionately institutionalize newly arrived immigrants whose behavior seemed unusual, abnormal, or irrational.

The listing of alleged causes of insanity developed in 1851 at Fulton served as the basic means of classification for the next three-quarters of a century, even though, beginning in 1899, these categories were subdivided into physical and moral causes. By 1929, state asylum officials in Fulton and elsewhere abolished this system of classification in favor of a new one based

---

30. Those released within twelve months as "recovered" were, between 1886 and 1888, 83.8 percent males and 86.3 percent females, and, between 1909 and 1910, 82.3 percent males and 76.3 percent females.

on principal psychoses understandable to medical professionals but much less clear to the layperson.

Among the physical causes driving admissions between 1886 and 1888, hereditary insanity accounted for 23.9 percent of male admissions and 19.9 percent of female. By 1919–1920, it had fallen to 3.2 percent for men and 4.9 percent for women. Intemperance remained a cause for male admissions but rarely so for females. Of males admitted between 1886 and 1888, 14.4 percent were due to intemperance, falling to 6.2 percent by 1919–1920. For women, intemperance admissions in 1886–1888 and 1899–1900 were not statistically measurable. In both 1909–1910 and 1919–1920, it became measurable at 1 percent.

Despite advances in treatments and a growing emphasis on scientific investigation and classification, physicians conceded that for a larger and larger percentage of newly admitted patients, they simply did not know the physical cause. In 1886–1888 "unknown cause" accounted for 15.4 percent of male and 15.2 percent of female admissions. By 1899–1900, those numbers were 27.9 percent and 27.6 percent; by 1909–1910, 28.3 percent and 36.3 percent; and by 1919–1920, 32.1 percent and 29.9 percent.

Normally the Fulton hospital admitted far fewer new patients, around 15 percent in the sample years between 1899 and 1920, for "moral causes" than for "physical causes." Moral causes consisted of categories such as "Adverse Conditions Such As Loss of Friends, Business Troubles, Domestic Troubles," "Mental Strain, Worry and Overwork," "Religious Excitement," "Love Affairs and Disappointments," and "Worry Over War."[31]

Stung by growing criticism at the turn of the century that the asylum had become a caretaker institution and that its medical personnel tended to be political hacks and second-rate physicians, mental health specialists, boards of managers, and the Missouri General Assembly embarked upon a program of review and renewal, drawing upon the experiences of institutions and physicians in both Europe and the United States. By reforms in administration adopted in the early twenties, the political patronage system's impact on top medical and administrative personnel had been significantly reduced. By the end of the 1930s, Fulton physicians embraced new treatments and therapies, emphasized professionalism and advanced training, published their findings, and presented their scientific observations and investigations to professional colleagues and societies. For the new leaders, these changes should lay to rest the earlier criticisms of asylums and the quality of their physicians and administrators.

---

31. This discussion of the traits of newly admitted patients is based on the Superintendents' Reports cited in note 29.

7

Bursting at the Seams
Growing Pains, 1890–1940

The dramatic growth of the patient population at Fulton between 1870 and 1940—from 303 patients in 1870, to 507 in 1880, to 547 in 1890, to 867 in 1900, to 1,133 in 1910, to 1,331 in 1920, to 1,584 in 1930, and to 2,476 in 1940—frequently required the institution to exceed capacity while pleading with the General Assembly to construct new buildings, upgrade and repair old ones, and add to the other infrastructure necessary to cope with additional patients. In 1881, for example, Fulton's superintendent reported that the asylum exceeded its patient capacity by over 35 percent, housing 507 patients in facilities designed for only 375. In 1909, Superintendent P. E. Williams warned the legislature that "if we do not provide more room for the accommodation of patients, I fear that before the end of the coming two years we will be forced to turn away many who apply for admission." Even after significant renovations and additions funded by the federal government's New Deal Public Works Administration and the Federal Emergency Relief Administration, together with a $10,000,000 Missouri bond issue in the 1930s, Superintendent Ralf Hanks observed that while overcrowding had been relieved, the construction and renovation program "does not provide much for future expansion." Since construction at the Fulton asylum generally lagged behind patient demand, whether in the 1880s, the 1930s, or the decades in between, it was not uncommon within a year or two of the completion of a major expansion project to hear renewed complaints about overcrowding. Indeed, Hanks reported to the legislature in 1941 that, despite the massive construction program just concluded, Fulton's patient population exceeded capacity by

The hospital staff prepares for a parade, circa 1930 (Fulton State Hospital).

10 percent, having jumped from 2,220 in December 1938 to 2,476 two years later.[1]

Two approaches characterized the response to overpopulation: physically enlarging the facility and its infrastructure, and rethinking the criteria for patient admission in order to be more selective. Both approaches had existed almost since the institution's formal opening in 1851. Throughout the first ninety years of operation, the first approach proved more palatable and practical for governors and members of the Missouri General Assembly. While the first approach also appealed to superintendents, many of them repeatedly urged consideration of the second approach, both to address the issue of overpopulation as well as the issue of most efficacious treatment.

A review of physical plant transformations between 1890 and 1940 reveals the nature and frequency of day-to-day problems confronting each superintendent-physician. Despite the major expansion overseen by M. F. Bell in the 1880s, by 1894, thirteen wards were in "very bad condition" and

---

1. Report of Superintendent, no date, *House and Senate Journals*, Appendix, 31st G.A. (1881), 37–43. Report of Superintendent, no date, ibid., 45th G.A. (1909), 12; Report of Superintendent, no date, ibid., 59th G.A. (1937), 27; Report of Superintendent, no date, ibid., 61st G.A. (1941), 3. The PWA and the FERA were but two of President Franklin Roosevelt's New Deal agencies established to create jobs and to lessen the impact of the depression on the unemployed and partially employed.

needed major renovation. Demand for admission prompted the superintendent and Board of Managers to request in late 1896 the construction of new wards, increasing patient capacity by three hundred to four hundred. While this new building opened in 1900, only the first floor and basement were ready for use. The two upper floors opened only after additional legislative appropriations had been received and after the unusual decision by the superintendent to utilize the labor of both patients and regular employees to complete the required work. Despite these additions, by 1911 another new dormitory was under construction. Two years later, to relieve overcrowding in the regular wards and to help ensure the health of the majority of inmates, tubercular patients were moved from the main wards to the newly constructed Hadley Building, described at the time as "one of the best and among the most modern buildings of its kind."[2] As had happened in 1900, a new east wing to the Fulton asylum remained unfinished in 1923 due to an insufficiency of legislative appropriation. One hundred fifty patients who were moved into that wing simply had to live amid construction on the remaining two-thirds of the building. When finally completed, an additional 150 patients joined those already housed in the east wing.

Building new wards, while critically important, was but one of the nonmedical administrative responsibilities of superintendents. Smaller building projects always demanded their time and attention, whether it was the construction of a chapel for two hundred in 1891, a new apothecary shop in 1893, a second icehouse in 1893, a new greenhouse in 1901, a poultry yard in 1905, or a mattress factory in 1913. Superintendents, working with the stewards, also oversaw farm operations, including the acquisition of additional farm and grazing lands and the opening of new orchards.

More mundane problems also required attention. In 1897, administrators and staff members sought—and discovered—a way to reduce the rat population in the wards. In 1903, the superintendent was responsible for overseeing the rewiring of the hospital. In 1908 and 1909, he reviewed literature on beds, selecting an iron model to replace the old wooden ones. In 1915, he had to prepare a memorial to the General Assembly requesting ninety-nine ceiling fans to be placed in the thirty-three hospital wards to enable patients to endure the particularly hot summers in mid-Missouri. In 1929, he engaged in discussions that led to the installation of a central radio receiving set, together with loudspeakers in each ward.

Superintendents also served as personnel officers, reviewing and evaluating employees, hearing grievances, administering discipline, or deciding on

2. Report of Superintendent, no date, ibid., 38th G.A. (1895), 20; Report of Superintendent, no date, ibid., 39th G.A. (1897), 14–15; Report of Superintendent, no date, ibid., 47th G.A. (1913), 18.

termination. They dealt with family members who alleged mistreatment and with scandals such as the embezzlement of $14,000 in 1905, allegedly by the asylum treasurer, W. D. Thomas.[3]

Superintendents were responsible not only for the identification of problems but also for securing funds necessary to address them. Obtaining funds from the legislature often required the lobbying efforts of superintendents over a period of years, sometimes decades. Three recurring problems bedeviled Fulton's hospital personnel between 1890 and 1940. First was maintaining a boiler system that was both safe and effective. Second was securing a water supply that not only was adequate to meet the needs of a growing population but also was free of contaminants. Third was insuring adequate fire prevention.

The boiler problem became acute as the hospital increased the number of wards and buildings on its campus and as it ran more and more heating pipes through its maze of tunnels. Although administrators alerted the General Assembly in 1893 that the thirty-seven-year-old boilers needed replacement, not until the Hartford Steam Boiler Inspection and Insurance Company refused to issue a policy on them were new ones authorized and installed in 1900. Within a decade these new boilers were "condemned" by a boiler inspector, requiring an emergency expenditure, authorized by Missouri's governor and state auditor, for new ones.[4] Despite a request in 1923, and again in 1931, that a new powerhouse be built because the old one was antiquated, poorly arranged, inadequate in meeting the needs of the institution, and in bad repair, the problems were not rectified until 1935–1936.

Clean water, whether for cooking, drinking, cleaning, or for therapeutic use, was essential to the successful operation of the asylum. But by 1901, the hospital's well, which produced about 100,000 gallons of water every twenty-four hours, could not cope with demand. Until that year, the asylum's farm animals drank their water from a creek. However, as the superintendent reported, "as the entire sewerage of the city of Fulton is emptied into [this creek], this water is impure and offensive and not suitable for milch cows or horses to drink."[5] To address the problem, the hospital built a 60,000-gallon cistern that was 39 feet deep and 22 feet wide to collect rainwater from the roofs of asylum buildings. The water, after passing through a double charcoal filter, would be used on the wards for drinking. By 1905, the hospital had also drilled a 908-foot well. Nevertheless, eight years later, due to the expansion of the facility and the increase in the number of patients, the

---

3. Report of Board of Managers, no date, ibid., 45th G.A. (1909), 5; Report of Board of Managers, no date, ibid., 46th G.A. (1911), 13.

4. Report of Superintendent, no date, ibid., 41st G.A. (1901), 12; Report of Board of Managers, no date, ibid., 46th G.A. (1911), 6–8.

5. Ibid., 15.

water supply once again could not meet demand. Administrators first consulted the City of Fulton to ascertain whether the asylum could connect to the city's water supply. Upon learning that Fulton could, at best, provide only one-third of the hospital's water needs, and then only for a few hours each day, the Board of Managers petitioned the governor and state auditor to authorize an emergency expenditure to immediately bore a new well, which was granted. Only after the new well came on line did the hospital have an adequate supply of clean water.

The fear of fire concerned every superintendent in the asylum's first one hundred years, but especially during the sixty years preceding World War II. By the last decade of the nineteenth century, superintendents repeatedly emphasized the absence of fireproofing and fire escapes in the wards, as well as the general absence of adequate equipment with which to fight fires. Without fireproofing, a small fire could quickly spread from ward to ward. Without fire escapes, attendants would have to lead patients down stairways, many of which were designed only for one person ascending or descending. Without fire equipment, even a small fire could not be easily extinguished. In 1893, an appalled Board of Managers immediately ordered the purchase of fire hoses when its inspection found no equipment capable of extinguishing a fire. Despite subsequent upgrades, in 1913 Superintendent George Williams reported that "should a fire occur here of any consequence we would be almost helpless to handle it with our present equipment." The institution only had one hose reel and a few hundred feet of hose, "not in the best of condition." Williams requested new hose, two more hose reels, a ladder truck, and hand fire extinguishers for the wards. He also noted that there was no firehouse at the asylum—that fire equipment, stored in the boiler room, "is very difficult to reach and . . . requires considerable time to get out."[6] Eight years later, Superintendent M. O. Biggs was still requesting hand fire extinguishers for the wards and for adequate firefighting equipment.

The demands for fire escapes in 1893 went unheeded by the General Assembly for over two decades. Even when it did authorize such construction in 1914, it provided appropriations for only three. As Superintendent Biggs revealed, these were too few to allow egress by patients and attendants in all the wards. Furthermore, it ignored a law that required an adequate number of fire escapes in public buildings.[7] Other superintendents over the next decades would continue to grapple with this issue.

The response of the General Assembly to the 1897 request that all build-

---

6. Report of Board of Managers, no date, ibid., 37th G.A. (1893), 7; Report of Superintendent, no date, ibid., 47th G.A. (1913), 25–26.
7. Report of Superintendent, no date, ibid., 48th G.A. (1915), 37.

ings at the asylum be fireproofed was slow, hampered by lack of funds. A quarter century later, the Board of Managers asked local architect M. F. Bell to submit an estimate of the cost of fireproofing the old wings of the hospital. Bell's report that the job could be done for $88,000 served as the basis for the board's subsequent request for legislative funding. By 1933, the General Assembly had funded the fireproofing of only half of the old wards. Not until the arrival of federal New Deal funds during the Depression were the other wards finally fireproofed, permitting the Eleemosynary Board of Managers' president W. Ed. Jameson to proclaim in 1937 that "within the next six or eight months this whole institution will be made practically fireproof."[8]

Just as a substantial portion of the cost of fireproofing had been underwritten by the federal government, so too was the most ambitious renovation and building program to occur at the hospital between 1880 and 1940. Between 1934 and 1939, drawing monies from a special $10,000,000 bond issue authorized by the state legislature as well as from various federal agencies created to cushion the impact of the depression by creating jobs, Fulton added a new wing to the Hyde Building and two others to the already massive central ward complex. Of particular pride was the erection of a new five-story hospital, housing a dental office, morgue, dispensary, examination and treatment rooms, laboratories, and X-ray and surgical rooms, as well as two floors devoted to the care of the acutely ill and one floor devoted to cancer patients. There was also a new building for incoming patients. After 1938, they would be funneled through this new three-story psychiatric clinic, designed to eliminate any resemblance to a jail or prison and to create a smoother, less stressful transition into the asylum.

Nor were those state and federal monies limited to new construction. They funded plumbing and wiring upgrades, painting, weather stripping, sewer repair and extension, fireproofing, road construction, and new tunnels. Civil Works Administration dollars built a new two-story addition to the laundry as well as a beauty parlor. Federal Emergency Relief Administration dollars built a new barbershop, and Works Progress Administration dollars moved and remodeled the asylum's cannery. Additional upgrades included the remodeling of the kitchen, cafeteria, dining room, and chapel, as well as construction of living quarters for some staff members and a new auditorium for the use of both staff and patients.

In 1939, the most expensive new building neared completion—a separate facility for the criminally insane. The demand for this building long pre-

---

8. Bell to W. P. Fulkerson, December 22, 1924 (Blueprints Section, FSHA); Report of Board of Managers, State Eleemosynary Institutions, no date, *House and Senate Journals Appendix*, 59th G.A. (1937), 7.

For many years, rocking chairs were a recurring approach to overcrowded conditions and lack of time for patient care; these chairs were in a tunnel hallway (Fulton State Hospital).

dated the appropriations' generosity of the 1930s. For well over half a century, Fulton's superintendents had complained about the state's decision to house the mentally ill with the criminally insane.

Superintendent Charles Hughes, in a personal letter dated August 2, 1871, urged Governor B. Gratz Brown to suspend the delivery of prisoners to Fulton and, instead, to support the erection of a secure ward for them on the grounds of the state penitentiary at Jefferson City. His rationale? "Our insane have a repugnance to being compelled to associate with the criminal insane."[9] The governor rejected the suggestion.

Superintendent R. S. Wilson in 1895 once again called for the removal of the criminally insane from Fulton to a special facility built for them at the penitentiary. "We all recognize," he wrote the General Assembly, "the baneful influence exerted by this vicious class; besides, the ordinary hospital is not sufficiently secure to insure their confinement."[10]

9. Governor B. Gratz Brown Papers, box 1, folder 29, MSA.
10. Report of Superintendent, no date, *House and Senate Journals Appendix*, 38th G.A. (1895), 22.

In 1905, both the superintendent and the Board of Managers urged a change in policy based on financial considerations. Fulton could not continue to accept such patients, since a criminal sent to the penitentiary lost his citizenship, and state law only compelled the counties to pay for the maintenance of their "citizens" in the state hospital.[11] Therefore counties simply refused to pay for the housing and treatment of the criminally insane.

Another call for change came in 1913 from Missouri's Board of Charities and Corrections, which reminded the General Assembly that "it is a comparatively easy matter to escape from the ordinary hospital for the insane, especially in the case of the insane criminal, who is the most cunning and dangerous of persons to guard." It also lamented the intermixing of regular patients at Fulton with this class of dangerous persons: "This practice is . . . unfair to the patients who are sent to the state hospitals for treatment with no more of disgrace or criminal taint attaching to them than to persons who go to the general hospitals for surgical treatment." Six years later, Superintendent M. O. Biggs complained that "association with this class is demoralizing to patients and attendants." Writing in 1931, Superintendent D. H. Young reported upon the "daily conflicts" between the criminally insane and the innocent insane.[12] Like his predecessors, he preferred that a separate facility be built to handle the criminally insane. While preferably such a facility would be constructed in a separate locality, it could be built on the Fulton campus, he conceded, although it must be located a considerable distance from the regular wards.

Despite repeated requests spanning over six decades, it was not until October 15, 1936, that the Missouri State Building Commission, using $420,000 in Federal Emergency Relief Administration funds, signed a contract to build a hospital for the criminally insane in Fulton, completed by 1939, although not furnished.[13]

Predating the flurry of construction in the 1930s, Fulton administrators had already identified three other classes of insane—epileptics, inebriates, and patients with a drug dependency—who, along with the criminally insane, might be removed from the asylum to make room for more traditional patients. Of these three groups, epileptics received the most attention. Writing in 1871, Superintendent C. H. Hughes concluded that epileptics

11. Report of Superintendent, no date, ibid., 43rd G.A. (1905), 9. See also Report of Board of Managers, no date, ibid., 5–6.

12. Report of Board of Charities and Corrections, no date, ibid., 47th G.A. (1913), 46–47; Report of Superintendent, no date, ibid., 50th G.A. (1919), 13; Report of Superintendent, no date, ibid., 56th G.A. (1931), 23.

13. Report of Superintendent, no date, ibid., 60th G.A. (1939), 30; "Construction Contract," October 15, 1936, State Building Commission Records, box 3, MSA.

exercised "a baneful influence over the inmates of an insane asylum."[14] He therefore recommended that they be segregated from the regular asylum population, being housed in wards, still located in Fulton, designed specifically to meet their needs.

Over the ensuing decades in both Britain and the United States, debate about the relationship of epilepsy to mental illness intensified. Beginning in 1873, the founder of British psychiatry, Sir Henry Maudsley, asserted that "the descendant of an epileptic parent [is] almost if not quite as likely to become insane as to become an epileptic, and one or other of the descendants of an insane parent not infrequently [suffers] from epilepsy."[15] By the 1890s, most simply considered epilepsy as a type of insanity.

By 1911, Superintendent George Williams urged the state to remove epileptics from all regular state mental hospitals, including his own at Fulton, and to place them in a special epileptic institution, which would of course have to be constructed. Likewise, he noted, inebriates were unsuitable patients for the state hospitals. If the state really wished to treat this "very undesirable and troublesome class" in public institutions, something he thought questionable, it should build and equip a special institution for their use. Two years later, he proposed that all patients admitted for drug dependency also be removed from the state hospitals.[16]

In 1923, the State Eleemosynary Board renewed the call for a separate institution for epileptics, although not for inebriates or those with a drug dependency. Such a facility, it reasoned, would better treat the needs of the epileptic, would be less disruptive of the treatment of nonepileptic patients, and would ease overcrowding at the four state hospitals where 445 epileptics were currently housed.[17] Despite such arguments, however, all three classes continued to be admitted into the Fulton institution in the prewar years.

Underlying the debate over the removal of these classes of insane from Fulton was the demand for admission by more "traditional insane" than the asylum could handle. As the chief administrator noted in 1937, while the major expansion and renovation projects of the 1930s, including the construction of a special facility for the criminally insane, had dramatically lowered the pressure due to overcrowding, it had not eliminated it entirely.

In the 1930s, Superintendent Ralf Hanks worried not only about overcrowding but also about the completeness of patient case histories prior to

---

14. Report of Superintendent, November 29, 1870, *House and Senate Journals Appendix*, 26th G.A. (1871), 32.

15. Quoted in Szasz, *Cruel Compassion*, 45.

16. Report of Superintendent, December 31, 1910, *House and Senate Journals Appendix*, 46th G.A. (1911), 27; Report of Superintendent, no date, ibid., 47th G.A. (1913), 15.

17. Report of Board of Managers, State Eleemosynary Institutions, January 1, 1923, ibid., 52nd G.A. (1923), 20–22.

their admission into one of the state hospitals. By early 1936, an asylum admissions form requested the answers to thirty-five questions, including "name, residence, nativity, age, number of children, mental state of children, occupation, education, habits when rational, habits at present, religious denomination, date of present attack, suicidal tendencies, known eccentricities of parents, insane relatives, probable predisposing cause, probable exciting cause, and additional history and insane manifestations."[18] But too often, Hanks believed, county courts that declared an individual insane did not ensure that these questions were answered fully by a physician knowledgeable about the patient's history.

He was also concerned that county courts, county clerks of court, and county prosecuting attorneys were not adhering strictly to law during the commitment process. In a lengthy September 1937 letter to these officials, Hanks laid out that process in detail. Any family member, citizen, or official who sought to have an individual declared insane had to submit to the local county clerk "a verified statement" alleging insanity. By law, the clerk was then required to schedule a judicial hearing before a judge who would weigh relevant evidence. Hanks emphasized that county clerks must notify the person alleged to be insane of the allegation and of the time and place of the judicial proceeding. Although he noted that it was legal to schedule a judicial hearing on the same day an allegation was received, he strongly recommended against undue haste. In his judgment, any individual alleged to be insane should have a minimum of five days before a court appearance to consult legal counsel, to find witnesses, and to prepare a refutation of the allegations. He reminded officials that any person alleged to be insane had to be represented by legal counsel at the judicial hearing. If he or she arrived at the proceeding without counsel, the court was required to appoint counsel before continuing. Hanks also reminded these officials that if an individual alleged to be insane, or his or her counsel, requested a trial by jury rather than the normal consideration by a judge, such a request could not be denied. Whether a judge or a jury determined the validity of the insanity allegations, Hanks emphasized that state law required "at least two witnesses to testify to facts showing the alleged person to be insane, one of whom must be a physician."[19] These rules applied regardless of the class of patient, their race, or their gender.

18. "Request for Admission of Patient, January 2, 1936," State Hospital No. 1, Patient Records, 1919–1938, reel LRP 713.54, Callaway County Archives, Office of County Clerk, Fulton, Missouri.

19. Ralf Hanks to Members of the County Court, County Clerk, Prosecuting Attorney of the Counties of the State of Missouri ("Admission of County Patients in State Hospitals"), September 30, 1937, ibid. For a case study of how the admissions process could be manipulated, see Andrews, *Insane Sisters*. Other states had experimented with extremely lenient patient admission policies. See, for example, Fox, *So Far Disordered*. For examples of petitions to the county court to

One class of patients who had arrived at the asylum received renewed attention in the first four decades of the twentieth century, although not because they were more dangerous or especially disruptive, or because their beds were needed to ease overcrowded conditions; this class was defined by color, not by type of insanity. Since Missouri's attorney general had ruled in 1865 that no law prevented the admission of African Americans into the state insane asylum, African American patients, at least in the facilities made available to them, had been treated as second-class patients even though, by the end of the century, they comprised slightly more than 10 percent of the patient population at Fulton. Superintendent W. L. Ray reported at the beginning of the new century that "quarters for the colored patients have long been inadequate for their proper care. The space is insufficient and their accommodations are necessarily poor."[20] The women had been segregated into a special ward on the fourth floor of the main hospital complex while the men had been crowded into "an altogether unfit" two rooms that had formerly been one of the institution's shops and, before that, a bowling alley.

The transfer of 120 patients to the new hospital at Farmington, which opened in the summer of 1903, allowed the Fulton asylum to house African American patients in more suitable, less crowded quarters. Promises that a new two-story red-brick building under construction would be made available as a modern segregated facility for African American patients were unfulfilled. When the building opened in 1907, it became the asylum's hospital. Nor did the opening of the state-of-the-art Hadley tubercular building in 1913 improve the lives of the hospital's tubercular African American patients, who were denied use of the facility, since a segregated building policy prevailed throughout the asylum campus. Not until 1925 did the State Eleemosynary Board encourage the General Assembly to provide a special facility to meet the needs of this tubercular group. Not until 1939 did a Fulton superintendent urge the legislature to appropriate $500,000 to construct a "building for colored patients" capable of housing 650 patients on the Fulton campus.[21]

Paralleling the turn-of-the-century debates surrounding asylum over-

---

assume the costs of institutionalization for indigent insane, see "Insanity Records, 1919–1936," reels LRP 713.54 and 713.55, ibid. For the costs of institutionalization, see "Patient Records, 1926–1938," reel LRP 713.54, ibid. Comparable costs for 1883–1885 are found in "State Hospital #1 Patient Accounts, 1883–1885," reel LRP 713.61, ibid.

20. Report of Superintendent, no date, *House and Senate Journals Appendix*, 41st G.A. (1901), 16–17.

21. Report of Superintendent, no date, ibid., 60th G.A. (1939), 35. For an example of how racism affected employment at the hospital, see Jack McBride, *The Search: A True Story* (1976; reprint, Jefferson City: Brown Publishing, 2003).

Wards for African American males were overcrowded throughout their history. This photo is from around 1930 (Kingdom of Callaway Historical Society).

population and its solution, as well as the housing and care of African American patients, was a four-decade pursuit of federal money to pay for damages to the asylum inflicted by Union troops during the Civil War. Ironically, reports by Superintendent T. R. H. Smith and the Fulton Board of Managers in 1863 downplayed the damage, emphasizing that the buildings were well preserved, although the trees, shrubs, and grass at the asylum had been mostly destroyed by cavalry horses. Nevertheless, by May 1875 the Board of Managers authorized members Thomas Harris and John Hockaday to hire an attorney to pursue compensation.[22] Not until March 1899 did the *Fulton Sun* report that the U.S. House of Representatives had passed a bill authorizing payment of $17,250 rather than the $40,000 claimed by the asylum. However, even that amount was not forthcoming, as the federal Court of Claims demanded additional evidence of loss. That evidence, when submitted, convinced it in 1907 to award Fulton only $14,000, with 25 percent to be paid to the asylum's Washington attorney. Only after asylum treasurer E. W. Dunavant traveled to Washington in 1915 to resolve a

22. See Chapter 3 for a discussion of their reports. Journal State Lunatic Asylum: Board of Managers Minutes (December 28, 1866–July 7, 1874), May 5, 1875, 298 (FSHA).

The earliest aerial photo of the hospital, taken in 1934, shows the sprawling campus and its surrounding farmland. The Administration Building has been renovated with columns—an improvement paid for by the belated award from the U.S. government for Civil War damages (Missouri State Archives).

dispute over attorney fees did the government transfer into his hands $11,200.[23] Within a year, those monies enabled the asylum to add a large porch and twelve Corinthian columns to the main administrative and hospital building.

Despite such aesthetic improvements, despite the more substantial nonaesthetic construction and renovation programs between 1890 and 1940, and despite the eventual victory in removing the criminally insane from the regular hospital wards, Fulton's asylum continued to feel the strain of overcrowding in 1940. As the new decade began, Fulton had also not satisfactorily addressed the needs of its African American patients. But at least the worst population pressures had been relieved, the buildings and patients were as secure from fire as technology allowed, the boilers worked well, the water was unpolluted, and the future looked surprisingly bright during the eleventh year of a stubborn depression.

---

23. "War Claim Allowed," *Fulton Sun*, March 4, 1899, 1; State Hospital No. 1 Treasurer's Report, no date, *House and Senate Journals Appendix*, 49th G.A. (1917), 57.

II

by Barbara Brazos and Margot Ford McMillen

8
Three Early Residents

In the early years, the asylum provided society with many services. By keeping mentally ill people behind its massive walls, the buildings protected the sane from dangers that delusional people might inflict. And because the causes for mental illness were poorly understood, the thick walls protected the mentally ill from an ignorant community that might humiliate or abuse a helpless person. These two services, indeed, may be seen as the primary reason for an asylum and, with this perspective in mind, the asylum's history is incomplete without personal stories. Mental illness is often a hidden disease and carries taboos that run deep in our culture because, unlike most disabilities, brain disorders sometimes cause the victim to behave in antisocial, bizarre, or dangerous ways that bring shame to friends and family. Also, because mental illness can affect anyone, when we hear about mental illness, we are apt to worry about our own mental health or that of close family members.

Thus, the hospital keeps patient records closed and works to insure patient privacy, both for the sake of the patients and for society at large. As a result, most of the personal stories from the Fulton hospital are lost forever. Occasionally, however, family stories preserve memorable incidents. One Fulton resident and hospital employee, for example, learned from her family that Dr. Marion O. Biggs, superintendent from 1913 to 1927, had taken special care of two of her great aunts. The eldest, at age eighteen, found a job at the asylum. Within the first month, she was bitten by a patient and contracted undulent fever (brucellosis). Her condition deteriorated, with high fevers, weakness, and muscle aches, over the course of only a few weeks. Dr. Biggs took a personal interest in her care. As she became gravely ill, he had her moved to a room across from his own family's apartment in the administration building so that he could attend her both day and night. Even under his watchful care, in an era without antibiotics, she died. The family lost not only their daughter, but her earning potential. So Dr. Biggs arranged for the younger sister to have work. She was only sixteen, too young to work with patients. The job she was given, at Dr. Biggs's behest, was to wait on the table of his family during their meals, in the administration dining room.[1]

While there is anecdotal information about the spirit of the place, formal patient records are closed forever to protect patient and family privacy. This policy is supposed to protect families and clients from the stigma that mental illness once carried. At the same time, however, many families have treated their afflicted members with dignity and abiding love. For many, the decision to bring a loved one to Fulton was wrenching indeed. Discovering stories about a patient's commitment and residence in Fulton's early years brings out details that both confirm and dispel the stereotypes. Three such stories have surfaced with enough detail to illustrate the complexity in the decision to remove a family member from home.[2]

The earliest of these stories concerns the wife of Missouri artist George Caleb Bingham. Eliza Thomas was the daughter of a University of Missouri professor, raised in a middle-class Columbia home when Columbia was little more than a village before the Civil War. As a family with roots in the South, the women in her family, including Eliza, were probably somewhat pampered, or at least their duties lessened, by the existence of slaves in the household. Eliza was twenty-one when she married thirty-nine-year-old Bingham on December 2, 1849, less than a year after the death of his first wife. In his portrait of Eliza from about this time, her gaze is steady and forthright, her gown simple and unadorned, her hair pulled back simply. Eliza was a religious woman and Bingham became a Baptist to accomplish the marriage.

Bingham was not an easy mate, however. He was the father of two youngsters—Clara and Horace—from his first marriage. Although she was of delicate health and began her married life by suffering a series of miscarriages, young Eliza soon was in charge of raising young Clara, and Bingham was often away from home. Driven by the desire for success as a painter and in politics, his obsessions led him on long journeys to market his paintings, create portraits of wealthy patrons, or study under masters of the time. As a portrait painter, he painted both men and women, but his interests were

---

1. Barbara Brazos, note to McMillen, June 29, 2005, in authors' collection.
2. Interestingly, the stigma and fear seem to have disappeared for some people closely affiliated with the institution. One family reported that a grandfather worked on one of the farms, but the family never knew if he was an employee or a patient.

Spending hours in a sunny dayroom, often with arms bound in straitjackets, there was little hope of cure for these patients (Fulton State Hospital).

stuck firmly in the male sphere. His most enduring paintings on river life, politics, and the law are almost bereft of females.

One author asserts that Eliza "had long suffered from mental difficulties." The nature of her early troubles is unclear from the records, however, and diagnosis at the time was imprecise. In his letters to his friend James S. Rollins, Bingham mentioned Eliza frequently and took pride in her activities. In January 1853, he wrote that she was on a trip to the South. He had "received a long letter" from her and reported that she had become "fat." A few months later he wrote from Philadelphia, where they were staying, that she "has a piano in her room for daily practice."[3]

Bingham returned to Missouri, but left Eliza and Clara on the east coast. In July, the mother and daughter spent two weeks at Cape May, enjoying the sea baths, which were supposed at the time to cure many ailments. He wrote that Eliza was much improved from the experience. The family spent much of 1856–1859 in Europe, where the artist studied under master painters and did some of his most enduring grand paintings of the Missouri frontier.

---

3. See Kenneth Winn, "George Caleb Bingham," in *Dictionary of Missouri Biography* (Columbia: University of Missouri Press, 1999), 73. Many of Bingham's letters are reprinted in C. B. Rollins, ed., "Letters of George Caleb Bingham to James S. Rollins," *Missouri Historical Review* vols. 32 and 33 (Columbia: State Historical Society of Missouri, 1937–1939).

Clara and Horace studied French and German, and Eliza's attention was "absorbed in the household." In the winter of 1858, he wrote, she "suffered much illness."

Returning to Missouri after the death of Eliza's father, the family found the state girding for the Civil War. They took up residence in Boonville. Their son, Rollins James Bingham, was born in 1861. Eliza and Rollins are most certainly the models for Bingham's only allegorical portrait, *Thread of Life*. She is posed as a classically draped Madonna figure, with child in arms, on a cloud supported by a flying angel. Despite the peace conveyed in this painting, the prewar time was difficult for Missourians. Bingham was torn between his Southern allegiance and a dislike of slavery. He was pressed into government service for the state, first for the pro-Southern state guard and then for the pro-Union provisional government. Following his political leads, Eliza's interests moved with her husband's. In 1863, she wrote to her sister that Bingham's opponents in a public legislative battle were angry "radicals" retaliating after Bingham had publicly embarrassed a Union colonel.[4]

Besides controversy, the war brought family tragedy. Union authorities commandeered a house Bingham inherited from Eliza's father. It collapsed, killing several occupants—the female relatives of pro-Confederate fighters. This accident touched off new battles and was a precipitating factor in the sack of Lawrence, Kansas, by Quantrill's Confederate guerrillas. And, to add to the family pain, Horace was killed while in service to the Union. With so much to occupy him, discussion of Eliza's health disappeared from Bingham's letters. She may have been living in Kansas City in 1873, as a letter from Mattie Lykins to the *Kansas City Star* thanked Eliza Bingham for toys and candy sent to Lykins's Confederate Orphans' home in that city.[5]

Their daughter, Clara, married and became the mother of five children by 1873. Then, in 1876, a letter from Bingham to Rollins reported that Eliza was in Kansas City, "very ill." A month later, still ill, she and son Rollins traveled to New York and Philadelphia for "the great centennial exhibition." Bingham was relieved after Eliza wrote him that the trip had been good for her. Bingham wrote, "I have been frequently uneasy on her account. We have lived together for so long and so harmoniously that her loss would be more than death to me." Less than four months later, after Rollins had entered Kemper Academy in Boonville, Eliza's health took a turn for the worse: "It has pleased God to visit me with an affliction which it will require all the fortitude which I can summon to my aid, to bear," wrote Bingham;

---

4. Nancy Rash, *George Caleb Bingham* (New Haven: Yale University Press, 1991), 178–79.

5. www.kcstar.com/millennium/part3/stories/mattie.htm, accessed July 10, 2005. The Lykinses were close family friends of both Binghams. Their effort to open the children's home was bitterly opposed by the husband of Eliza's sister, dividing the family. Then, after Eliza's death, Bingham moved in with and soon married Mattie Lykins.

> I have ascertained that the opinion of the phicician whom she called in to examine her lungs was erroneous, and it has turned out that the mental shock which it gave her has deranged her upon the subject of religion, and a few days experience has convinced me that I will be compelled to take her to an asylum . . . she is inexpressibly happy. Her derangement exhibits itself in brilliant visions of Heaven and her departed relatives and friends who are inhabitants thereof. She is certain that her Savior visits her and converses with her, instructing her what to do, and she cannot bear to hear the slightest doubt expressed as to the actual fact of all that appears to her in these visions of her disordered brain.
>
> Her heart overflows with love to me and all her relatives and friends, but she requires impossible things of me, which she thinks I can easily perform, and my not performing which distresses her very much, making her sometimes believe that I do not love her, although in fact I would willingly die for her, if by so doing I could restore her to health.[6]

Bingham traveled to the asylum in Fulton to view the accommodations and satisfy himself that Eliza would be comfortable there. T. R. H. Smith was superintendent at the time, and he agreed to take Eliza. The trip by train was publicized well enough that it drew a writer when the train stopped in Moberly. The *Moberly Monitor* ran a story on October 21, 1876, which was reprinted in the *Boonville Weekly Advertiser* on November 3 under the headline "Driven Insane by a Thoughtless Physician, Adjutant General Bingham's Wife Taken to Fulton." The article explained that a physician had told Eliza that her disease was incurable and "The gloomy talk drove the poor woman mad." The story "will be read with deep sadness by many friends of Mrs. Bingham," said the writer:

> The two passed through Moberly on the St. L, KC & N R'y . . . one of the saddest spectacles our reporter ever witnessed . . . for many a weary year have this twain traveled life's weary journey hand and hand, and the aged partner of this painter-statesman has cheered him in adversity and rejoiced with him over his triumphs. But suddenly as if the sun were stricken from the heaven at noonday the light of his life went out and the partner of his joys and his toils became a hopeless lunatic.[7]

The article concludes that the two were "accompanied on the trip by quite a party of friends."

A few days later, Bingham wrote from Fulton, "I came over . . . this morn-

---

6. "Letters of Bingham to Rollins," vol. 33, 351.
7. *Boonville Weekly Advertiser*, November 3, 1976, 8.

ing, having last night received an unfavorable letter from Doct [T. R. H.] Smith . . . I have the consolation of knowing that my wife suffers no pain, but seems to be gradually and peacefully traveling to the home of the blessed. She imagines that she is already in Heaven and speaks of herself as no longer a tenant of earth." She died soon after and, a month after her death, Bingham wrote to Rollins, "I have a sad and lonely life now which finds its chief solace in the society of those who knew and loved my dear wife."[8]

About twenty years after Eliza's death, a family in Vienna, Missouri, brought their twenty-three-year-old epileptic son, whom we will call Anthony, to the asylum. Author Joan Gilbert of Hallsville discovered several rare letters from asylum superintendents and from Anthony. In an unpublished manuscript, Gilbert explores the family's situation.[9]

Coming to Missouri in 1831 with several related families, Anthony's grandparents came from successful Tennessee farm stock. His grandfather had inherited a 640-acre farm in Tennessee, and, in Gilbert's words, "brought considerably more money than the average settler." In the estate of Anthony's mother were "many cancelled notes," indicating that some family income came from lending money. His mother had lovingly kept the letters regarding Anthony, her eldest, in a collection along with other family records, letters, and clippings about family events like birthdays, weddings, deaths, and births. The collection, passed down to one of Anthony's sisters, included clippings about a successful father: He was elected to the school board and, at his death, his funeral was one of the largest in the area's history. Only about half the mourners were able to get into the church.

The family clearly valued education. One sister was a schoolteacher and another a Sunday School teacher. A brother became a minister, following in the footsteps of an uncle who was a Methodist minister. Another cousin became president of a state banking association. Local lore states that the family members were large, strong people. To demonstrate his strength, the minister uncle once hoisted a 150-pound hog under each arm and jumped a fence. Anthony was apparently similarly large, which would have made his epileptic seizures menacing to family members, especially to his mother and sisters alone much of the day on an isolated farm. At the same time, the family kept Anthony in their hearts even during his institutionalization. A family photo taken on the lawn shows members gathered around his portrait.

We do not know exactly when Anthony went to the asylum. The earliest

---

8. "Letters of Bingham to Rollins," vol. 33, 375.

9. All the original documents referred to in the story of "Anthony" are referenced in Gilbert's unpublished manuscript and in her private collection. While she has generously shared the manuscript, the rights to the story remain her own.

Three Early Residents   125

Patients took their meals together in dining rooms like this (Missouri State Archives).

letters in the collection, from Superintendent Coombs, were an effort to make respectful reports to the loving family. The first, written January 3, 1898, says:

> Dear Sir:
> This is to inform you that your son's condition is decidedly better than it was several months ago. His mind is much clearer and his epileptic seizures are less severe and at longer intervals. At times he is a little demonstrative and shows a combative tendency but all in all he is much brighter and we are necessarily more hopeful.
> Very truly yours, etc.

In August the same year, Coombs advised the parents that the boy's seizures were "not so violent as they used to be, nor are they so frequent," and he added, apparently in response to a letter from the boy's mother, "We have no objection to his mother coming to see him, and believe it will do him good." The next February, Coombs reassured the family that Anthony was "much improved." In the meantime, Anthony had written home twice:

December 21
   Dear Father and Mother I will rite you a few lines to let you know that I would like to see you and I hope that I will be well to get there before long. . . . This is a very good place. I hope to god that all of you are well and stay that way I can't think of much to rite now and you answer as soon as you can. I want to know how you all are getting along tell duglas to come out here I want to see him awful bad so I will close for this time goodby . . .

A letter six weeks later asks again for "Jim Duglas" and says, "I am better than what I was I hope to god that I will be back there after while." Another letter, written four months later, asks about "uncle Alex and ant Mary uncle jake and ant emly . . . monrow and fany." After this letter, there was apparently a long silence. A new superintendent, W. L. Ray, took charge of the asylum in 1901, and on January 28 of that year had the responsibility of sending a telegram: "Anthony your son is dead have banker to wire money here for shipping expence otherwise we will bury him here." To this brief message, the Maries County Bank replied, "We guarantee shipping expense on body . . . Ship to Dixon."

In claiming the body, the family reached out as well as they could. Rather than hiding the story, the *Maries County Gazette* ran an extensive obituary:

   Anthony, eldest son of [parents' names] of this place, breathed his last at the Fulton Asylum of which he was an inmate, last Monday. He has been afflicted from infancy and during the 26 years of his life was a constant sufferer. His remains were shipped to Dixon and from there conveyed to the home of his parents. Services were conducted in the M.E. [Methodist Episcopal] church by Rev. Fryer Wednesday morning and a large concourse of sorrowing friends followed the departed one to his last resting place. The *Gazette* extends its earnest sympathy to the bereaved parents and relatives.

Soon after, the *Gazette* ran a mournful Victorian-style poem in Anthony's memory, signed "Sister."

>   Dearest Brother, thou hast left us
>   And now we mourn for thee;
>   But alas, we soon will meet you
>   In that land so good and free.
>
>   Yes, indeed, we all are numbered,
>   One by one we're gathered home;
>   And the time is swiftly coming
>   To meet you at the throne.

> Father, mother, sister, brother
>> Now in sadness weep for thee;
> But dear brother, we are coming
>> To that land so good and free.
>
> Oh, dear brother, thou hast suffered,
>> How, not even thee could tell;
> But now thou art an angel,
>> And with Christ forever dwell.

The final pieces of the correspondence saved by Anthony's mother come from W. L. Ray, who reassured the family that Anthony's final days passed with "little suffering." In his last two days, Anthony experienced "an unusual number of fits and sank rapidly." Ray praised Anthony as a "kind-hearted and obedient patient" and called his death "deeply regretted by all who knew him." A few days later, Ray wrote that, in a separate package, he was returning Anthony's watch to the family.

While Eliza's story is one of lost hope and Anthony's story is one of compassion, a later set of narratives illustrates how commitment to the asylum may have been used as punishment for actions against the dominant society. Twenty years after Anthony's death, the actions of sisters Mollie and Feemy (née Sykes) resulted in declarations of their incompetence and Feemy's commitment to Fulton by the Ralls County Court. Gregg Andrews has painstakingly documented the struggles of the Sykes sisters in *Insane Sisters: Or, the Price Paid for Challenging a Company Town*. He writes that four Sykes sisters and one brother came of age in northeast Missouri in the years after the Civil War. The family came into the Little Dixie area from the north during Reconstruction, when the traditional leading families, mostly with Southern allegiances, were clinging to power and tradition. The Sykes family, arriving in this area, found themselves on the wrong side of every cultural battle line.

At the same time, the suffrage movement urged women to pursue education and to try new roles. One sister, Laura, found satisfaction in fundraising for the church, a socially acceptable activism. Emma was beginning a life of intellectual pursuits when she died in childbirth at age twenty-four. The lives of Mollie and Feemy would take less orthodox directions. In her early years, Feemy married but petitioned for divorce after thirteen months to pursue life as a writer. Although she helped provide some care for her family financially, she rejected traditional roles. For example, she refused to become the direct caretaker for her brother's six children after the miscarriage and death of their mother.

A picture of Mollie shows her dressed in lacy Victorian splendor with tiny heart-shaped earrings dangling from her ears. Feemy cuts a fine figure in a dark dress and dashing hat. It is hard to know what kind of impression they made on society, but it is certain that their intellectual strength helped them use the few rights the law had granted. Supporting herself partly by buying and selling real estate, Feemy managed to remain independent. She had a fascination with the law and studied vigorously. Had she been a man, her independent study could have led to a career and political appointments. She was not a man, however, and her resulting anger with the male-dominated legal profession became worse when she was disappointed by the male-dominated medical profession. A botched face-lift left her in constant pain, and she sought relief through hypnotism from a mesmerist in Nevada, Missouri. Soon, she was involved with "a variety of flamboyant magnetic healers, folk doctors, herbalists, snake-oil salesmen, and other itinerant lecturers and healers."[10]

While Feemy was independently broadening her horizons, Mollie was pursuing a place in society by marrying a succession of men. Having survived a brutal alcoholic, she wed a kind but penniless cousin. After pursuing careers in various crafts such as china painting and dressmaking, she ended the marriage in divorce. A third, brief marriage ended in her husband's death, but in her fourth marriage she found respectability and security. Her husband, John Scott, died within a few years but left her in possession of an eighty-acre farm, some other real estate, and a contested life insurance policy. Mollie was now cynical about marriage and advised Feemy to marry a wealthy man, advice that Feemy ignored. Instead of marrying, Feemy used her law background to help Mollie satisfactorily settle the life insurance and the estate of John Scott.

Mollie next married Sam Heinbach, an alcoholic in the habit of going barefoot, a man in poor health who owned a lot of property. Much of his land lay beside the thriving Atlas Portland Cement Plant. As a village called Ilasco sprang up next to the plant, he collected modest rents on 106 lots. Mollie pursued Heinbach into marriage, and they set up housekeeping in December 1908 in the rough cabin he had occupied. Soon they had purchased and moved into the nicest house in Ilasco. Heinbach remained alcoholic and difficult, but Mollie cared for him until his death just over a year later. His land, of course, had become increasingly valuable. He had paid ten dollars per acre and had seen it increase to an estimated five hundred dollars per acre. Heinbach had refused to sell it. It is unclear whether Mollie would have sold it if asked. Andrews believes that she had become comfortable as a major landlady of Ilasco and enjoyed the prestige that came

---

10. Andrews, *Insane Sisters*, 43.

with the position. At any rate, rather than offer to buy, lawyers began a campaign to discredit Heinbach's will, force a bargain sale, and vilify Mollie.

From the beginning, the newspapers reveled in the sensational case and fed the public curiosity. The time was one of moral turmoil when issues of temperance and women's rights brought angry supporters and opposition to town meetings. The main argument to discredit Mollie was the assertion that the alcoholic Sam was not of sound mind when he married and when he drew up his will. Attorneys produced Sam's agent, who said that he sometimes had to wait several days for Sam to sober up to transact business. Another argument was the fact that Sam collected rent at all. The lawyers asserted that, rather than rent the land, a sane man would have sold when it more than doubled in value over a four-year period.

Forty Ilasco residents signed statements in support of Mollie, and several women testified on her behalf. All were ignored or discredited, as lawyers asked questions about their sex lives, drinking habits, or the legality of their marriages. The all-male jury, closely aligned with the community's principal families who, of course, profited from the Atlas plant, decided against Mollie. At this point, Feemy became more involved. Her fee would be ownership of the increasingly valuable land after Mollie's death, and the deed was rewritten to reflect that association. Over the next ten years, Feemy pursued the case relentlessly, in a partnership that found the sisters frequently opposed and increasingly indebted. For two years, Mollie disappeared from Ralls County, and there was speculation that she was fleeing Feemy out of fear for her life. After her return, attorneys pursued a new suit to prove that Mollie was insane. The trial lasted two days and was settled when Mollie, who was completely deaf by this time, broke down and consented to be placed under her brother's guardianship.

Feemy continued the fight. All along, her disdain for lawyers and doctors was interpreted as rebelliousness. Cultural attitudes of the time put forth explanations of insanity that included theories such as "utromania," in which a "tipped" uterus caused insanity and made a woman become convinced of her own importance. Feemy's actions became increasingly desperate, and she grew more vociferous in her disdain of lawyers. It was inevitable, perhaps, that the Ralls County Court would accuse her of "monomania," a fixation with one subject. In her case, the symptoms were her fixation on money and lawsuits. Feemy had demanded that the court hear her views about spiritualism and alternative medical cures, and the prosecutor quickly pursued and dwelled on her unorthodox beliefs. Thus, Feemy's short talk about the medical profession did not help her case.

She lost the case but won the right to appeal after a change of venue to Hannibal. However, to pay for their debts, the sisters' land was appropriated by the county and sold at a sheriff's sale to Atlas. With Feemy's funds cut

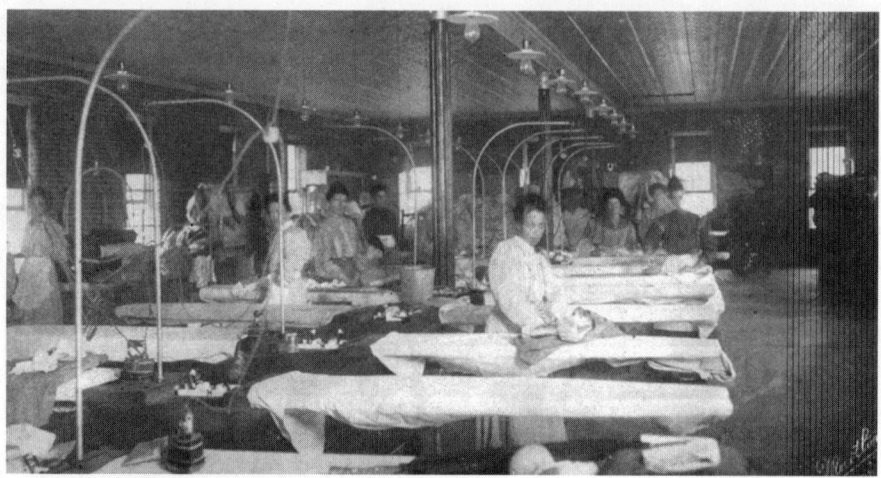
Rather than enduring long days of boredom, patients worked in the laundry that took care of the needs of staff as well as patients (Missouri State Archives).

off, she was allowed to remain in Ilasco but reduced to living in filth. The proud and beautiful Feemy now wore dresses made from gunnysacks. Not surprisingly, she began to lecture neighbors about how powerful players had manipulated the law. In 1921, the state created the Eleemosynary Board and put one of Feemy's old adversaries, attorney Charles E. Rendlen, on the board. The lines of communication to the hospital were now established, but the county still had the problem of who would pay for Feemy's care at the asylum.

On April 5, 1927, the Missouri General Assembly passed a law to allow county officials to recover expenses from the estate of the insane. Giving her a week to prepare a defense, the same judge found her incompetent and a danger to "her own person and the lives and property of others." Feemy was committed as a "private" patient in August 1927. As a private patient, she paid forty dollars a month for her confinement at the same time that county patients were charged eighteen dollars per month. She died at the hospital in 1930, probably after a fall that resulted in a broken hip and led to pneumonia. This was, however, during a period of one of the asylum's frequent abuse scandals when overcrowding resulted in several mysterious deaths. Mollie died in 1928 at home, after catching on fire at the stove.

Gregg Andrews argues persuasively that the corporate-financed and male-dominated legal system fueled Feemy's anger, leading to desperately erratic behavior and eventually wearing her down: "The outcome . . . raises questions about the use of guardianships and insanity as methods of social control against unconventional women." In fact, he writes, "doctors, politicians, and other male professionals had insisted that women such as Feemy who pursued education, autonomy, and independence did so at the risk of their own emotional and physical well-being." The *Ralls County Record* announced Feemy's death with a "benevolent tone of paternalism," Andrews writes. After calling Feemy "brilliant . . . well-educated, refined," the editor wrote: "Peace to her troubled soul."[11]

11. Ibid., 12, 193.

9

Dramatic Changes in Treatment, 1940–1949

With the nation just recovering from the Great Depression, Hospital No. 1 rang in the 1940s with a patient census at 2,476.[1] The new five-story Hospital Building with medical clinics and sick wards was fully operational, the top story dedicated to treating Missouri's indigent cancer patients. In the Hadley Building nearby, long ramps allowed attendants to push wheelchairs bearing tubercular patients to sunrooms on the second floor. The building for the criminal insane had finally been finished. The dairy farm, meat locker, and garden were providing most of the food for the hospital and a surplus for other state institutions. Under the direction of Superintendent J. R. Bunch, the hospital was fairly self-sufficient, with its own deep wells and a new powerhouse providing electricity. The self-sufficiency was important for the state to afford the growing number of residents. A new building provided space for an auditorium, kitchen, and an especially welcome cafeteria. One report noted, "The advantage the patient has of selecting his own food has a very salutary effect in developing his initiative."[2]

One worker took special interest in the history of the hospital. Louis Bratton started work as an aide in February 1941 at age twenty-seven and retired in 1979 as a Maintenance Supervisor II. His starting salary of forty dollars a month was supplemented by housing, meals, medical care, prescriptions, and laundry. From the beginning, every day at work was an adventure, with the possibility of being called to assist at any part of the hospital, even helping on tasks that were not listed in his job description. The hospital was a busy place; besides the farms and orchards, where patients

---

1. Report of the Superintendent (Jefferson City: Department of Mental Health, 1941).
2. Dwight H. Brown, *Missouri Manual, 1939–1940* (Jefferson City: Secretary of State, 1940), 623.

The 1940 Medical Building today is in partial use as office space (McMillen photo).

cared for the animals, there was a locker plant where patients helped with butchering. They also preserved produce when it came out of the fields. Bratton remembered that there was a potato barn for storage and that potatoes were heaped up in a mound three feet from the walls to prevent freezing. A patient tended a wood-burning stove to keep the crop from freezing. At harvest time, there were long tables set up in front of the administration building, where patients shucked corn, cleaned string beans, and peeled tomatoes, then preserved them in gallon cans for winter use. Thousands of gallons of produce were preserved each year.[3]

In the power plant, a patient kept the books and knew how much water was pumped and electricity was generated each day. The patients "took care of the wards, cleaned the wards, waxed the floors [using] big wooden drags with carpeting on them to polish the floors . . . did the cooking. . . . The employees just supervised." Early in his career, he was asked to replace the head cook, a position he knew nothing about. He soon learned that the patients did the actual cooking while the staff sat on stools and watched. It was easy for lawmakers and administration to justify the patient labor as paying for their room and board while increasing the patient's sense of usefulness and self-esteem.[4]

3. Louis Bratton, interview by Barbara Brazos, January 29, 2000, tape recording in authors' collection.
4. Ibid.

Yield from the land made a $5,000 profit in 1944, and swine were slaughtered to provide $16,800 worth of meat for the state. Milk production was 924,645 pounds. In a meeting at the Kingdom of Callaway Historical Society, one former maintenance worker remembered that the hospital's orchard stretched from the cemetery to the road. Seaman Field was a garden. Two patients drove mule teams to haul manure from the dairy to the garden all day long.[5]

Bratton was drafted into the army a few months after he started and served for "four years, eight months, and eight days," then returned and received training on the GI Bill for a job in the hospital tin shop. His first jobs in the hospital shops were making such things as metal bread pans, pots, and wind turbines for the calf barn. Echoing the sentiments of many employees, Bratton remembered that the hospital was "a good place to work" and that it was more self-sufficient than most small towns. Employees and patients took pride in the buildings and grounds, which were enhanced by flower beds and a goldfish pond in front of the administration building. The fish spent the winter in the hospital greenhouse.[6]

The status of the superintendent and business manager was reflected by the location of their parking places. While the superintendent and business manager parked in front of the administration building, most employees parked by the kitchen. In bad weather, they walked to their jobs through the underground tunnels that had been constructed to connect the buildings as they went up. The tunnels were useful in many ways. Besides providing safe passage for aides to walk patients to the main buildings, the tunnels provided a way for food from the kitchen to be easily transported to dining rooms in various buildings. The tunnels also afforded space for electrical cables and water and heating pipes as the campus was modernized.

In the 1940s, the potential for cure was slim, and the strategies for handling violence were primitive. When a patient became unruly, workers on the floor called out and maintenance men from as far away as the power plant came to help. A nurse working at that time remembered her first days on the wards. To control violent patients, she was equipped with a towel and a sock with a bar of soap in the toe. Staff could wrap the towel around a violent patient's neck and twist until the patient passed out. One aide remembered that she wore a wet towel over her shoulder on some wards of the hospital: "Then they'd leave you alone." A sock with a bar of soap in the toe could be swung at a patient's head to knock him or her out. Neither the sock nor towel method left lasting marks on the patients.[7]

---

5. Bill Clevenger, interview by Brazos, August 2000, tape recording in authors' collection.
6. Louis Bratton interview.
7. Staff knew that violence was always a possibility. One nurse remembered a patient who at-

Tunnels carried water, electricity, and heat to hospital buildings and provided safe passage from living units to dining and treatment areas (Fulton State Hospital).

There was no money to train staff in better strategies. Missouri was nearly four million dollars in debt. Newly elected Republican governor Forrest C. Donnell (1941–1945) had not promised expansion of the mental health budget. He did promise, however, an end of the patronage system of hiring state employees. At the time, patronage meant that government jobs, including many of Fulton's, were awarded according to political affiliation and loyalty rather than training. Even the low-paying positions came with housing and other benefits. In an interview, one power plant worker remembered living in a dormitory and receiving room and board as part of his pay. The hospital pharmacy filled his prescriptions, and the hospital laundry did his laundry. Work took all his time, though, with shifts of "seven twelves," or seven twelve-hour days and one day off with an extra half-day off once a month. With little time to call his own, he was also expected to socialize with patients when they had dances and events. While he called the system "paternalistic," he said that patients and staff all felt they were being taken care of.[8]

---

tacked and tried to kill her. The patient was later released but readmitted after trying to kill herself. Meeting the patient later, the nurse remembered: "I walked in there . . . '———, how are you?' She knew my voice." And the patient apologized: "I hurt you bad" (Julia Davis, interview by Brazos and McMillen, January 10, 2000). The soap-in-sock and towel strategies for staff protection were common at the time. Marle Woodson, a reporter hospitalized in Oklahoma, describes the same treatment in Robert Whitaker, *Mad in America: Bad Science, Bad Medicine, and the Enduring Mistreatment of the Mentally Ill* (Cambridge: Perseus Books, 2002), 69.

8. Bill Clevenger interview. Reorganization of the Public Welfare Department had been suggested by welfare workers as early as 1937. The first federally funded commission in Missouri was on Unemployment Compensation in 1938. For more on the campaign to replace patronage with a merit system, see the Missouri Association for Social Welfare (MASW) papers, archived at the

The patronage system also resulted in "perks" for some Fulton businesses with politically connected owners. Workers remember the special relationship between Jameson's Ford dealership and the hospital. Buying a car at the dealership could result in a job recommendation at the hospital.[9] There were also perks for the county, in terms of services. The State Hospital morgue served as the county's only morgue. And the State Hospital physicians, whom state workers knew and trusted better than the doctors in town, treated staff and family members as well as patients. The system provided housing, including luxurious housing for those in the highest positions. In the main building, doctors' apartments were spacious, with large windows and sweeping views of the grounds. Yet the beautiful apartments were just a short walk from the patient hallways, so the sounds and smells of the grim reality of mental illness were always nearby.

With job security based on political connections, it was a frequent occurrence that, the morning after an election, workers hired during the previous administration woke to the news that they had to find new jobs. One worker at the state hog farm had been hired in the Democratic administration at the rate of fifty dollars per month plus housing that included a place to keep chickens and a milk cow. When Forrest Donnell the Republican was elected, the worker and his wife, with two young daughters, had to quickly find another farm where they could move with their livestock.[10]

The new governor pledged to change hiring practices from political affiliation to merit. To judge merit, applicants would take exams that evaluated expertise and experience. A brochure from Donnell's office noted, "By April 1, 1942, twenty states of the union had each enacted a state-wide civil service law. . . . In Missouri, pursuant to a Federal law, a merit system is in effect in certain departments in which federal funds are employed." By this time, the Social Security Commission, Unemployment Commission, State Highway Commission, and State Liquor Commission all used merit examinations, although the Highway and Liquor Commissions were also obliged to hire half their appointments from those "affiliated with the political party casting the highest number of votes for governor."[11]

The first advantage of hiring according to merit would be economy for the state, because a skilled new employee would need less training. There would also be fewer turnovers and more security for employees regardless

---

Western Historical Manuscript Collection in Columbia, Missouri (Collection #3475, f. 3927–31).

9. Doris Brown, interview by Brazos and McMillen, July 25, 1999, tape recording in authors' collection.

10. Julia Davis interview.

11. "The Merit System" (Jefferson City: Office of the Governor, 1943), 4–5. MASW Collection, f. 3931.

of their political affiliation. To make the changes, a new state constitution was needed to replace the Constitution of 1875. In 1942, Missourians voted for a constitutional convention. In overseeing the convention, Donnell kept his campaign promise and, in 1945, was elected U.S. senator. His successor as governor, Phil M. Donnelly, a Democrat, oversaw adoption of the new constitution and the creation of a new body of law for Missouri. Among other changes, the new constitution recognized that the state was becoming increasingly urban. Urban areas, therefore, received more Senate seats, while rural citizens still had a larger basis in the House.[12]

The new constitution also reorganized the state's various divisions and departments, partly to bring them into compliance with federal guidelines as federal money became important to running state agencies. This reorganization had significant impact on the Fulton facility. In 1947, the Eleemosynary Division was disbanded, and State Hospital No. 1 became part of the Department of Health and Public Welfare's Division of Mental Diseases. The governor still had the power to appoint directors of state departments, so the new department was not totally politics-free, but for the most part the statewide merit system replaced the patronage system. Twelve new laws brought the Division of Mental Diseases and its institutions into compliance with the new constitution and federal regulations. One law made it possible for Missouri to benefit from federal "postwar reserve funds," which provided money for communities to build their own general hospitals. Other new laws also enabled state hospitals to remove indigent patients back to their counties or granted the director of the Department of Health and Public Welfare the right to take over property of deceased patients to defray expenses.[13]

Just as discussion of the constitution and new laws brought public attention to the relationship of the state and its mentally ill citizens, so too did a series of books and movies. In the spring of 1940, Fulton and the hospital received unexpected attention after the publication of *Kings Row*, a novel by Fulton son Henry Bellamann, who had had a successful career in music and poetry and lived in New York as a full-time writer. *Kings Row* depicted small-town life as corrupt at best and terrifying at worst. Westminster professor emeritus Jay Karr points out that the town and asylum in the book were based on Fulton and that many characters were thinly disguised versions of Fulton residents.[14]

As soon as it came out, the *New York Herald Tribune*, the *New York Times Book*

---

12. Duane Meyer, *Heritage of Missouri* (St. Louis: River City Publishers, 1970), 684–86.
13. Ibid.
14. Jay Miles Karr, introduction to Henry Bellamann, *Kings Row* (Fulton: Kingdom House, 1981), xi–xxv.

Review, Time Magazine, and the *New Yorker* reviewed *Kings Row.* Clifton Fadiman, reviewer for the *New Yorker,* summed up the cast of characters as "a sadistic surgeon who likes to cut off people's legs, a doctor who's too fond of his daughter, a town hangman who loves his work . . . a mystically mad priest, a girl violinist who is slated for the booby hatch . . . and a village idiot, too." The book was in the top ten of the bestseller list through July. According to Karr, "all [the reviewers] were telling their readers to read it, and printing pictures of the author, and using lots of space to discuss the story."[15]

At the time of publication, and even today, Fulton residents could name the models for most of the characters, and they could even describe details of the incidents in the book. Henry Bellamann's sister, still living in Fulton, told the *St. Louis Post-Dispatch,* "one half of the town is angry because they think they see themselves in *Kings Row* while the other half is angry because they were left out." Although the portraits were stretched to provide drama, the novel replayed the stories of Bellamann's own life. A musically gifted child, he had been born in scandalous circumstances and rejected by the town society. To those similarly injured by small-town sensibilities, the novel was vindication; others felt differently. The *Mexico Ledger,* from the county seat of the adjoining county, always on the lookout for signs of moral weakness in its imagined competitor, noted smugly, "It might have happened to us." To Fulton's credit, the town embraced the novel. Ovid Bell Sr., the local newspaper editor, reviewed it in print and was invited to at least three club meetings to discuss his impressions. Even though most residents had bought a copy, the newspaper ran a serialized version. The town also invited Bellamann to its annual "Kingdom Supper," an event that celebrates a native son who has left town and made good, but Bellamann had a lecture invitation for the date and did not return to Fulton before his death.[16]

When viewed as a document about the asylum, the novel illustrates clearly how the destinies of the town and the hospital are intertwined. The asylum was the major employer. Merchants, landlords, politicians, and professionals all owed their respectability to the hospital, even if they never visited it and were even slightly embarrassed by its presence. To underscore that fact in *Kings Row,* Bellamann devised a scene wherein asylum doctor Parris Mitchell makes $100,000 by selling land to the state, reinforcing the widely held belief that those connected with the asylum used their connections for financial gain at the taxpayers' expense.[17]

---

15. Jay Miles Karr, "Rediscovering the Author of *Kings Row:* The First Bellamann Lecture, Oct. 18th, 1979" (manuscript at Kingdom of Callaway Historical Society), 10.
16. Ibid., 41.
17. Bellamann, *Kings Row,* 474.

Dramatic Changes in Treatment 139

The images of corruption were expanded in a blockbuster film adaptation starring Ronald Reagan in 1942. The book reappeared on the bestseller list for seven more months. Six years later, in 1948, Henry Bellamann's widow, Katherine, finished Henry's second novel, *Parris Mitchell of Kings Row*. One of the few books to disclose the predicaments of a doctor at an asylum, the book traces Parris's relationships with the patients: "Living and working among the monstrous phantoms, the distortions, the violent tensions and grotesque exhibitions of sick minds could never be a happy experience, but it could be immeasurably exciting," the book's narrator asserted, adding, "you can expect a higher percentage of mental illness in the small town."[18]

Kings Row and *Parris Mitchell of Kings Row* were early entries into the literature of mental illness, but it was not long before a string of books and movies fascinated the public with the wonders and mysteries of the mind and provided hope that cures for mental illness would soon be available. *Spellbound*, a 1945 Alfred Hitchcock film, opened with a written prologue: "Once the complexes that have been disturbing the patient are uncovered and interpreted, the illness and confusion disappear . . . and the devils of unreason are driven from the human soul." In this early entry into psychological films, a psychoanalyst (Ingrid Bergman) counsels an accused murderer: "Open your mind and the pain will leave." Through dream analysis (with the dream sequence designed by Salvador Dali), the memory of the guilt-ridden amnesiac (Gregory Peck) is restored and a mystery solved.[19]

The same year *Spellbound* appeared, *The Lost Weekend* swept the Oscars, winning Best Picture, Best Actor, Best Screenplay, and Best Director with a script that declared that alcoholism was an illness that could be cured. In the film, actor Ray Milland, playing a disappointed writer, spirals into hopelessness, is committed to and escapes an alcoholic ward, and suffers through the vividly depicted DTs. He is finally rescued by the love of a woman who believes, "One cure didn't take. There's another."[20]

In 1948, a sensitive and realistic entry in the canon of mental health literature hit the silver screen. *The Snake Pit* starred Olivia de Havilland as a young woman who has suffered a break with reality. The screenplay was based on a true story by Mary Jane Ward, and Ward's story is presented as the young woman encounters crowded wards and overworked staff at the state institution: "We haven't got enough of anything but patients," says the superintendent, a line that entered the vernacular of mental health profes-

18. Henry Bellamann and Katherine Bellamann, *Parris Mitchell of Kings Row* (New York: Simon and Schuster, 1948), 65, 153.
19. *Spellbound*, motion picture, directed by Alfred Hitchcock (Los Angeles: United Artists, 1945).
20. *The Lost Weekend*, motion picture, directed by Charles Bracket and Billy Wilder (Universal City, Calif.: Universal, 1945). Based on a novel by Charles Jackson.

sionals. Less romantic than Hollywood's earlier efforts, *The Snake Pit* took viewers behind asylum walls to see shock treatment, a continuous water bath, a straitjacket, and occupational therapy. Finally, a sympathetic doctor with a picture of Freud on his office wall discovers the truths about the patient's past through psychoanalysis.[21]

As *Snake Pit*'s sobering portrayal of mental health care revealed, the promise of a cure was elusive. In the 1945–1946 *State of Missouri Official Manual*, the eleemosynary institutions' board of managers statement pointed out, "Since the entry into World War II, the institutions have been confronted with numerous problems. Doctors, nurses, technical and general employees have been called into the service. High wages in war industries brought about a continual employee turnover. Food rationing, priorities, food and material shortages, partial shipments and delayed shipments have added to the difficulties of operation." Meanwhile, they added, "In spite of these perplexities, the institutions are giving the patients the best possible care and treatment."[22]

New treatments were being developed all over the world, and Fulton used them all. Besides hydrotherapy, patients were treated with insulin shock therapy, Metrazol convulsive therapy, artificial fever therapy, electroshock, and X-rays. An outpatient clinic served nondangerous people who could be treated without coming in contact with the chronically or acutely ill. This also helped alleviate the staff shortage, which was so acute that there were only five nurses for the 2,500 patients. As nurse Jane Wallace told the *Fulton Sun*, "You'd just have to go flying from one end of campus to the other."[23]

Some treatments were used for years, then later discarded because they were dangerous to the patients. Insulin shock therapy, for example, was a treatment given to physically healthy patients in early stages of schizophrenia. Each patient was given an intramuscular shot of insulin, with dosages increasing each day, decreasing the blood sugar until the patient reached shock, a condition that was maintained for thirty minutes to two hours before administration of glucose or a saline solution. Shock included loss of contact with surroundings accompanied by "primitive movements" like kissing, sucking, thumb sucking, writhing, and eyes floating "up and down." The procedure was repeated for twenty to fifty days, with Sundays off. The treat-

---

21. *The Snake Pit*, motion picture, directed by Frank Partos and Millen Brand (Hollywood: Twentieth Century Fox, 1948). Ward's true-life experience with the system made her an effective advocate, and she toured the nation for the next decade to talk to mental health professionals. In 1954, she delivered the keynote address at the Mental Health Association of St. Louis annual meeting.

22. Wilson Bell, *Official Manual State of Missouri, 1945–1946* (Jefferson City: Secretary of State, 1946), 774.

23. Pat Mosher, "Nurses Reflect on Changes in Profession," *Fulton Sun*, May 6, 1990.

Dramatic Changes in Treatment 141

In 1955, the hospital sponsored this float in the annual Fulton Christmas parade. The "Lollipop Land" banner makes a sly reference to the lollipops given to patients after insulin shock therapy (Fulton State Hospital).

ments were thought to eliminate toxins and revive normal responses to stimulus.[24]

Insulin shock therapy nurses were to watch for violent attack, falling pulse, absent corneal reflexes and secondary shock. To guard against slipping back into coma, patients were given lollipops, a high-calorie lunch, and something to do.

As early as 1941, a U.S. Public Health survey found that nationally, 5 percent of all insulin-therapy patients in state hospitals died from the treatments and 80 percent of those released came back to the hospital. Only 6 percent did well enough to live in society three years after treatment. Manfred Sakel, the Viennese psychiatrist who had pioneered the treatment and reported 70 percent cure rates, explained that he had selected patients carefully: They were strong, young, only recently diagnosed with insanity, and had no other physical ailments such as kidney disease or cardiovascular disorders.[25]

Other therapies, like Metrazol convulsive therapy, began to replace in-

---

24. Helen F. Hansen, *A Review of Nursing with Outlines of Subjects, Questions and Answers* (Philadelphia: W. B. Saunders, 1944), 655–57.
25. Whitaker, *Mad in America*, 90.

sulin shock therapy. Metrazol was a drug intended to induce seizures and allay the symptoms of "depressive psychoses, schizophrenia, involutional melancholia and depressed manic-depressive syndrome." It was given intravenously for an average course of five convulsions. The treatments triggered such violent seizures that patients ended up with fractured and dislocated bones, loosened teeth, and hemorrhages in various organs. As with other shock therapies, the idea was to shock the patient out of delusions and into lucidity, and when the treatment was unsuccessful the answer was to shock again. Once patients had endured this therapy, they became increasingly resistant and afraid of the injections and were reduced to pleading or violence in resisting the staff. Some doctors opined that the fear itself was the curative factor in the treatment.[26]

Artificial fever therapy, or pyrotherapy, used heat to relieve mental illness. Fever could be induced with an injection of malaria or typhoid; this procedure was used to treat syphilis. One Fulton resident remembers heat treatments she received at Fulton State Hospital as a child, when she developed unexplained spasms described as Saint Vitus' dance. She was placed in a box of lights, or a "radiant heat cabinet," for several hours and recovered to be symptom-free, except for a burn on her back where the skin touched a light.[27]

Electroshock came to the hospital in 1941, just a year after the machines were introduced in the United States, bringing a relatively untested but promising therapy to Missouri. It was used almost indiscriminately on patients with many diagnoses. By jolting the brain with electricity, the treatment put patients into seizures, after which they were dazed and amnesiac but usually sociable. The fatigue, disorientation, and submission that resulted made patients easier to manage on the wards. For some patients, the memory loss was permanent, which was sometimes viewed as helpful when patients could not recall the anguish-causing incidents in their lives. Unfortunately, however, symptoms of insanity returned as the brain healed, so the therapy was repeated.[28]

Vesta Binkley, a former patient at Fulton, penned a memory of electroshock treatment for *Hospital Highlights,* the hospital newspaper, in 1957:

> Patients were generally on treatment twice a week—two days for the women (Mondays and Thursdays) and two days for the men (Tuesdays and Fridays). Promptly at 7:30 treatment patients were rounded up by the cry "Treatment patients *git* to the door." Begging, pleading crying and resisting they were herded into the gymnasium and seated

---

26. Ibid., 93–95.
27. Barbara Brazos, interview by McMillen, June 5, 2003, tape recording in authors' collection.
28. Whitaker, *Mad in America,* 99–100.

around the edge of the room. Between them and the shock treatment table was a long row of screens. The table on the other side of the screens held as much terror for most of these patients as the Electric Chair in the penitentiaries did for criminals. . . . In order to save time, one or more patients were called behind the screen to sit down and take off their shoes while the patient who had just preceded them was still on the table going through the convulsions that shake the body after the Electric Shock has knocked them unconscious. One attendant stands at the head of the table to put the rubber heel in their mouth so they won't chew their tongue during the convulsive stage. On either side of the table stand three other attendants to hold them down. . . . The only comforting thing from those times was the sight of some of the quieter and more controlled patients comforting the terror-stricken ones. I can remember many a friendly hand placed on mine—many a comforting shoulder I leaned against while I waited my turn. . . . This has been changed somehow now I am glad to say, and treatments are not quite so inhumanely administered—but I hope to see the day when they will be entirely replaced by the new drugs now coming into use as tranquilizers.[29]

A nurse who started at the hospital in 1938 remembered nursing electric shock patients: "Terrible," she said. "I used to feel so sorry for them, really and truly, it's the only thing that calmed them down, really, it was for their good, too." Another hospital employee, a social worker, reflected that although shock treatments had been good for some patients, "people get on bandwagons, and they think if it's good for one, then it's good for the whole group. Shock treatment . . . was overused." Alzheimer's disease patients and schizophrenics were often treated unsuccessfully with shock treatment, but this social worker said that shock treatment was the only thing "that could bring people out of a deep depression."[30]

In this era, there were no drugs specifically for the treatment of mental illness, but doctors were desperate to try new strategies to effect cures. Magnesium sulfate was an early entry into psychopharmacology and was used as a cathartic. It was thought that magnesium sulfate—Epsom salts—could deplete excess spinal fluid in encephalitis and other states associated with cranial or spinal pressure. One worker remembers going to the railroad depot and unloading boxcars of magnesium sulfate for the hospital. The salts were dissolved in water and given by the cupful, a treatment that survived through the 1950s.[31]

29. Vesta Binkley, "They Help Us to Live Again," *Hospital Highlights* 8, no. 6 (July 1957): 3.
30. Doris Brown interview; Jane Bierdeman-Fike, interview by Brazos and McMillen, July 1999, tape recording in authors' collection.
31. Unidentified speaker at meeting with authors at Kingdom of Callaway Historical Society, January 6, 1999, tape recording in authors' collection.

One aide described that using magnesium sulfate as a cathartic had a useful purpose in that it wore the patients down. She described a ward where most patients went to physically demanding work every day and received routine doses of magnesium sulfate every night. Because they had diarrhea all the time, they were too tired to be violent.[32]

Doctors were hopeful that psychoanalysis would become the cure-all therapy, and popular works like *Snake Pit* and *Parris Mitchell of Kings Row* described institutions where doctors and patients interacted freely, without the constraints of time and overcrowding. In truth, however, psychoanalysis requires a one-on-one relationship between a trained therapist and the patient, and this was barely possible in a state institution. Therefore, the most frequently used therapies at Fulton, as at other state institutions, were those that called for little staff time. Various therapies were adopting professional standards. Music therapy, which had the advantage of bringing patients together in a social activity under the guidance of one staff person, was earning recognition as a path to emotional well-being. The hospital had long employed music as a pastime and amusement, but researchers had recognized that music created emotional responses in both listeners and players. As researchers endorsed the profession of music therapy, practice rooms were established in every hospital building. Music therapists found talent among the patients and also brought musicians to the hospital from the outside.

Another promising therapy was occupational therapy (OT), which taught skills, like weaving, woodworking, sewing, and leatherwork, that might be useful outside the hospital as occupations. Initially, there were no merit-system standards for OT therapists, so it was difficult for the hospital to hire such specialists.

For the most part, staff and patients were committed to making themselves content in their situations because patients often entered the hospital as young adults and stayed for the rest of their lives. In the continuing search for a cure, special-interest groups such as the Missouri Association for Social Welfare (MASW), founded in 1901, became important advocates for the mentally ill. From the beginning, members had lobbied actively for better laws regarding health and social welfare, and they had been especially active to bring the end of patronage. The September 11, 1947, minutes of their Health Committee noted a particular concern for senile patients with chronic conditions who, because of changes in the law, could be evicted from state institutions. The committee wondered "whether they would be just dumped back on their communities and perhaps be cared for in county homes with poor standards or even in jails." The committee suggested,

---

32. Barbara Brazos, note on draft manuscript, August 7, 2006, in authors' collection.

"Information could be furnished the legislators concerning . . . social service departments in State Hospitals in order to plan for the total welfare of the patients rather than build so many new hospitals or more buildings."[33]

Thus began a movement away from institutionalization and toward treating mental illness in the community. Suggestions from MASW brought voices outside the government to play a role in influencing patient care. Over the years, MASW and other professional organizations would become powerful advocates for their clients and also promote their own profession. While MASW was growing in importance, faculty members in the School of Social Work at University of Missouri–Columbia started a professional social work program. The earliest Fulton hospital social workers came from that department.[34]

These first years after World War II brought several forces together to change mental health care. The new constitution opened the way to hire professionals rather than political cronies, and the attention from media created a newly receptive public that demanded skill and training. In 1948, William J. Cremer, M.D., became the new hospital superintendent. Born in Jefferson City, Cremer had been educated at the University of Missouri–Columbia and Washington University. He had worked at institutions including St. John's in St. Louis and the State Hospital at Nevada before assuming the job of psychiatrist at Fulton in 1946.[35]

When he arrived at the hospital, its main building housed administrative offices, living quarters for some staff, a drugstore, a cafeteria, and a dining room. Male patients lived in the North Wing and females in the South. "Outlying" housing on the campus provided a male infirmary, the Hyde Building that housed 250 elderly women, the Hadley Building, for patients with tuberculosis, a building for the acutely ill, a "psychopathic clinical building," and the Marion Oley Biggs Memorial Building, which had "recreational and therapeutic devices suitable to the class of individuals that cannot be entrusted with more liberal or parole privileges." There were also utility buildings: a laundry, a powerhouse, cold storage and creamery, a can-

---

33. Minutes of the Health Committee steering committee, September 11, 1947, MASW Collection f. 3111, Western Historical Manuscript Collection–Columbia.

34. The university's Department of Social Work was established in 1946 in the College of Arts and Science as a one-year graduate program that led to a Certificate of Social Work. An undergraduate program was also created in the College of Arts and Science. In 1949, a two-year master of science program was added (www.system.missouri.edu/sswmain/history.shtml). The first social worker at Fulton is thought to have been Harriett Wilmoth Clark Wise, born April 1, 1907, in Mexico, Missouri. A graduate of Hardin College, she also attended the University of Wisconsin and the University of Missouri. After working in Fulton, she moved to the Nevada State Hospital, where she worked for twenty years and retired in 1972 (obituary, *Fulton Sun*, May 25, 1994).

35. "Dr. William Cremer," obituary, *Fulton Daily Sun-Gazette*, December 8, 1976, 1.

Since treatments were experimental and primitive by modern standards, many patients were in the hospital for life (Fulton State Hospital).

nery, a greenhouse, storerooms, a carpentry shop, and a dozen other specialized structures, including a mattress factory.[36]

The doctor-to-patient ratio in the 1940s was 1:300 at the asylum, a figure set by law. The salary of Superintendent Charles Carter Ault, who had served from 1943 to 1947, was $3,600 per year. A day attendant or a night attendant, each working twelve-hour shifts, was paid $828 per year. Most nonprofessional staff salaries were less than $1,000 per year, but supervisors, electricians, stenographers, and others made from $1,200 to $1,600. I. C. Marquette, the dairy herdsman, was paid $1,800, just slightly less than three assistant physicians, who received $2,000. In contrast, Dr. Cremer's salary started at $6,000 in 1947 and by 1951 had risen to $7,872. Other salaries increased, too, so that by 1951, the lowest-paid attendants made $1,452. These new salaries emphasize the new sense of professionalism and pursuit of cures in mental health care. While in the past the hospital had touted its agricultural output as part of its ability to provide for its inhabitants over the long term, reports filed by Cremer did not mention the hospital's food production.

36. Bell, *Official Manual, 1945–1946*, 774–75.

One Cremer initiative ended the strict segregation of all patients by sex. While sleeping quarters were still male or female, the patients got together at meals and for activities. Putting the two sexes together meant that female staff now worked with men and vice versa. One nurse who had worked at the hospital for ten years said she had a hard time getting used to working side-by-side with men, but, she said, integration of the sexes "was a good thing, because it reflected people's lives as they got better. . . . They'd fall in love with each other . . . just human nature when men and women [are] together. . . . You'd be surprised how well things went."[37]

Farmwork, kitchen work, and work in the shops helped the hospital meet its budget and gave patients working skills. For patients, the activity also relieved the boredom of sitting in a day room for hours on end, and the diversion was worth more than a paycheck. In fact, for many years, patient labor was unpaid or paid with small wages of a few dollars a week. Occasionally, families sent spending money to the patients, so the hospital had a banking system. Money was paid out in the form of coupon books worth one to five dollars that could be spent at a canteen—a store where patients and staff could buy snacks, cigarettes, gifts, and grooming products. With one employee supervising, the managers and clerks came from the patient population.[38]

The first canteen was in the administration building, and there was soon a second in Biggs. Eventually, there were five, each located convenient to residents and staff. All canteen profits were spent for patient entertainment and activities—trips to the zoo, the state fair, ball games, the St. Louis Muny theater, and other outings. Fulton residents also benefited when canteen profits were spent on firework displays and carnivals, which the public also enjoyed.[39]

When patients and staff worked together, there was ample room for delight. One running joke concerned the institution's first-time visitors, who often were unable to tell patients from staff. Such outsiders opened themselves to ridicule when they spoke to staff members in particularly solicitous tones, thinking that they were patients who might become upset easily. Another joke concerned a patient who worked at the canteen and came up ten cents short when he figured up the day's receipts: "Oh my God," said the patient. "I hope I'm not losing my mind."[40]

Despite the adoption of new therapies, the rise in salaries, and the adop-

---

37. Doris Brown interview.
38. Betty Steinrauf, "Fulton State Hospital Canteen," undated note to McMillen, 1999, in authors' collection.
39. Ibid.
40. Bill Clevenger interview.

tion of new work relationships, Missouri's mental health care came up short in almost every national study—Missouri was one of only eight states that still required a judge's opinion before a person was committed to a state institution, thus stigmatizing the patient as if mental illness was a criminal condition. Another study showed Missouri's expenditures for health were the lowest in the forty-eight states. World War II had focused national attention on mental health issues, partly because of the number of men who had failed the military. According to one source, 1.75 million American men were rejected or discharged because of mental and emotional disabilities, and three-quarters of a million more were prematurely discharged from service for the same reasons, bringing the need for mental health care to the nation's attention.[41]

Perhaps in reaction, the 1948 legislature appropriated $361,000 for new occupational therapy and bakery buildings. To build the OT building, according to the *Sun-Gazette*, the state razed an "old rough-hewn oak barn that was put up in 1880 and in later years has been used as a garage." The lumber was reused for a new large barn for the hospital's dairy. The newspaper noted that the 68-by-50-foot, one-story barn with loft had been built without nails, the framing held together with pegs. Another old brick building that dated back to 1875 was taken down to make way for the new bakery. The legislature had also appropriated $600,000 for a new dormitory for employees, five cottages for doctors, a house for the superintendent on farmland on Route Z, and repairs for the other buildings.[42]

The legislature moved forward with a resolution to study mental health: "There is not enough of anything but patients in mental hospitals throughout the country," said the study published by the House of Representatives, echoing the words of *Snake Pit*. The study concluded that while the medical profession now saw hope for the mentally ill, the public still believed that mental illness was disgraceful and incurable, striking "only those who are inherently weak."[43]

It was true that newspaper writers often played on the public's fear about mental illness. On June 6, 1949, Teddy Alva Lane, committed to the hospital for killing his mother, used a meat cleaver and a knife to kill two other patients and wound a hospital cook. The victims had been peeling potatoes and, as Dr. Cremer explained, "had knives in their hands." The attacker thought they "intended to kill him. . . . Of course, that was a delusion." The Associated Press story, carried by the *St. Louis Post-Dispatch* and distributed

---

41. Donald Peterson, interview by McMillen, March 15, 1985, tape recording in authors' collection.
42. *Fulton Daily Sun-Gazette*, March 22, 1948, 1.
43. H. R. 75, "The Mentally Ill: Their Care and Treatment in Missouri," November 1948.

nationally, described one victim as "decapitated" and the other as "chopped and hacked to death."[44]

Despite the sensationalism, the decade closed with dramatic new hope for the mentally ill. New drugs made it possible to sedate patients at night, so that the ward could sleep. Hospitals wanted to get away from the use of restraints, straitjackets, wristlocks, and bed chains. At Hospital No. 1, Dr. Cremer seemed determined to create a new era of openness about mental health. As the decade closed, OT launched a mimeographed newspaper featuring patient work. Dr. Gus S. Waraich, the clinical director, enthusiastically declared that the newspaper had "an important role" in giving patients "pride and self-respect." The newspaper, *Hospital Highlights*, also allowed patients to share their situations. One item in the first edition noted that someone had visited a patient who was "much surprised . . . since no one had visited her for fifteen years."[45]

Also in the 1940s, partly because of the labor shortage, women took an increasing number of state jobs. This meant that, for Fulton at least, the hospital became a more familiar place. Some neighborhood kids remember riding bikes around the circle drive. One Fulton woman remembers: "We used to go out there when I was in high school. Go out there and go through the tunnels. Go up and visit a friend's mother, ride the elevator up in the hospital building, then we'd go have a little snack in the cafeteria." She remembered also that there were swings on the grounds where patients would go to relax.[46]

With a native son, Harry Truman, as president of the nation from 1945 to 1953, Missouri felt a surge of pride. With its new state constitution, Missourians were focusing on and preparing for the future. The end of World War II had seemed to settle the question of what nation would dominate the world. Everything seemed possible, even a cure for mental illness.

---

44. "Insane Killer Chops Two Other Men to Death," unnamed newspaper (probably *Fulton Sun-Gazette*), clipping at the State Historical Society of Missouri.
45. Quoted in *Mexico Ledger*, September 15, 1949, magazine section.
46. Shirley Payne, interview by McMillen, December 30, 1999, tape recording in authors' collection.

10

Missouri's Mental Health Care Comes of Age, 1950–1959

In the 1950s, mental health care in Missouri changed more dramatically than in any previous era. This was partly because of the national change in public attitude. Thanks to print media and radio, movies, and television, Missourians could no longer consider themselves isolated from the rest of the nation. At the same time, the American public felt that mental health was in crisis. A study released in 1950 by the Council of State Governments revealed that while the U.S. population had increased 2.6 times between 1880 and 1940, the numbers in state institutions had increased 12.6 times.[1]

Indeed, this was the peak of population at Hospital No. 1. The Missouri *Official Manual* for 1949–1950 reported that the institution's average population was 2,565, with a capacity for 2,677. These patients were served by about 530 employees, with salaries ranging from $1,260 per year for custodial workers to $7,872 for Dr. Cremer. Doctors' benefits included housing in new homes on hospital grounds. Many other workers also had housing on the hospital campus. "Hospital Attendant I," the largest category of employment, had the most contact with patients and stayed with them night or day on twelve-hour shifts. They earned a yearly salary of $1,380.[2]

For taxpayers, care was still a bargain. Thanks to the farm, the dairy, and all the thrift inherent in a self-reliant institution, the cost per day per patient was $1.65.[3] The hospital owned 1,068 acres and leased 200 more for pas-

---

1. Rael Jean Isaac and Virginia C. Armat, *Madness in the Streets* (New York: Free Press, 1990).
2. Esther Downs Bishop, ed., *1949–1950 Official State Manual, Walter H. Toberman, Secretary of State* (Jefferson City: Mid-State Printing, 1950), 577.
3. Sara Thomasen, "History of FSH," manuscript, 1989, 7 (FSHA).

ture, and operated its own "power house, laundry, storehouse, and general repair and maintenance shops."[4] Despite the seeming self-sufficiency, making ends meet was a constant problem, and the hospital depended on patient labor. One patient wrote: "Many of these patients work hard all day at necessary jobs within the hospital—kitchen, cafeteria, peeling room, mending room, sewing room, laundry, dairy barn, greenhouse, and many others. Many work at jobs that require considerable responsibility and skill. They receive no pay whatsoever for their work."[5]

The hospital functioned as a separate community, apart from the town beyond the front gate. A patient interviewed in 2002 reported that she had borne two babies while a resident. Indeed, in the *1953–1954 Annual Report of Mental Diseases*, there is a notation among surgeries of one delivery. There may have been others, as annual reports vary in the language they use to categorize medical events. Because the hospital was Fulton's largest employer, everyone in town had direct experience with it through their own jobs or those of close friends and relatives. The contact gave Fulton residents special insight, which often found outlet in humor: "The Fulton population was 10,000, and 2,000 would be insane . . . that we knew of," said one Fultonian, repeating an old Callaway County joke.[6]

For some Fulton kids, a visit to the hospital provided a cautionary warning. One woman said that her grandfather took the family on rides to the hospital, "and the image of the hospital it was not good. Those buildings—Hadley and Hyde—you could see through the windows to padded rooms and at times there'd be somebody just absolutely bouncing off the walls, and he [grandfather] would say something like, 'You need to straighten up, or . . .' and it worked, but not seriously. It was kind of frightening." Despite these observations, the woman telling this story grew up to work as a professional at the state hospital.[7]

Another woman, who began work in the early 1950s as a hospital night aide, reported that with more than thirty patients in the ward, she and a nurse worked a ten-hour shift. On the first day, she learned to mix medicines, read the charts, and take the patients to breakfast. She said that the staff depended for help from patients who were able to give it. The second night, the supervisor was very careful in demonstrating how to measure and dispense the medicine. "Tomorrow night, you'll have to give the medicine. You'll be working alone." The young worker protested that she wasn't ready

4. Bishop, *Official Manual, 1949–1950*, 577.
5. Binkley, "They Help Us to Live Again," 3.
6. Mary Virginia Baker, interview by McMillen, December 30, 1999, tape recording in authors' collection.
7. Jamesetta Van Buren, interview by Brazos, summer 2000, tape recording in authors' collection.

and that she didn't even know the patients well enough to avoid mixing them up and giving the wrong medical doses. Her protest made no difference to the overworked supervisor. On the third night, the young woman telephoned and quit her job—although her mother thought she should have stayed, saying that it was a good ward.[8]

It was challenging to find good workers and to make them competent caregivers. Training was a new idea, so nurse Doris Brown received permission to start a nursing education program. She explained her plan to Dr. Cremer: "I'll just take the new employee . . . and I'll take them on the ward, work with them, teach them. Well, they didn't know how to take a temperature reading. They didn't know how to take blood pressure. They didn't know how to turn a patient. . . . I'd take three or four at a time. . . . They didn't know how to make a patient's bed. They'd never worked in a place like that. We had some real good people, and we had some that weren't worth a darn."[9]

Dr. Cremer was acutely aware of shortages and shortcomings. In 1953, he gave extensive interviews to Lew Larkin of the *Kansas City Star*, who was writing a series called "The Mentally Ill in Missouri." The series was reprinted and widely distributed in the state. Cremer asked, "Why don't we have even one registered nurse here?" and added that the American Psychiatric Association recommended that the hospital hire twenty but they were not available. The hospital was also short nine physicians and 160 attendants. New attendants were trained with a one-hour lecture per week for four months. The shortages and lack of training, said Cremer, resulted in patients having to be in restraints or in "rocking chair brigades . . . Rocking the hours and days away."[10]

Just as the institution sought to increase staff training, it also sought new treatments. Studies were casting doubt on the effectiveness of insulin shock therapy. For one thing, experts could not explain what was happening in the therapy to cure the patients. The insane person, put into a coma, awoke in a helpless, often infantile state. Some guessed that the regression indicated that the coma killed the brain cells that caused the insanity. The death of the faulty cells would allow the brain to heal. Others guessed that sinking into a coma gave the patient a chance to vent all problems, clearing the brain of disease-causing conflicts.[11]

When old treatments were discontinued, new ones took their places. On

---

8. Mildred Sparks, interview by Brazos, October 17, 1999, tape recording in authors' collection.
9. Doris Brown interview.
10. Lew Larkin, "The Mentally Ill in Missouri," reprint from *Kansas City Star*, January 6, 1954, MASW Collection f. 3877, Western Historical Manuscript Collection–Columbia.
11. Whitaker, *Mad in America*, 86.

October 22, 1954, the Missouri Association for Social Welfare sponsored a panel to discuss the needs of patients and changes in law. The panel discussed the movement to treat mentally ill people in their homes rather than bringing them to institutions. Thinking that this treatment would be more humane, effective, and economical, the General Assembly had given permission for outpatient treatment, and Hospital No. 1 devoted one day per week to outpatients. But when staff were working at the outpatient clinic, they were not on the wards, which exacerbated the shortages there. A "Mrs. Levers," chairman of the Kansas City Mental Hygiene Society Legislative Committee, noted the reason for the shortage: "Dr. Johns, out at Fulton, said that he has money for a psychiatrist, not too attractive, but there is money in the budget, but he cannot find the psychiatrist." The end of the patronage system meant that state agencies could go outside the state for new hires, but this required more money for salaries.[12]

Obtaining extra money was difficult. Dr. Edwin P. Gildea of St. Louis noted that the state hospitals were all fairly powerless in the legislature when weighed against highways, schools, and other needs. Dr. Thaddeus Clark, president of the Mental Health Association of St. Louis and a Unitarian minister, summed up the three conflicting arguments—the humane versus the economy versus political expediency. The panel drafted a statement for the legislature. First, they asked for an increase in appropriations, especially for personnel and training. Second, they asked for money for outpatient care. Third, they asked for adequate facilities.[13]

The MASW requests reflected the public's growing acceptance that mental illness and accompanying delusions were beyond a person's control. By this time, the metal cages that restrained violent patients had been an enduring symbol of the terror of insanity. One Fulton resident remembered seeing them at a display: "some of those iron beds out there that looked like a box . . . like a cot, but there was a top . . . a metal or wire top . . . like a cage that you would lie down on."[14]

New treatments, especially one new medication, held promise that restraints like cages could become a thing of the past. In May 1954, Thorazine (chlorpromazine) appeared on the market; it promised to be a medication to stop a patient's unruly behavior. Within eight months of its appearance, Thorazine had been given to over two million patients. A nurse who re-

---

12. "Panel Discussion Presented under the Auspices of the Missouri Association for Social Welfare," MASW Collection f. 3160, Western Historical Manuscript Collection–Columbia.

13. Ibid.

14. Anonymous Fulton resident, interview by McMillen, December 30, 1999, tape recording in authors' collection. In the metal cages described, the patient could be made to stand for periods by simply tipping the box on end (Brazos, note on draft manuscript, August 7, 2006, in authors' collection).

membered the introduction said: "Before Thorazine, all you could do was restrain violent patients. People would be in restraints for years. In violent episodes, patients and aides both got hurt."[15]

Sometimes called "chemical restraints," Thorazine did not treat a specific illness like schizophrenia or depression but rather it offered peace for the ward and safety for the staff. At least one attendant had a personal experience taking Thorazine by accident. On the first day of work, he saw a pitcher of fruit drink, unmarked, in the refrigerator. Thirsty, and too broke to buy a soda, he took a drink. Soon, "I was just getting all stiff . . . Contractures and drooling. And I'm talking to one of the charge nurses. . . . 'I don't know what's wrong. I feel so bad.'" The nurse asked what he had eaten during the day, and the answer was nothing except the fruit drink, which, he now learned, had been mixed with Thorazine and intended for the patients. "So they had to give me a shot and take me home and check on me after work. . . . It was a good experience because I know what they feel like. It's an uncomfortable feeling."[16]

Besides sedating patients, Thorazine was thought to be therapeutic. French psychiatrists Jean Delay and Pierre Deniker used it to induce "artificial hibernation," where patients could be "moved around like puppets" and would lie "quietly in bed, staring ahead." They called the drug "neuroleptic," from the Greek for "take hold of the nervous system." Side effects included thirst, clouded thinking, swollen tongue, stiffness, pain, and a sense of alienation. Psychiatrist Nathaniel Lehrman of Brooklyn wrote about this experience with Thorazine: "I couldn't stand up straight. My eyes weren't focusing properly, and walking—or anything else, even thinking—became a terrible effort. I couldn't even read. The medication was robbing me of my will, and of any control I had over my own fate."[17]

Smith, Kline and French, the patent owner in the United States, sponsored television programs and coached a speakers' bureau to promote the drug. Their optimistic sense of possibility was recorded in *The Nurse-Patient Relationship,* a training film recorded in a New Jersey institution and distributed by Smith-Kline. The film followed a young RN, a "psychiatric nurse," as she worked with a severely withdrawn patient. The story shows the effects of the drug—patients sit trancelike or walk in a sedated shuffle. The film also expresses the boredom and inactivity of life on the ward and gives realistic advice: Therapy will take a long time, and progress is slow. The young nurse is encouraged to be aware of her own anxiety and to send a message

15. Doris Brown interview.
16. Norbert Giesing, interview by Brazos, October 22, 1999, tape recording in authors' collection.
17. Whitaker, *Mad in America,* 143–44, 178.

As medicines became more precisely adapted to psychological conditions, the pharmacist became an important part of the hospital (Fulton State Hospital).

to the patient, "You are important, respected, accepted." At the same time, the film suggests that, with a caseload of sixty-four patients, a nurse could find fifteen minutes a day to spend with each of the most needy: "The problem of violence has been solved, but she [the patient] is still sick and still needs help to find her way to mental health." At Hospital No. 1 and at other state institutions, staff—"the most sensitive instrument" in the words of the script—was always in short supply.[18]

In 1949, Portuguese neurologist Egas Moniz received the Nobel Prize for developing the technique of lobotomy. The operation, which dated back to Moniz's early experiments in 1935, had later been named and widely promoted by Walter Freeman, who traveled the nation to demonstrate the technique. After surgery, "The delusional idea is still there, but it has no emotional drive," Freeman said, "I think we have drawn the sting, as it were, of the psychosis or neurosis."[19]

Jack Ferguson, a doctor at Traverse City State Hospital in Michigan, adapted the procedure so that it could be performed in three minutes, by

---

18. *The Nurse-Patient Relationship* (film; New Jersey: Smith-Kline, 1958). Critics would later say that Thorazine had not been properly tested and that its acceptance into use was an early example of how drug companies with large public-relations budgets gained power over doctors.

19. Isaac and Armat, *Madness in the Streets*, 20.

inserting a tool like an ice pick through the eye sockets to sever nerve fibers at the base of the frontal lobe. While lobotomies stopped the patients' violence, results varied widely. Lobotomies left many patients helpless, sometimes even to the extent of being unable to determine when they needed to eat or to relieve themselves. The return of such patients to their families was obviously difficult for the families. Most hospitals banned lobotomies by 1960. At Fulton, the procedure continued until 1966.[20]

A much less invasive but very interesting therapy of this same era was psychodrama. Psychodrama was listed as a therapy for patients at the Biggs Building in the hospital's 1964 publication for the Midwestern Governors' Conference, and it was named as a treatment for juveniles at Fulton in the *1962–1963 Annual Report*, where a psychodrama room is noted in a 1963 floor plan. The psychodrama stage at the St. Louis State Hospital, which had several levels, lighting, and seating for an audience, was important enough to be noted in therapy literature. In psychodrama therapy, patients and therapists take roles and reenact stressful situations to help explore the dynamics of conflict. Therapists hoped the reenactment would be more useful than simply talking about the situation. It is hard to judge the effectiveness of the therapy, but it should be noted that psychodrama provided material for artists and brought mental health issues to the public.[21]

Perhaps because he wanted to test some of the theoretical treatments, on February 1, 1956, Dr. Cremer retired as superintendent but stayed at the hospital as a psychiatrist. He finished his career as clinical director of acute intensive treatment, a position he held from 1973 until his death on December 7, 1976, at age sixty-seven. To replace him as superintendent, the Department of Health and Public Welfare hired Dr. Alfred K. Baur from St. Elizabeth's Hospital in Washington, D.C., a mammoth federal facility with seven thousand patients. St. Elizabeth's was the nation's oldest mental institution and had a huge infrastructure of buildings, a complicated hierarchy of staff, and a network of overlapping programs. At the same time that Baur was hired in the middle 1950s, Business Manager Robert J. Seaman moved from State Hospital No. 4 at Farmington to Fulton. With a dedicated manager in that position, the superintendent was able to focus more completely on patient and staff matters. Seaman stayed at the hospital un-

---

20. Ibid., 178–80.
21. Adam Blatner, *Acting In: Practical Applications of Psychodramatic Methods* (New York: Springer, 1988), 1–4, 9–11. Psychodrama therapy led to a new theater form. Building on the 1920s work of German Jacob Levy Moreno's "Theatre of Spontaneity," the "Theatre of the Absurd" was evolving. *The Bald Soprano*, by Eugene Ionesco, was produced in Paris in 1950, followed by many works by Harold Pinter, a British playwright. Seeing these works, the audience witnessed conversations and activities of everyday citizens who found it impossible to communicate. The playwrights made ordinary conversation seem impossible, then hilarious, but as audiences laughed, they saw the thin line between sane behavior and insanity.

til 1976. Hiring a professional business manager and an esteemed psychiatrist sent a message: Missouri was committed to bringing the best physicians and most modern therapies to the mentally ill.[22]

Dr. Baur would only stay in Fulton a few years, but he brought the hospital to a new stage of service for its patients. An undated Baur document, perhaps addressed to hospital staff, described the housing and rehabilitation of the criminally insane and suggests that the term be changed to "some less offensive name; such as, 'The Division for Conduct Disorders.'" Describing the criminal mind, Baur wrote: "The criminotic individual sees himself as a self-conscious actor in a brilliant setting in which he attempts to deny his failure and to dramatize his own psychic conflicts. . . . The result . . . is self-destructive, self-defeating, self-betraying and self-denying . . . a tendency for a fixed type of crime, a predictable modus operandi." Baur noted that rehabilitation depended on understanding the "inmate," ensuring that he relates in positive ways to the hospital and staff, "occupational therapy and vocational experience" to learn to work with other people, group therapy as often as twice a week with individual therapy as a follow-up to help the inmate understand and correct his behavior, "education and cultural opportunity," "custodial control," and finally, development of "a full tolerance of the general frustrations and anxiety which occurs as the result of environmental pressures and resistances."[23]

One enduring legacy of the Baur administration was the Clinical Pastoral Education Program. In August 1956, Baur hired Reverend Dr. William Rogers, a minister of the United Church of Christ, whom Baur had known as a chaplain at St. Louis City Hospital. At Fulton, Rogers found that only one retired minister was working with patients. Chaplain visits and church services were irregular with such a small staff, but Rogers says Baur was "a firecracker" in demanding that patients get service from the chaplaincy department. "I had to run to keep up with him," said Rogers. Rogers's wife, Ruth, was also an ordained minister, but according to Rogers, Baur did not believe in women ministers. Ruth was hired for a position in occupational therapy, but when patients found out Ruth was a pastor, she did counseling from her OT position. Rogers held chapel services in Biggs and in the auditorium on the second floor in a building behind the administration building. He also had services in the Hyde Building. He learned to visit with people of all theologies, counseling, not preaching, so "they all thought I agreed with them."[24]

What began as the "Clinical Training Program" soon had pastoral stu-

---

22. According to records in the *State Manuals*, Cremer's salary was $12,500, and Baur's was $15,499.
23. Alfred K. Baur, "Marion Oley Biggs Memorial Building," 1, 2, 4 (FSHA).
24. Reverend Dr. William Rogers, telephone interview by McMillen, January, 2000.

dents and interns working at the hospital for twelve-month educational programs. The program soon became known as the Clinical Pastoral Education Program, or CPE. Every patient got regular visits from chaplains, who represented many faiths. They were instructed not to evangelize, but to approach patients as humans. Chaplains added to the feeling of community and ministered to some chronic patients for many years: "The satisfaction was that, after a year, you could see a big change, and that was your reward," said Rogers, adding that it was especially wonderful when patients were able to return to the community.[25]

Another new hire, Nina Davis, began work as a nurse in 1956. She later told the *Fulton Sun* that when she was hired, the hospital was "beginning to change." They were so anxious to hire nurses that they created a position of photographer for Davis's husband. Forty-five days after her arrival, Davis was asked to open a surgery ward in the hospital building and to train staff to care for surgical patients. In this ward, surgeries normal in the larger population would be performed as well as lobotomies. As Davis began to make a list of needed items, she was told the first surgery would be the same afternoon at one o'clock.[26]

The shortage of supplies and staff was acute, and existing staff were underpaid and overworked. It was not until August 1, 1956, that the hospital was able to hire enough staff to achieve a forty-hour week for most workers. For attendants, the forty-hour week did not begin until October 15, 1956.[27] Staffing at Biggs, the maximum security unit, was especially problematic. A shortage of personnel meant that the building was "chiefly run by attendants, and restraint was excessive." There was only one physician on call, sometimes part-time, and no psychologist, psychiatric social worker, or other professionals. As the only maximum security unit in Missouri, Biggs had nine wards, each with a capacity of thirty-five patients. In each ward there were eleven single rooms and a large dormitory with twenty-four beds, two and four beds to a cubicle. Each ward had a large day room, a nurse's office, lavatory, and a utility and clothes room. The goal was to provide security for the public but, at the same time, to have the setting be conducive to therapy for the mentally ill people who may recover and rejoin society after a time.[28]

---

25. Ibid.
26. Pat Mosher, "Nurses Reflect on Changes in Profession," *Fulton Sun*, May 6, 1990, 5; Barbara Fairchild, "She Confronted the Challenges," *Fulton Sun*, July 20, 1991, 9.
27. Alfred K. Baur, "State Hospital No. 1," *Annual Report of the Division of Mental Diseases, 1955–1956* (Jefferson City: Division of Mental Diseases, 1956), 30.
28. Francis J. Tartaglino, "Maximum Security Unit: Fulton State Hospital, Fulton, Missouri, Prepared for the Midwestern Governors' Conference Interstate Workshop on The Care and Treatment of the Socially Hazardous Mentally Ill Offender," 1964 (FSHA).

Again, the population had quickly outgrown the facility. The ten-bed ward planned for surgical and acutely ill patients had been converted to house the most dangerous patients. After the conversion, the building had no room for therapies and education, but only enough room for, as one report said, "the usual mental and physical examinations made on admission, the necessary routine laboratory procedures, sedation, isolation and restraint as indicated . . . A moderate amount of electric convulsive therapy and sub-shock insulin."[29]

For recreation, Biggs had only two outdoor spaces—"bull pens"—each 75 by 125 feet. A fourteen-foot wall enclosed the entire complex, and the ground was covered by cinders, making it dusty and hot: "One can readily see that under the circumstances described, there was very little meaningful communication between patients and personnel, and . . . the general atmosphere must have been a rather rigid and restrictive one." Attention was given "chiefly to security measures . . . none to occupational therapy, recreational and industrial therapy, educational classes, music therapy or any organized type of activity necessary in the re-socialization of a patient back into a community."[30]

After Baur's arrival, he converted the ten-bed ward into administrative offices, a staff room, and rooms for therapies. Employee bedrooms were turned into classrooms and a dentist's office. Space was refigured to create a canteen, library, barbershop, and visiting room. The basement area, formerly used for storage, was remodeled to create an occupational therapy department and recreational services area. A ten-foot wire fence enclosed a softball diamond. Patient escapes over this fence, however, were frequent—there were two major breaks of seven men in 1959–1960—so a new fence was later added.[31]

In the 1950s, Americans recognized a new category of behavior disorders. The hospital was getting "frequent requests from distraught parents and community agencies that do not know what to do with certain children who are severe behavior problems."[32] Indeed, three boys aged "0–14" had been admitted in the 1950–1951 fiscal year, along with twelve boys and ten girls aged 15–19.[33] In 1956, the staff formally agreed to admit juveniles, and by July 1957, the population of 8–16-year-olds had stabilized at "some 20." The hospital reported that they were curtailing admission of children,

29. Ibid.
30. Ibid.
31. Ibid.
32. Alfred K. Baur, "State Hospital No. 1," *Annual Report of the Division of Mental Diseases, 1956–1957* (Jefferson City: Division of Mental Diseases, 1957), 46.
33. *Annual Report of the Division of Mental Diseases, 1950–1951* (Jefferson City: Division of Mental Diseases, 1951), 29.

"both because of lack of space as well as lack of staff adequate to cope with any larger number."[34] In 1958, the Children's Code commission rewrote the Children's Code, providing for individual treatment, including psychiatric treatment, for children and adolescents under seventeen and a half years old.[35]

Child labor laws had been tightened to keep employers from exploiting youth, but there was no compulsory school attendance past eighth grade, so juvenile delinquency had crept into the news. Juvenile laws had not been written to handle young delinquents, so young criminals, including murderers, were sent to Fulton. The first children's unit was in the old South Wards, in a brick building constructed before the Civil War: "They were not air-conditioned," said one person interviewed. "Working there in the summertime was really grim because it was so hot. At any given time, we had maybe about sixty kids there, seventy kids . . . and it was a total mix. We had retarded kids, autistic kids, kids with psychiatric disorders, kids with behavior problems . . . all mixed together."[36]

The old buildings looked menacing from both the outside and the inside. One social worker remembers the young people taking advantage of their horror-movie accommodations: "The kids used to go into the bathrooms and turn off the lights and scare each other . . . probably any ghosts would run away." Next door, in the North Ward, was the rehab unit for the Biggs Building. The social worker remembers: "The girls' unit had this window . . . that faced the rehab building . . . I had young ladies who liked to do striptease . . . in fact those rehab guys slipped my girls a whole set of keys to the whole building."[37]

As this incident illustrates, it takes a sense of humor as well as an ability to stay on top of situations to work in a state institution. In spite of the challenges, Superintendent Baur managed to enjoy himself. During his tenure, he initiated annual fairs that brought entertainers and rides to the residents, paid for by the earnings of the canteens. One Fulton resident observed, "I remember Dr. Baur during one of his fairs in July—that was always in the big circle—would get dressed up in some kind of funny costume on the monkey dunk and patients could throw balls and dunk the superintendent."[38]

---

34. *Annual Report, 1956–1957*, 46.
35. The state's first "Children's Code," written in 1919, adopted twenty-five recommendations, such as requiring school attendance for children age seven through fourteen and eliminating child labor except for at home or in agriculture. *See* Peter Romanofsky's "The Public Is Aroused: The Missouri Children's Code Commission, 1915–1919," *Missouri Historical Review* 68 (1974): 204–22.
36. Tom Lezon, interview by Brazos, January 13, 2000, tape recording in authors' collection.
37. Anonymous former worker, interview by Brazos, tape recording in authors' collection.
38. Anonymous Fulton resident, interview by McMillen, December 30, 1999, tape recording in authors' collection.

It was easier for Dr. Baur to enjoy his tenure because the social welfare movement was by now in full swing. The files of the MASW in 1958 show 2,400 memberships from unions, caseworkers, hospitals, churches, health organizations like the American Heart Association, and service agencies like the Salvation Army. MASW had limped along for more than fifty years with little support or income. Now, with headquarters in Jefferson City, the MASW was poised to lobby the legislature for new programs and funding.

Despite the gains of the 1950s, the decade is best remembered in Callaway County for the fires that destroyed several buildings in the county. A café near McCredie, then another restaurant in Kingdom City, and then the Millersburg School were all destroyed. On March 15, 1956, the administration building of the Fulton State Hospital went up in a blaze so spectacular it was reported all over the nation. One Fulton woman saw the fire on television in Oxnard, California, where she was visiting. Another remembered: "We were living on East Sixth Street; you could see it from our house. So we called Mother, and she came over to stay with the children while we went down to watch it. I remember David was up and looked at the fire, and we got Nick up, and he was fussing, and I said, 'You look out there and see that fire, 'cause you're going to hear about it the rest of your life.' And he said, 'I see it. Let me go back to bed.' But the thing I remember the most was, of course, we were all so concerned for the people out there, and a lot of town people helped move people from one building to another."[39]

The most enduring story about the fire is a humorous one that several Fulton residents remembered. One said: "Two of our leading citizens were locked up with the inmates. One of them was Brooks Ann Cole, who . . . wrote for the Fulton newspaper, and the other was Mrs. [Orfa] Nichols, whose husband was the radio station owner. And they'd been helping move them [the patients] from one building to the other, and when they got to the place where they were going to put the people, they locked them up." The women protested, of course, but the tired workers thought the two were delusional, especially since one claimed to be a newspaper reporter, which was an unusual job for a woman in 1956. Residents can laugh about the situation now: "It took some time for them to release them."[40]

Louis Bratton could already see the fire from his bedroom window when he received a call. As a ladderman for the hospital's brigade, he went to fight the fire. It had started in an elevator shaft and smoldered for hours as attempts were made to save property and documents before the blaze erupt-

---

39. Martha Clapp, interview by McMillen, December 30, 1999, tape recording in authors' collection.

40. Ibid. This story gets better with each telling. According to Ron Lutz, longtime KFAL radio personality, Brooks Ann Cole worked for the radio station and had gone to the fire to cover the story, dressed only in her nightgown and robe.

ed and was visible across town. Bratton said the flat slate roofs, part of the earlier fire prevention modifications, made extinguishing the blaze impossible because the water just made puddles on the tiles.[41]

The fire was a tragedy in many ways: an important historic building was lost, and people were endangered although no one was killed. Patients and townspeople reacted heroically. In his annual essay, Baur reported that young men from Westminster College saved "almost all of our records and equipment," but many records were still lost. There is no record today of who is buried in the cemetery, because those papers were lost in the fire. Worse, the fire destroyed many of the records of current residents: "When I worked there, from 1988 to 1992, several geriatric patients had no known next-of-kin to contact," wrote one nurse; "the fire had destroyed the old charts where that information was listed."[42]

Besides losing the administration offices and living space for patients, many staff apartments were in the main building. A grandfather clock, which is now in the lobby of the administration building, was saved when somebody carried it out and laid it in the grass. Unfortunately, it was wet to the point of ruin when a supervisor gave it to a worker who collected clocks. This worker took it back to the hospital shop with the intention of fixing it. After about forty years, the hospital recognized the clock's importance and restored it.[43]

As confirmation of the hospital's commitment to the chaplaincy, among the first supplies ordered were five cartons of Bibles on September 10, 1956. And, because so little survived the fire, the hospital issued a list of needs so the public could respond appropriately. "Since we are such a large family," says the bulletin, "anything new needs to be of good quality, as so many people use it. Used articles, too, should be in good condition, with all their pieces intact, as our busy staff has little time for repairs." The bulletin was signed by Evelyn Berry, a longtime volunteer supervisor. The volunteers solicited an accordion, art supplies, books, craft supplies, electric irons, desks, card tables, chairs, radios, framed pictures, garden tools, kitchen utensils, magazines, records, games, sewing machines, sheet music, tape recorders, typewriters, holiday decorations (fireproof), and a variety of other goods. They also invited volunteer groups to entertain with choral groups or variety programs.[44]

---

41. Brazos, note on draft manuscript, August 7, 2006, in authors' collection.
42. Brazos, notes on first draft of manuscript, 2002, in authors' collection.
43. Louis Bratton interview.
44. See Evelyn Berry's "A Volunteer Program Penetrates a Maximum Security Setting," *Mental Hospitals*, 1963, 503 (FSHA). The quoted memo is signed Evelyn Berry.

The Administration Building was inaugurated in 1958. This view shows the oldest building on the campus, a pre–Civil War ward that survived the fire, peeking over the new Administration Building (Fulton State Hospital).

Volunteers were a big part of life on the wards. In July 1957, *Hospital Highlights* brought readers up to date on the doings of the staff and volunteers. There was an announcement of a Fourth of July picnic, the visit from Will Freund (instructor of art at Stephens College in Columbia), a conference for volunteers, Employees of the Month in every department, and news of the volunteers. For the volunteers, interacting with patients was interesting as well as helpful. One volunteer remembers bridge games organized by a man who had taught a group of patients. The club was affiliated with the American Contract Bridge League and met every Monday night with both volunteers and patients. The organizer was in the hospital for killing his wife. Our informant joked: "Wouldn't you have hated to trump his ace?"[45]

Volunteers adopted wards, remembering birthdays. They helped with music therapy and other therapy programs, planned chapel programs, and gave evening parties for the patients. Patient Vesta Binkley summed up her feeling after returning to the ward after a volunteer-sponsored program:

45. Mary Virginia Baker interview.

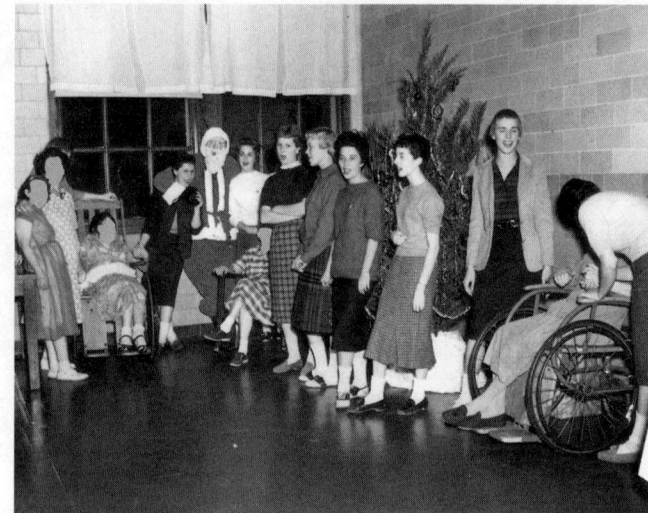

Game nights brought town and hospital residents together (Fulton State Hospital).

I felt a warm glow inside me—and I felt so proud of them [the volunteer workers]! When you are in a place like this for years on end and you seem to be lost to all the world you grow to feel that you belong to the place and everyone here belongs to you. In place of the loved ones who no longer seem to care you learn to feel a kinship and sympathy with all the lonely shadows among whom you move.[46]

46. Binkley, "They Help Us to Live Again."

11
Enlightened Leadership, 1960–1969

By 1960, the *State Manual* reported the patient census at "approximately 2,300," with an official daily population during 1959 at 2,253, including 90 children. There were three buildings under construction for geriatric patients. With completion of those wards, with 336 new beds, the hospital planned to empty wards in the basements of other buildings. The Division of Mental Diseases' *Annual Report* for 1959–1960 reported that the cost at the hospital per capita had risen to $4.68 per day. While Biggs and the children's unit served the entire state, in 1959 the division had created geographical "zones" of service for state hospitals. Fulton's "zone" included thirty-two rural counties, the northeast section of the state. State Hospital No. 1 continued to encourage public education about mental illness. The division's *Mental Health News* reported that 2,500 people had visited State Hospital No. 1 during National Mental Health Week in 1960. The visitors represented seventy-three towns. At the carnival on June 28 and 29, 1,500 patients enjoyed the festivities, which included an appearance by the bluegrass show *Ozark Opry*.[1]

Dr. Baur's leadership extended into areas other than public education. In 1960, he made the bold decision to hire Dr. Elmer C. Jackson, the hospital's first African American doctor and a man remembered fondly for his humanity and wisdom. Jackson had graduated from Langston University in Oklahoma and had received graduate education in chemistry at the University of Wisconsin and basic medical training in the army during World War II. Completing his medical degrees at the University of Colorado, he interned at Homer G. Phillips Hospital in St. Louis and then went into prac-

---

1. *Mental Health News*, Department of Mental Health newsletter, July 1960, MASW collection f. 3869, Western Historical Manuscript Collection–Columbia.

Perhaps the most popular attraction during carnival days, the dunking booth provided a chance for patients to dunk good-natured staff members (Fulton State Hospital).

tice. Upon arrival in Fulton, Dr. Jackson started out as the physician for the black patients. While Dr. Baur welcomed Jackson, other staff members turned a cold shoulder, and nurses even refused to carry out his instructions without confirmation from another doctor. Fulton restaurants at that time refused to serve blacks. When he was offered local housing only at extravagant prices, he settled in Jefferson City. He earned the respect of colleagues, however, and eventually worked in every part of the hospital, including the children's ward and Biggs, retiring in 1989. When he died in 1999, colleagues attended three tribute services. "Clearly, Dr. Jackson was Fulton's grand old man," said the superintendent at the time, Felix Vincenz.[2]

In addition to breaking racial barriers, Dr. Baur's tenure was marked by caring for all in the hospital community, from residents to staff. He launched the first "Employee Recognition Program" in 1960, awarding employees with long service records and those who had performed outstanding service. The state hospital was still Fulton's leading employer. A group of former workers remembered the 1961 dress code: Men wore black pants, white

2. Linda Hall, "Dedicated Psychiatrist Remembered," *Jefferson City Post Tribune*, June 7, 1999, 1.

Enlightened Leadership 167

In the days of the dress code, it was easy to tell staff from patients (Fulton State Hospital).

shirts, black shoes and socks, and a black bow tie; women wore a full slip, girdle, hose, and a white uniform. They recalled, "If you went to work dressed any other way, you were sent home."[3]

Dr. Baur retired in 1961. Before his brief tenure ended, he witnessed the completion of the administration building in 1958 and a new geriatrics building in July 1961, which created an isolated space for elderly patients with tuberculosis and an isolation ward for those with infectious skin problems. The choice of Baur's successor should have been in the hands of Dr. Addison Duval, director of the Division of Mental Diseases. Duval was an active leader, and had issued a ten-year plan for the department, including changes in the sex offender law, and a request that the courts help decide when to discharge dangerous persons rather than leaving it to the superintendents. Duval also had proposed children's facilities at each state hospital, suggesting that the Hadley Building would be the most appropriate site at State Hospital No. 1.[4]

Duval, however, would not see his suggestions adopted, nor would he participate in a search for Baur's replacement. Duval was a newcomer to the

---

3. Unidentified Fulton State Hospital worker speaking at meeting with authors at Kingdom of Callaway Historical Society, January 6, 1999, tape recording in authors' collection. The group agreed that as dress codes relaxed, it became increasingly hard to tell staff from patients. Maintenance men, who worked in all parts of the hospital and had contact with hundreds of people, had an especially hard time.

4. Addison Duval, "A Ten-Year Mental Health Program for Missouri, 1961–1971," MASW f. 3898, Western Historical Manuscript Collection–Columbia.

state. Having no idea about longtime political unions and feuds, he made the mistake of praising the chair of the appropriations committee, a Republican, for increasing the budget for the division. Governor John Dalton, a Democrat, was miffed that he did not get credit. Therefore, he fired Duval and hired Dr. George A. Ulett, M.D., who had been director at Malcolm Bliss Mental Health Center in St. Louis and had taught at Washington University. Ulett later called the firing and hiring "a great brouhaha in the State Division of Mental Disease."[5]

When Dr. Baur retired, Ulett approached Donald Peterson, then superintendent at Anoka State Hospital in Minnesota. Ulett and Peterson had a longstanding personal and professional relationship going back to 1946, when both were in the military. They had testified together at a court-martial hearing of an officer who had made up bogus orders, toured the country collecting pay, and then gambled away the money. Peterson later said that as a seasoned veteran with ten years of service at that time, he gave Lieutenant Ulett his "first lesson in psychiatric diagnosis" and instructed him in giving testimony in court. They successfully argued that the man was not insane, was trying to cheat the government, and deserved a dishonorable discharge.[6]

Peterson had traveled the world, serving at General Headquarters Far East Command in Tokyo, Japan, and in the Office of the Surgeon General in Washington, D.C., holding the highest-ranking psychiatric job in the army. Throughout his army career, Peterson was bothered by what he later called "the stunning figures of rejections and discharges from military service during World War II" caused by mental illness.[7]

At Ulett's request, Peterson visited the campus. He later remembered:

> It was . . . dreary . . . we found some places still segregated. We found certain wards eating with no silverware except a huge spoon, on the theory that you can't give psychotic people knives and forks because they'll kill you. . . . The place was filthy dirty, which was likely to happen if you have no central, organized housekeeping with a boss. . . . In nursing services, there was some question over who was in charge of a ward—was a nurse in charge or was an aide in charge? There'd been no money expended on buildings and grounds.[8]

Arriving at his new post, Peterson immediately began to make changes, and these changes were not always popular. When he arrived, workers came to the hospital in three shifts. Hours were 7 a.m. to 3 p.m., 3 p.m. to 11 p.m.,

---

5. Quoted by Donald Peterson (interview).
6. Donald Peterson interview.
7. Ibid.
8. Ibid.

and 11 p.m. to 7 a.m. "The three shifts passed like ships in the night," Peterson said, noting that one shift didn't report to the next. Each shift, therefore, had to operate without knowledge of what had happened before they came in. For patients in seclusion, this was a particular problem. Patients were put in seclusion after violent incidents, and those who were attacked helped decide when the patients were released. A staff person could be assaulted and put the patient in restraints, then finish the shift and go home. The patient would still be in restraints when the staff person came back. Occasionally, patients were in restraints over an entire weekend. Because of half-hour lunch breaks, Peterson argued, the workers were being paid for eight hours work but only working seven and a half. He announced that shifts would be extended by a half hour so that workers could communicate. His announcement angered the working staff: "There's always the feeling when a new superintendent comes in that the local people will outlast him, he'll go home . . . [and that] people in charge have to have the authority to execute their responsibility, and they have to use it." One nurse remembered that in an early staff meeting Peterson announced, "You will first hate me, then you'll learn to love me."9

There may have been less anger if Peterson had been able to give raises, but the budget was rigid. The legislative appropriation had authorized money to work on the physical plant but not for raises. Peterson told the story:

> We had some detractors out in the community, and we had a very good, energetic man, a psych aide, who had two troubles. He was energetic and a troublemaker, and he organized what was known as the "Club." And they held rallies, meetings, and, frankly, they didn't like me. They sought to get rid of me. . . . I had pretty much of a mutiny on my hands one day. And of course they had real grievances. I caused the nursing services to overlap by half an hour. As a means of one shift letting the other shift know what the hell it had done. This went over not very well, you know, because these kids were used to working seven and a half hours and getting paid for eight hours. . . . Well, things were getting pretty tense.
>
> [As to the] *Fulton Daily Sun-Gazette*, well, I can't say they weren't friendly, but they printed the allegations without checking with me if they were true. Anyway, this day they [the Club] were going to have a motorcade and see the governor, also, they were going to block the entrance of Fulton State Hospital so that anybody who was not going to Jeff City could not get to their jobs. . . . This trouble continued off and on for a few months.10

---

9. Nina Davis, interview with Brazos and McMillen, December 6, 1999, tape recording in authors' collection.
10. Donald Peterson interview.

At the time, St. Joseph State Hospital was also having problems, which led the state legislature to investigate both institutions. At a town meeting in the Callaway County courthouse, there was testimony from members of the "Club" and from Peterson's supporters. One supporter, a nurse, spoke persuasively in Peterson's defense and managed to defuse the situation. "Operating a state hospital is a complicated business," Peterson said, "pressures . . . arise from the legislature, the personnel of the hospital, various organizations . . . and these pressures are not always at the same time pushing in the same direction."[11]

Some problems at the hospital were solved by personal initiative rather than by legislative action. One example is the desegregation of wards by race. Until Peterson's arrival, according to one estimate, "90% of black patients" were in basements, including eighty-seven black women in the basement of the Renn Hospital building. This basement ward for black women had been in operation since the early 1930s and perhaps earlier. When "Miss Willie" Samson Edwards came to Fulton in 1933, she was offered and accepted a job as an attendant in the ward. According to Fulton author Jack McBride, she found that the patients "often wallowed in their own waste if they were incontinent or could not control their bowels. Some went without baths or decent hair care for months at a time." She left the job, worked at the Missouri School for the Deaf and public schools, and finally labored as domestic help for families; she lived most of her years in a pair of tents erected on a town lot. In January 1974, she disappeared and was found dead in a pond in northeast Fulton.[12]

There was a large number of African Americans at Fulton because there had been a race riot at the Farmington asylum in the 1930s and black patients had been transferred to Fulton. To effect desegregation in the 1960s, Peterson hired Jane Bierdeman-Fike, who had started her career in 1944 as a caseworker in St. Louis and had received a master of social work degree from St. Louis University in 1949. From 1955 to 1962, she had worked at St. Louis State Hospital when it was desegregated. At St. Louis State Hospital, the clinical director had directed the transfer of African Americans to white wards in groups of three to avoid the problems of isolation of one patient or "pairing up" of two. Bierdeman-Fike and Peterson used the same system.[13]

11. Ibid.
12. McBride, *Search*.
13. Jane Bierdeman-Fike, interview by Brazos and McMillen, November 15, 1999, tape recording in authors' collection. On May 19, 2003, a building in the Hearnes Center was named for Bierdeman-Fike; the program for the ceremony included an abbreviated list of her accomplishments, which included a 1971 Alumnae Professional Achievement Award from Maryville College, a 1997 award from the National Association of Social Workers, Washington, D.C., "for

After desegregation in the 1960s, black and white patients enjoyed entertainment together (Fulton State Hospital).

In the 1960s, racism flourished in Callaway County, and, indeed, most of Missouri. When a hospital resident, a white woman, was walking around town on a pass and was seen talking to some black men, the hospital received a phone call from a Fulton resident, who warned the staff not to let the patient out on a pass again.[14] To change attitudes, Bierdeman-Fike asked a professor from Lincoln University, the historically black college in Jefferson City, to launch a black studies program in Biggs. Although the program ended when the professor moved away, Bierdeman-Fike remained committed to building a program to replace it: "I think that racism is a mental illness, if you define mental illness . . . as 'a break with reality.' In other words, if you think you're better than other people based on race, that's a break with reality. That's delusional."[15]

Besides accomplishing desegregation, Peterson approached the treatment of mental illness aggressively, by using all available medications, lobotomies, and shock treatment. The goal was to send patients home in an

---

exceptional contributions," and a 2001 Honorary Doctorate of Humane Letters from William Woods University (FSHA).

14. Anonymous former employee, interview by Brazos, tape recording in authors' collection.

15. Jane Bierdeman-Fike interview, November 15, 1999. The challenge of a diverse population continued, and in the 1990s the staff adopted a program called "Winning Balance" to help staff anticipate and adapt to various points of view, whether rural or urban, or based on gender, race, or religion.

acceptable condition that they could sustain. Hydrotherapy treatment was being phased out, and Peterson relied heavily on shock therapy. He believed that "if you didn't give a person shock treatment that was in a deep depression, they would suicide," said Jane Bierdeman-Fike. "And then you gave them mood elevators . . . but the most emergency treatment was shock treatment." Lobotomy was a last option only used after other treatments failed. According to one employee:

> Dr. Peterson was pretty much a proponent of it . . . and I think many of the more progressive places in the state had stopped doing it. They [the doctors at Fulton] were still doing it, and they had an elaborate system of checks to make sure you didn't do it erroneously or too precipitously. . . . A couple of social workers, a couple of psychologists, a couple of psychiatrists, maybe that surgeon, . . . Dr. Ritterbusch. . . . New psychological testing . . . Medication reviews . . . Extensive interviews with the patient . . . And based on review of that, would they go and do the lobotomy or not? . . . It was a big, serious process.[16]

Dr. Peterson's preferred method of lobotomy consisted of small cuts. The results were less globally damaging and, if the problematic aggressive behavior persisted, the procedure could be repeated. One patient had multiple lobotomies at the state hospital, and her sense of humor and ability to play the mandolin and sing remained intact.[17]

At Fulton, the end of lobotomies came in 1966 when the hospital was under review for accreditation by the Joint Commission on Accreditation of Hospitals. Although procedures to resume lobotomies were announced in 1973, with the explanation that the new form of surgery was less damaging and more precise, the operation was not performed.[18]

Whether using old techniques or adopting new ones, Peterson sought therapies that would give patients the best possible chance at living a full life back in the community, rather than keeping patients in the hospital. Joe Mangini, who started his career as a social worker in the Biggs unit in 1969, told a newspaper reporter that it was a challenge to change staff attitude to accept that patients could work toward release: "To get people that had worked in an environment that was primarily custodial for years and try to tell them, 'Yeah, custody is a part of it, but we're also going to do treatment here, fellas,' was not an easy thing to do."[19]

16. Jane Bierdeman-Fike interview, November 15, 1999; Tom Lezon interview.
17. Brazos, note on draft manuscript, August 7, 2006, in authors' collection.
18. Jerome P. Curry, "Fulton State Hospital to Resume Lobotomies," *St. Louis Post-Dispatch*, June 3, 1973.
19. Jim Herweg and Ann Yow, "By Reason of Insanity," *Kingdom Daily News*, special section, July 27, 1980, 5.

Because mental illness is so hard to assess, it is difficult to decide exactly when a patient is ready for release. To facilitate that decision, Peterson involved a number of staff members:

> Every morning at five minutes after eight I had a meeting. . . . [I] heard what had happened throughout the last twenty-four hours. The meetings often dissolved down into little committees. . . . Someone thinks this patient is ready for discharge. Someone else does not. . . . In the end, I do make the decision. . . . This takes the doctor off the hook. . . . But if I participate, he can't be made a scapegoat.[20]

When Peterson met with patients who were about to go on their own, he would give them frank advice: "Let the neighbors get used to you . . . because they remember you as the guy with the shotgun."[21]

Peterson was a hands-on administrator. When a patient took a psychologist as hostage and holed up in the Biggs Building, Peterson went to the spot and talked to the patient quietly, perhaps applying his theories on hypnosis and applied suggestion. He had a deep, authoritative voice, which he knew how to use to good effect. After three hours, the patient released the hostage and gave up. After that incident, Peterson instituted a "no hostage" policy in the Biggs Building that has lasted into the twenty-first century. The policy calls for an instant lockdown as soon as a hostage is taken because, under lockdown, nobody leaves the building under any circumstances. Patients with hostages have no hope of using the hostage to demand escape. Justifying the policy, Peterson explained, "Once outside with a hostage, the hostage becomes deadweight, and would probably be killed."[22]

At the time, the Biggs Building was in especially bad shape, even having windows out. When Peterson finally convinced the Division of Mental Diseases that he needed to rehabilitate and expand Biggs, they offered him $700,000. Peterson found this unacceptable: "I told George Ulett that . . . there was just no way . . . that I'd get anything for $700,000 that would be useful. I don't like to waste money, but I don't want $700,000. . . . He said I'd better take it, but I said I'm just not gonna do it, George, this is a trap." Peterson asked Dr. Francis J. Tartaglino, the clinical director, to prepare a detailed report on Biggs for the Midwestern Governors' Conference Interstate Workshop. He passed the report to the state legislators. It included detailed plans for expansion "and I did get . . . a mess hall, got a swimming pool, got a gymnasium." The building program was completed in 1968–1969.[23]

20. Donald Peterson interview.
21. Ibid.
22. "Peterson Tells of Sept. 20, 1971," *Kingdom Daily News*, April 14, 1972, 1.
23. Donald Peterson interview.

With the expansion came new staff. A consultant in forensic psychiatry—the treatment of criminal insanity—came two days per week, and there were also new psychologists, psychiatric social workers, recreational, occupational, and music therapists, chaplains, teachers, and volunteers, who all helped move Biggs from a security-obsessed facility to one employing more therapy. Tartaglino reported that rather than calling the patients "criminally insane," "we prefer 'the more dangerously insane' because many non-criminals are housed in maximum security and many criminals are in the general population." And, Tartaglino said, "It is indeed surprising to see how much can actually be done for the so-called criminally insane patient . . . if one has a well-planned organized program and is fortunate enough to have an adequate and sufficient staff."[24]

The restructuring and renovation allowed Biggs to house 280 patients, or thirty-five patients in each of eight wards. A new admission lived in either Biggs 7 or Biggs 8, two wards that were isolated from the others. After patients stabilized, they were moved to a ward with more freedom, moving in the building from the top floor to the bottom. Such transfers could be made without a court order, but the patients were carefully screened before moving, and the superintendent was consulted if there was any question about a move. Trustworthy patients could move to wards that participated in activities and dances, and they were allowed to socialize while in the dining room. They might work in a sheltered workshop or even in the community, as preparation for returning home some day. In 1962, the program had resulted in fifty-five patients being finally discharged; in 1963, that total had risen to sixty-two.[25]

As one nurse points out, the concept of a maximum-security hospital is "strange and unwieldy." A hospital, after all, is a place that seeks to cure and release patients rather than punish, but the public wants criminals punished and may not accept rehabilitation: "The Department of Corrections controls the front door [admissions]. The Department of Mental Health controls the back door [discharge]."[26]

Some older patients, although not allowed to go home, were eventually moved to the geriatrics building and stayed the rest of their lives, but the goal was for Biggs patients to make a smooth transition back into life in a community. Making that move, however, was admittedly difficult: "I would like to emphasize," wrote Tartaglino, "that the success of a program in any Maximum Security Unit is keeping as many patients as possible usefully occupied and providing opportunity for improving their station in life."[27]

24. Tartaglino, "Maximum Security Unit," 4.
25. Dickson Terry, "A Hospital or a Prison?" *St. Louis Post-Dispatch*, October 18, 1964, 1.
26. Brazos, notes to McMillen on first draft of manuscript, in authors' collection.
27. Tartaglino, "Maximum Security Unit," 4.

Besides the authorized patient departures, there was also the risk of unauthorized escape. Four patients ran away on August 17, 1964, after performing the play *The Caine Mutiny Trial* with a hospital theater group. One patient was stopped before leaving the grounds. Two others stole a station wagon and were tracked down in a residential neighborhood. The final escapee, a sexual psychopath, entered a women's dormitory at Fulton's William Woods College. After a few such incidents and the accompanying media stories, community unease increased. Interviewed by a reporter, Judge Hugh P. Williamson claimed that "People in this town are in a constant state of apprehension."[28]

Despite occasional escapes, doctors and their families in homes on the hospital grounds were generally not worried about breakouts. One family moved to one of the doctor's cottages in the mid-1960s. With one son, they had "lots of sleepovers . . . Some people would not give their children permission to sleep over—very few—but because they were afraid. However, we sort of had the philosophy that if anyone were escaping they would not choose to be so close. They would try to get away."[29]

The conviction that escaping patients would leave town was widely held. However, many "walkaways" were discovered in Callaway County barns, nearby woods, or hitchhiking. Some went south along Stinson Creek, an area nicknamed "Dark Hollow," and Hams Prairie. Others went north toward I-70. Escapes were reported on local radio KFAL-KKCA, and residents were urged to lock their doors, phone neighbors, and remain watchful until the radio reported that the escapee had been caught. Community fear also fueled a rumor mill revolving around the concern that hospital residents were having affairs and becoming pregnant. Peterson responded to the criticism by saying that hospital policy was "not to be subjected to pressure from either employees in the hospital or the townspeople outside."[30]

Despite the criticism, public acceptance of mental illness had come a long way in the 110 years of the hospital's existence. This acceptance was crucial because many experts believed that success depended on treatment within a community rather than in a hospital. In the late 1960s, the social work department pioneered the establishment of outpatient mental health clinics in Mexico, Hannibal, Rolla, Lebanon, and Eldon. Jane Bierdeman-Fike remembered: "They had a doctor, and usually our social workers would travel out to the clinic. . . . We worked with the communities and set these

---

28. Terry, "Hospital or a Prison?"
29. Anonymous Fulton resident, interview by McMillen, December 30, 1999, tape recording in authors' collection.
30. Ibid.

up, and therefore they were more accepted. Most of the people knew that there was mental illness in the community."[31]

One of the new local clinics built with federal dollars was the Mid-Missouri Mental Health Center, which opened in January 1967 next to the University Hospital in Columbia. With beds for 30 children, 73 adult psychiatric patients, and 17 alcoholic patients, "Mid-Mo" was designed to serve 52 mid-Missouri counties with intensive, short-term treatment. Peterson complained that the opening of new mental health centers was a mixed blessing for stabilizing patient numbers. While some people could be treated in their home communities, the centers ultimately added to the burden of the state hospital rather than helping it, because the centers identified new cases of mental illness and sent them to the state hospital.[32]

Public acceptance of mental illness and the increasing understanding that it could be treated made many families hopeful, but as in the 1800s, the realities of expanded treatment taxed the system. As early as 1960, civil rights activists had proposed that the mentally ill had a right to treatment. A 1966 court ruling stated that if no treatment was available within a prison system for a person found "not guilty by reason of insanity," then the system had to release that person. A few years after the 1966 decision, there was recognition of the right of mentally ill persons to refuse treatment, medication, or both. The court decided that the mentally ill could demand a hearing to ask for their release every six months. This "patients' rights" movement made it clear that the legal system was increasingly willing to address mental health issues.

Dr. Peterson saw the hospital as a part of the larger community. In 1969, State Hospital No. 1 was renamed Fulton State Hospital, a change of nomenclature bringing the community and hospital together. George Ulett would credit Peterson with another positive linguistic change, reflecting a "greater hope for patient recovery," when the department changed its name from the Division of Mental Diseases to the Missouri Department of Mental Health. The close relationship between Ulett and Peterson continued, to the extent that they coauthored *Applied Hypnosis and Positive Suggestion*, published in 1965 by C. V. Mosby in St. Louis. Their rapport was certainly beneficial to Fulton and to the hospital. Ulett later wrote about visiting Don and Catherine Peterson at home:

> I would arrive about 7 a.m. and drop in presumably for a cup of hot tea. In reality I dropped in for advice. It was the wisdom of Don and Catherine that directed our council of superintendents to decisions that accounted for many of the successes. . . . During this time the pa-

---
31. Jane Bierdeman-Fike interview, November 15, 1999.
32. Donald Peterson interview.

tient population of the overcrowded five state hospitals dropped from 10,000 to 5,000 patients and at the same time the work force rose from 5,000 to 10,000 mental health personnel.[33]

By the end of the 1960s, many hospital staff agreed that the place was "just like home" for patients, with its own society, mores, and rules. One staff member said it was an "asylum" in the true sense of the word, a place of refuge for people who might otherwise be living on the streets. The hospital staff could feel a sense of pride in accomplishment and optimism about the future. In a departure from the serious institutional style of annual reports, the department's annual report for 1968–1969 sports a bright cover and is titled *Psychiatry in the Space Age*. The document discusses the bright future for technology in mental health, including the use of EEGs, computers, and the new technology of "video . . . useful in many phases of treatment and training."[34]

Reflecting on the hospital's history since the Civil War, one staff member could hardly believe that a single century could show so much change:

> I used to take graduate students down into the tunnels to show them the old Civil War cells, and holes in the wall where the rings were to secure the lunatics. . . . It's kind of like under the kitchen, or a little bit beyond that . . . there was one metal door. It took a special key. You open that, it's like stepping into the past . . . stone, unfinished walls, it's like a basement dungeon. It's divided into little cell-like rooms. There's no gates or bars or anything like that. . . . If you were standing against one of the walls, at about shoulder height, there's indentations in the wall where they had pins to secure the chains for holding patients. All these little cubicles . . . about eight feet by four feet. And it's a special sealed-off area. . . . Back in the sixties, the old Civil War buildings . . . were still standing. And this was a particular area that some of us had keys to . . . under one of the old Civil War buildings . . . It's history.[35]

---

33. George A. Ulett, "Colonal [*sic*] Pete," undated memoir, perhaps given at Peterson retirement (FSHA).
34. "Psychiatry in the Space Age" (Jefferson City: Missouri Division of Mental Health, 1969), 13.
35. Tom Lezon interview.

12
New Strategies, New Challenges, 1970–1979

In the 1970s, the ability to diagnose disorders had advanced. While many patients were chronically ill and were expected to live out their days as geriatric patients, others were admitted with the hope that they would be released. In the Biggs Building, forensic, or criminaly insane, patients were admitted under the following fourteen categories: schizophrenic reactions (various types, with the paranoid type predominate); involutional psychotic reaction; inadequate personality; schizoid personality; passive-aggressive personality; sexual deviation (some of these were diagnosed as psychotic); dissocial reaction; antisocial reaction; alcoholism (addiction); psychoneurotic reaction, anxiety type; adjustment reaction of adolescence; chronic brain syndrome associated with convulsive disorder; chronic brain syndrom, all others; and mental deficiencies.[1] A few residents were admitted without diagnosis. Even with the sometimes vague categories, treatments for each disorder were becoming specific and new medications were given for each one. Partially due to the new medications, Robert Seaman, business manager, estimated in a 1972 speech that cost of care had risen to $20 per day.[2] In 1967, the cost per day had been an estimated $9.09.[3]

The hospital was particularly innovative with its program for rehabilitation of the criminally insane patients. The *Official State Manual* in 1970 lauded the facility's efforts that allowed "a gradual progression toward increased liberty for those patients originally maintained in maximum security." Therapies that emphasized noninstitutionalized treatment brought the inpatient

---

1. Tartaglino, "Maximum Security Unit," 36–37.
2. "Fulton State Hospital Leader in Treatment of Juveniles," *Kingdom Daily News*, May 5, 1972, 1.
3. Thomasen, "History of FSH," 7 (FSHA).

census down to about 1,550, but the staff was following "more than 2,000 patients on leave status, including more than 1,000 . . . in licensed nursing homes."[4]

Among the new strategies for treatment was an Alcohol and Drug Abuse (ADA) program that specified only twenty-eight days in the hospital for detoxification and therapy before release to outpatient care. Indeed, regional centers for alcoholism treatment had been one of Dr. Ulett's goals as director of the department. However, he had met resistance from all the state hospitals, where administrators insisted they had no time, staff, or facilities to establish such centers. As a result, until the ADA program began, alcoholics had been housed in locked units with other mentally ill patients.[5]

The Fulton facility continued to refine its outpatient strategy. Experience had demonstrated that in order to succeed, outpatient programs required excellent communication between the hospital, the family, and the patient, since the patient quickly returned to the community. The hospital developed a series of booklets that answered questions about patient rights, privileges, rules, how to make phone calls, how to arrange for visits, and other issues. What clothes does the patient need? What should be done with the patient's valuables? The booklets, adapted for patients and families, opened with the word "Welcome" and ended with "Good luck!"[6]

The brochures also contained a discussion of fees, which were based on a sliding scale. Upon arrival at the hospital, the patient would visit the "Resource Investigator's Office," where application could be made for help such as Social Security, veterans' benefits, railroad pensions, military allotments, and so forth. The office arranged to receive benefits and would deposit an allowance into an account for the patient's spending money. From two to five dollars per week could be held in the patient account. The list of staff members at Fulton State Hospital had grown, so that a patient was likely to have contact with a variety of aides, nurses, psychologists, and therapists. The ward aide, a patient learned, was "your primary link to the other peo-

---

4. Ibid.; Thelma P. Goodwin, ed., *1969–1970 Official Manual*, James C. Kirkpatrick, Secretary of State (Jefferson City: Von Hoffmann Press, 1970), 794; Thomasen, "History of FSH," 7.

5. "Alcoholism: The Missouri Experience," a video produced by Missouri Department of Public Health, explained that Ulett's interest began after the 1958 suicide of an alcoholic Marine veteran who had received the medal of honor in World War II. The mayor of St. Louis and governor raised $96,000 to start an experimental "open-door" unit at Malcolm Bliss Hospital in St. Louis. The unit opened on February 6, 1962. Dr. Ulett was involved with the treatment, which brought patients to the inpatient unit for twenty-one days and then placed them in Alcoholics Anonymous groups in the city. Follow-up after one and two years affirmed that 60 percent stayed sober, 20 percent were drinking less, and 20 percent were unchanged. One member of the team said the clinic was "the only place just for alcoholics other than the State Hospital, where you might get a frontal lobotomy." The center drew national attention to Missouri.

6. "Fulton State Hospital: A Guide for Patients" (Fulton State Hospital, 1970).

ple on the staff who are involved in your treatment." Aides were with patients more than other staff, and a patient's success in treatment often depended on the aides.[7]

A registered nurse provided skilled nursing care and supervised the aides, and a social worker handled the intake interview, worked with families, and made discharge plans. After discharge, the social worker kept up with patients by finding a clinic or agency to continue treatment in the patient's hometown. A ward doctor was the physician in charge of medical and psychiatric treatment. The booklets given to patients explained that some mental health conditions were the result of medical problems. Each patient received a complete physical upon admission, including a skin test and chest X-ray for tuberculosis, blood and urine exams, and dental and eye exams. A clinical psychologist ran tests and conducted therapy individually or in groups. A vocational rehab counselor could help patients learn about job training and gave tests to discover patient job preferences and skills. Additionally, there were four groups of activity therapists: Occupational therapists taught patients leatherwork, weaving, ceramic glazing, sewing, embroidery, or other handicrafts. Music therapists taught them how to make music and arranged for musical groups from the hospital and from the outside community to play. Recreation therapists provided "the use of a game room or swimming pool at certain times weekly." Industrial therapists provided daily scheduled work.[8]

Chaplains who were specially trained to work with people with mental illness visited each patient, conducted group therapy, and were available by request. Indeed, the 1970s witnessed employment of the largest number of chaplains in hospital history. Dick Rummel was director of chaplains, Don Stassel served as chaplain for the youth center, and Bernie Lischway, a Catholic priest, was chaplain of Biggs. Ralph Galbraith, who started work at the hospital in 1966 and received his doctor of ministries degree in 1972, served the acute and chronic populations. In addition to these ministers, three interns worked in the Clinical Pastoral Education Program.[9]

Mental health physicians were focusing increasingly on medications for overcoming depression or anxiety. The general public had not become accustomed to the regular use of medications, however, and patients were warned against quitting their medicine when they felt better. This was difficult for patients who had problems with organization skills and confusion. The patient's guide warned: "One of the most common reasons a per-

7. Ibid., 6, 12–15.
8. Ibid., 14–15.
9. Bob Vegiard, interview by McMillen, January 10, 2000, tape recording in authors' collection.

son returns to the hospital after going out on trial visit or being discharged is that he stops taking his medication." The hospital's goal was to stabilize a patient and to send the patient home with a medication schedule if medication could be helpful. Patients would go home for visits lasting from a week to a year before being officially discharged.[10]

However, some chronically mentally ill patients were never discharged, so Fulton continued to have "chronic" wards for patients in the hospital longer than ninety days. One attendant started working on the wards in 1971, when she was twenty-two. Her preliminary training took six months, including classes in anatomy and physiology, medications, psychology, and patient interaction. Life on the wards had a predictable rhythm: "Back then, we did the medications and it was nothing to get called to geriatrics and give meds to fifty patients, because the wards were large. And the medications were interesting. Now we have the neat little unit dose, [but back in 1971, we had] the milk of mags, the cascaras, the Thorazine came in gallon jugs. . . . I hated laxative night." She eventually went back to school, became a nurse, and built a career for herself at the hospital.[11]

Some patients were locked in their wards, while other patients had ground privileges. Patients with ground privileges found a variety of ways to make a little pocket money. One set up a watch repair shop in one tunnel, and others ran little stands where townspeople bought fishing worms, blackberries picked on the grounds, or hickory nutmeats. For a time, a patient ran an animal shelter under the water tower, starting with one dog and then acquiring more. To build pens, he scavenged pallets and scrap materials. To keep them fed, he raided the hospital kitchen for leftovers. The operation was so successful that Fulton residents started dropping animals off and adopting them at the hospital. The animal shelter ended during the cleanup prior to an inspection by the Joint Commission of Hospital Accreditation (JCHA), a commission of the American Psychiatric Association and American Medical Association. Meanwhile, the JCHA apparently did not object to—or perhaps discover—the fact that patients and staff gathered to gamble with dice in a shady spot behind the power plant. The craps games were so popular that they drew players from town. It is said that the stakes reached well into the hundreds, even thousands, of dollars.[12]

Long-term patients worked side by side with staff, and fond relationships developed. In interviews, several workers reported that they thought pa-

---

10. "Fulton State Hospital: A Guide," 15–16.
11. Jamesetta Van Buren interview. While most medications were given according to need, laxatives like milk of magnesia and cascara were scheduled for the entire ward.
12. Anonymous worker, interview by Brazos, summer 2003, tape recording in authors' collection.

tients would have protected staff if there was trouble: "If you found a friend out there as a patient, you had a friend."[13] Starting work in 1970, one man was assigned to the food storage area and drove a food truck. He remembered a special friend:

> M. C. . . . was in his seventies. He came out here when he was twenty years old for killing a couple of guys that kept bugging him . . . knocking his hat off . . . he just grabbed them by the shirts and mashed their heads together, and, of course, killed them. So they sent him out here. . . . He helped me in '71 and '72, until he broke his ankle. He didn't know what money was. The first year, I gave him five dollars for helping me on the food truck, and he carried it around for two months.

Rather than thanking the patient with money, one aide had recommended that M. C. be rewarded with coupon books to use in the hospital canteen, or with candy bars and sodas. Another aide adopted a variation: "I carried boxes of tobacco so I could pass it out."[14]

Patients like M. C. were "institutionalized." That is, they had adapted to institutional life and had created opportunities within that environment for themselves. One patient, J. B., was renowned for his business sense. He sold watches and cigarettes from a suitcase to employees and patients, making a small profit on each item. He kept track of hundreds of accounts in his head and got paid once a month, telling customers what each owed. He also had a car-washing business and would offer to wash cars for fifty cents, and then he would subcontract the work to other patients for a few nickels. He carried rolls of money, but it was said that he hid some of it in the tunnels. Eventually, his sister came for him and took him to Florida. One worker remembered, "I wasn't the only one running those tunnels looking for the money." After a month, the patient came back. "He came on the grounds at night, went through the tunnels . . . and picked up his money."[15]

J. B. was well known for other reasons. He stopped traffic one day when he sat in front of the hospital with his head buried in red-painted rags, as if he had been hit by a car and was hurt. One staffer "fell all over himself to help," but when he found out it was a prank, he got mad and locked up J. B. for three weeks. One Fulton woman remembered fondly this patient "with a sense of humor." She remembered seeing a lady's pocketbook on the walk: "I reached down to pick it up, and it moved . . . there was this 'tee-

---

13. Unidentified Fulton State Hospital worker, meeting with authors at Kingdom of Callaway Historical Society, January 6, 1999, tape recording in authors' collection.
14. Anonymous worker, interview by Brazos, summer 2003, tape recording in authors' collection.
15. Ibid.

hee-hee-hee-hee,' and he popped up from behind a bush. He played that trick on a lot of people."[16]

Another patient well known to the community was originally from Yonkers, New York. "He was paranoid. He heard voices. And he had a garden out there [on the hospital grounds]. . . . That was when patients were allowed to have gardens. And he had tomatoes and watermelons. . . . He did some work for us when we lived out in the country. We would pick him up and bring him back to the hospital grounds. He would be on the crew. Very strange, but very respectful."[17] The patient eventually died and was buried in Pioneer Cemetery on Fourth Street. Another well-known character was "Taxi," who pushed a mail cart from one building to another, making engine sounds and shifting gears with his hands as he "drove." Folks said he was left at the hospital as a baby and lived there until he died.[18]

With people so adapted to life in the mental institution, it was hard to draw the line between competence and incompetence. As early as the 1950s, sociologists and psychologists looking at life inside the asylum saw patterns that were similar to those in normal society. As people settled into life on the ward, there were rites of passage, hierarchy, and the struggle to maintain individuality and personal space. The patterns sociologists reported were the same as in other institutions—monasteries, the military, even college campuses. The patterns seemed so predictable that they challenged the idea of the erratic behavior of insanity. Erving Goffman, author of *Asylums: Essays on the Social Situation of Mental Patients and Other Inmates*, published in 1961, was perhaps the best-known proponent of this view. He argued that mental hospitals encouraged behavior that others called "psychotic" because institutions took away the patients' abilities to assert themselves in ways that were "normal." Losing their ability to express themselves "normally," they became unable to live outside the asylum.[19]

For many residents, the hospital was home, where they felt comfortable. Indeed, a major problem was the high amount of patient relapse and readmission due to the inability to adjust to live outside. National studies revealed that 47 percent of all people admitted had been in a mental hospital before. In 1972, Fulton State Hospital received a three-year grant by the National Institute of Mental Health for $100,000 per year to grapple with readmissions. Two factors were blamed for the recidivism: inability to handle stress and failure to take prescribed medications. John J. Harris, a social

---

16. Anonymous worker, interview by McMillen, December 30, 1999, tape recording in authors' collection.
17. Ibid.
18. Luci Hess, interview by Brazos, December 1, 1999, tape recording in authors' collection.
19. Isaac and Armat, *Madness in the Streets*, 48.

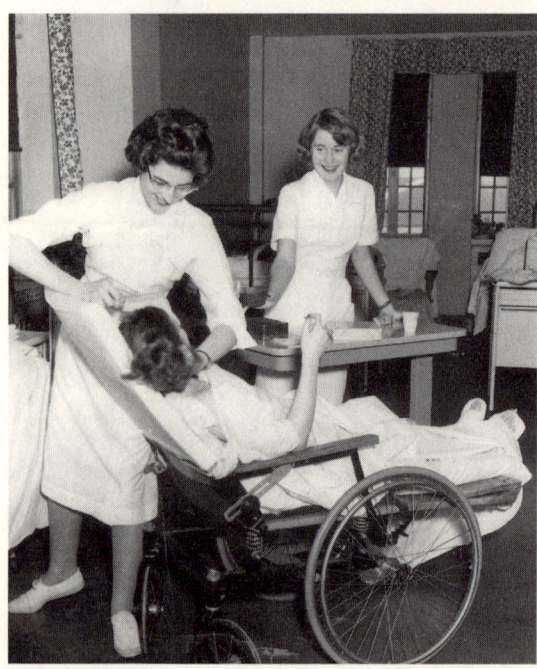

When a beauty parlor was added to the hospital, it was an innovation that helped to provide a more normal life within the institution and to prepare patients for life in society. For those with multiple disabilities, however, staff was often called to provide everyday care that normalized patients' lives (Fulton State Hospital).

worker, was hired to set up a ward that would duplicate life in society. The program focused intently on chronic patients, including work schedules and taking care of oneself. Jane Bierdeman-Fike described the program: "We had a Hospital Improvement Grant on readmitted patients. And that became a really intensive program for really chronic patients." As part of therapy, she remembered, Peterson thought that every person should work, "not to the point of trying to exploit them, but to stay away from idleness."[20]

Even though patients felt secure in the hospital, mental illness meant that patients could be unpredictable. A grim reminder came on September 20, 1971, when patients captured psychologist Kay Mohatt, one of the few women allowed in Biggs at the time. They dragged her to her office, taped her hands behind her back, taped her eyes shut, and gagged her. George Chase, a Protestant chaplain and part of the Clinical Pastoral Education Program, was beaten to death with a mop handle when he rushed to Mohatt's rescue. Psychologist Dave Jannick later told reporters,

> There was quite a lot of resentment toward the psychology department in particular because we were the department that had the bad taste to have a female employee. The attitude was, "If we hadn't had her, these guys wouldn't have broken in, tried to rape her, tried to use her as a hostage, and then poor George wouldn't have gotten blud-

---

20. Jane Bierdeman-Fike interview, November 15, 1999.

geoned to death." Which probably isn't true. They wanted out, and we just happened to be the people they had access to a little easier.[21]

There are two conflicting stories about Mohatt's rescue. One story, repeated by hospital staff, claimed that another worker, called the "White Knight," talked the criminals into releasing her. The other story, recorded by reporters in court during the patients' trial, claimed that one of the criminals called Dr. Peterson to demand a car. When Peterson arrived, he talked the men into giving up.[22] Three patients were charged with Chase's murder; one was committed to Biggs with catatonic schizophrenia. The professional staff, however, would not sit in a room with him; hence he got no treatment. He later told reporters: "If you're a sex psychopath, they take you to films, give you notebooks and books to read on sex and stuff like that—try to straighten you out. If you're up here for murder or something, you're just lost."[23]

This murder was just one incident in a string of highly publicized events at the hospital. Seven months after the murder, a lawsuit claiming "inadequacy of care and treatment" was filed in April 1972 in the U.S. District Court of Western Missouri by the St. Louis Legal Aid Society. The lawsuit, *Eckerhart v. Hensley*, had three parts: Count 1 condemned the treatment and conditions at Biggs, count 2 challenged patient placement without due process; and count 3 sought compensation for patient labor.[24] A second "patient rights" suit was filed a few months later, demanding that patients be given the right to register and vote. This suit was settled so quickly that the first registration for qualified voters was held in October 1972.[25]

On December 15, 1973, Judge Elmo Hunter addressed count 2 of the Legal Aid Society lawsuit, ruling that patients could not be transferred to Biggs from other buildings without a hearing, that patients already in Biggs were entitled to an immediate review, that the hospital needed to provide for religious expression by Black Muslims, and that patients could convert to one religion or another without institutional interference.[26] The Biggs professional staff took on the review, while the chaplains added a new religion to those they already counseled.

In 1974, however, another lawsuit accused the hospital of negligence.

---

21. Jim Herweg and Ann Yow, "By Reason of Insanity," *Kingdom Daily News* insert, July 27, 1980, 32.
22. For the official version, see "Peterson Tells of Sept. 20, 1971," *Kingdom Daily News*, April 13, 1972, 1. The in-hospital version of the story has a sweet ending, with "The White Knight" later proposing and marrying Mohatt.
23. Herweg and Yow, "By Reason of Insanity," 36.
24. "Treatment at Fulton Attacked in Suit," *St. Louis Post-Dispatch*, April 30, 1972, 27A.
25. "Hospital Voter Signup Held," *Jefferson City Capital Daily News*, October 7, 1972, 8.
26. "Judge Supports Patient Rights," *Columbia Daily Tribune*, December 15, 1973, 5.

The National Juvenile Law Center contended that a nine-year-old boy had been sent to Fulton for evaluation in 1962 and had been "lost" for twelve years. "Poppycock . . . worse than irresponsible," Peterson told reporters. "There are a bunch of bleeding hearts these days, and things are getting a little dangerous with the federal courts practicing psychiatry and trying to keep others from practicing it." Further investigation showed that the allegations were indeed false.[27]

Some blame for the communications problems was due to budget restrictions at the hospital. Low wages meant staff shortages, and low maintenance budgets contributed to a deteriorated physical plant. To reduce expenses, Division of Mental Health director Harold Robb, who had replaced Dr. Ulett in December 1971, announced that "more than half of the 4,500 patients" in the state's mental hospitals would be released. The newly released people would go to group homes, nursing homes, communities, and families, leaving only the truly mentally ill at the hospital.[28]

The staff shortage had become such a problem that on September 22, 1974, the Joint Commission of Hospital Accreditation revoked Fulton State Hospital accreditation, citing its shortage of physicians and failure to meet fire and safety standards. Since the revocation could have meant loss of important federal payments, including Medicare and Medicaid, which had started in 1965, the hospital administration filed an appeal.[29] At the state level, Governor Christopher "Kit" Bond and the Department of Mental Health were rethinking delivery of care to the state's mentally ill. On July 1, 1974, the Omnibus State Government Reorganization Act had established the Department of Mental Health as a cabinet-level state agency. Governor Bond supported Missouri Senate Bill 300, which would take money from state hospitals and shift funds to a number of community mental health clinics that would be created throughout the state.

Health professionals at the existing hospitals vigorously objected to the proposal. One mental health nurse, Harriet Cave, gave up her job and worked full time to defeat the bill. "When there is not enough money to decently care for the patients in the hospital, I simply do not understand how you can claim that [moving care from institutions to clinics] will not result in harm to the helpless people now in the state schools and hospitals," she said, pointing out that similar plans in other states had resulted in large numbers of homeless persons on the streets.[30]

27. "Dr. Peterson Blasts Allegations," *Fulton Sun-Gazette*, December 6, 1974.
28. Betsey Solberg, "State Hospitals Plan Mass Release," *Kansas City Star*, September 9, 1973.
29. "Fulton Hospital Not Accredited, Newspaper Says," *Columbia Daily Tribune*, December 25, 1975, 1.
30. "Former FSH Employee Voices Dissatisfaction with Senate Bill 300," *Kingdom Daily News*, February 17, 1975, 1.

Superintendent Donald Peterson was equally enraged: "I made kind of a tactical error. I was walking down the hall in the Capitol, and the governor (Kit Bond) came out from some place. He was happy to see me and asked what I was doing. I said, 'I was lobbying against that stupid Senate Bill 300 that's so dear to your heart.' He didn't like that."[31] When the Senate bill failed, Department of Mental Health director Harold Robb put money into the plan through administrative action, and the regional centers were built anyway, taking money from the hospitals.

Nor was Fulton State Hospital alone in facing tough times. The state hospital in Nevada, Missouri, had also lost accreditation and, like Fulton, it had no money for new staff. In fact, the state's fiscal situation was so bad that the Missouri budget office had announced that the hospital needed to save 3 percent before the end of the fiscal year. Business office director Robert Seaman figured that if 90 percent of the staff agreed to work without pay for four days, the institution could save the required 3 percent and avert layoffs. Otherwise, twenty-six employees would lose their jobs. After a vote, 536 of 1,400 employees agreed to work without pay.[32] Almost immediately, department director Robb announced that, according to the Fair Labor Standards Act, the voluntary pay loss was illegal. Fortunately, Peterson's appeal to the JCAH had won, and accreditation was reinstated.[33]

The budget crisis and the dramatic vote to forgo pay renewed public interest in the hospital. The *Columbia Daily Tribune* ran a three-part series, "Fulton State Hospital: Another World," which gave Peterson and other administrators a forum to explain their program and the need for funding. The series revealed to the public the department's suggestions to save money by delaying maintenance projects, cutting back on food selection in the cafeteria, disconnecting electric lights, and not replacing staff who retired.[34]

By the end of 1975, newspapers announced that Dr. Peterson would be forced to retire when he reached age sixty-five on February 29, 1976. Peterson had asked for an extension of his retirement date, and staff members supported an extension, too, especially since Dr. Patrick Gannon of St. Louis State Hospital had resigned rather than serve as Fulton's superintendent. Still, Peterson's request was denied. The *Columbia Daily Tribune* obtained notes "taken surreptitiously" at a March 1975 meeting of the Mental Health Commission that "reveal the pressure which obviously has caused Dr. Robb to sacrifice two of his most able Superintendents," Gannon and Peterson.[35]

---

31. Donald Peterson interview.
32. "Work-without-Pay Plan," *Columbia Daily Tribune*, December 18, 1975, 10.
33. "Fulton's Appeal Nets 1-Year Accreditation," *Columbia Daily Tribune*, December 20, 1975, 1.
34. Cynthia Felts, "Fulton State Hospital: Another World," *Columbia Daily Tribune* January 11, 12, and 13, 1976, 8.
35. "Group Backs Hospital Officials," *Columbia Daily Tribune*, January 24, 1976, 8.

Peterson was vocal about his forced retirement, both to the papers in 1976 and in a 1983 interview: "In the last few years, Dr. Ulett resigned. Under pressure, I'm pretty sure, and he was succeeded by . . . Dr. Robb, who was succeeded by Duane Hensley, who was an educator. Ph.D. Of course, he [Hensley] couldn't please either." Peterson summed up his tenure, one of the longest runs by any superintendent at Fulton State Hospital, by saying the era of residential state hospitals was over. In his opinion, chronically ill patients would eventually be put in nursing homes, their assets to go to the nursing home. On the other hand, Peterson was hopeful that each generation of drugs would make it more possible for patients to become truly well. With new treatments, mentally ill people could keep their jobs and keep their families going. "And," Peterson said, "it's immensely less costly to the state."[36]

After Peterson's retirement, thirty-five-year-old Dr. Richard Jacks was named superintendent. His tenure began, happily enough, with a statement by Tom Evans, Jacks's assistant superintendent, that there would be "less typewriters and more wheelchairs" at the Fulton facility, which staff hopefully interpreted as less paperwork and more help for the patients.[37]

In 1976, the hospital celebrated its 125th anniversary with a parade. The maintenance department built a float that featured a revolving cake with 125 electric candles. The cake was five feet around and three feet tall, revolving with power from a generator. One maintenance worker remembers that administrators said, "We want this. Can you build it?" and the maintenance workers had answered, "If you've got the money, we can build it."[38] While there may have been money for a giant revolving cake, Jacks's administration was plagued by the same budget crisis that faced his predecessor. On April 19, 1976, he was compelled to announce that administration buildings would be heated only to 50 degrees in winter, air conditioning would be cut, and half the hospital vehicles would be "moth-balled."[39]

Many employees found these drastic measures unacceptable. Jacks's popularity suffered further when he missed a banquet for retired employees, attended by three hundred people and the press. The *Kingdom Daily News* reported that Paul Cooper, a cook for 48 years, and his wife, Alice, a staff member for 44 years, had been honored as employees with the longest tenure. Other hardworking couples were honored, including Johnnie and Virginia Payton (31 and 23 years, respectively) and Emmett and Frankie

---

36. Donald Peterson interview.
37. "Jacks Addresses 'Town Meeting,'" *Fulton Sun Gazette*, July 23, 1976, 1.
38. Unidentified worker at Kingdom of Callaway Historical Society, January 6, 1999, tape recording in authors' collection.
39. "FSH Initiates More Austerity Moves," *Sun Gazette*, April 20, 1976, 1.

Wefenstette (17 and 19 years). The hospital also recognized Millie Kemp (45 years) and Veta Dickson (42 years) for their service.[40]

Tom Evans, the assistant superintendent, had resigned without explanation the day before the celebration, making Jacks's disappearance even more mysterious. When a search failed to find Dr. Jacks, his disappearance began to look like a scandal. The department immediately appointed Dr. James K. Ritterbusch to replace him, calling Jacks's replacement "a personnel matter" and saying the reason would not be disclosed. A few months later, Jacks was hired to work at St. Joseph State Hospital.[41]

It is interesting and perhaps significant that this dysfunctional year came just a few months after a popular new film made mental hospitals look like relics of an unenlightened past. In 1962, Ken Kesey's novel *One Flew over the Cuckoo's Nest* had been published to great acclaim; a powerful film starring Jack Nicholson followed in 1975 and swept the Academy Awards. Kesey had based his book on his time spent working as an aide at a veterans' hospital but made the story into an argument for freedom and against institutionalization. The incidents in the story, which involves one patient who has been locked up against his will and others who are in the insitution by choice, have been convincingly interpreted in terms as varied as an allegory against communism or a misogynist rant. For Fulton viewers, the events at their state hospital almost seemed to outdo the film.

The appointment of Dr. Ritterbusch quickly restored the calm. He was well-known in the hospital and the community, a graduate of Westminster College who had gone on to medical school at the University of Missouri–St. Louis and who had been the hospital's chief surgeon since 1958. Ritterbusch respected the skills of every category of worker and, as if to illustrate his respect, changed the top-to-bottom chain of command that had put doctors in charge of other staff members. He established "units" with social workers, nurses, and psychologists participating equally to create treatment plans. One doctor, accustomed to being in charge of treatment, transferred away from a team rather than being reduced to one of many votes. Another doctor, Dr. Henry Bratkowski, told the *Fulton Sun-Gazette* that the unit approach was necessary in order to make up for lack of medical staff: "It is extremely difficult to recruit doctors to . . . state institutions at the salaries being paid."[42]

Ritterbusch also encouraged staff to try new treatments, even to disagree. For Kay Brandt, RN, a unit leader, the goal was to change behavior and get

---

40. J. G. Paroline, "FSH Honors Ex-Employees," *Kingdom Daily News*, December 6, 1976, 1.
41. "Ritterbusch Named Superintendent of Fulton State Hosp," *Columbia Daily Tribune*, April 27, 1977,.1.
42. J.J. Maloney, "Too Many Who Do Not Belong," *Fulton Sun-Gazette*, February 12, 1978, 8.

the patients out of the hospital. For other unit leaders, forensic patients had to show that they understood and felt remorse for their past behaviors.[43] In spite of the disagreements, and even with major problems of funding and staffing, Ritterbusch insisted that the hospital staff try new programs, always geared to the hope that mentally ill people could return to society and live a normal life. In 1976, staff, under the guidance of Bill McReynolds, developed the first experimental "token economy" on the wards. A "token economy" rewards positive behavior with tokens that can be used to buy desired items. Tokens were awarded for activities like attending classes or dressing appropriately but withheld after episodes of bizarre behavior or noncooperation.[44]

Although new programs emerged, much stayed the same. Fulton State Hospital still had its dairy and grain operations. The hospital staff still included doctors that performed medical procedures and nurses that cared for medical patients with an understanding of psychological as well as physical needs. There was still a dentist and an ophthalmologist. The morgue was still functioning. Patients working in the sewing room still made and repaired clothes for the patients. The Hyde Building functioned as a group home where residents enjoyed a degree of freedom. They did their own laundry, had a game room, had day passes, and worked downtown. They walked outside to the cafeteria for meals, but in rainy weather, they took the tunnels: "We even had dances in the administration building. Every Friday night."[45]

One new aide, who started work in 1977, was assigned to an "acute" ward on the fifth floor of "the old buildings," that is, the white brick North Ward and South Ward buildings erected before the Civil War. His first impression was of dark rooms with patients huddled in a corner. A patient walked by and said, "This place smells like snake shit." The worker remembered, "I will never forget it . . . and I thought, 'I am not working here.'" He needed a job, however, and soon found he enjoyed the work. He stayed sixteen years, worked on his nursing degree and transferred to Mid-Mo, and then returned to Fulton.[46]

Hospital workers were particularly touched by the situation of women in the Geriatrics Building. Some wives had been left at the hospital when they were experiencing postpartum depression. Even if they recovered, if the women had no skills and their husbands had divorced them, the hospital was their only home. One social worker remembered a catatonic lady who perched on chairs like a bird and another that called all day for her husband.

43. "For Some It's a Long Road Home," *Kingdom Daily News*, July 16, 1978, 8.
44. Gerald C. Davidson and John M. Neale, *Abnormal Psychology* (New York: John Wiley and Sons, 1994), 558.
45. Norbert Giesing interview.
46. Ibid.

At least once, a nurse tried to reassure an elderly woman who had been depressed and had been dropped off by her husband. In that case, the patient was terrified to learn—the morning after her abandonment—that her name was on the list for electroshock; a social worker stressed how "we did the best we could for the ladies."[47]

The Biggs unit, a world unto itself, continued to function like a prison, where the dangerous mentally ill lived side by side with the mentally retarded. One of the most dangerous groups consisted of pretrial inmates, sent by courts for evaluation. Courts needed such evaluations in order to determine whether the accused knew right from wrong at the time of the crime and whether mental illness was to blame for the crime. If that was the case, an insanity plea could send the accused to the hospital rather than to prison. In the 1977–1978 legislative session, the Sexual Psychopath Law was under discussion. Kay Brandt, Fulton's director of acute intensive care, criticized any mixing of "dangerous and nondangerous" patients.[48]

In response to such criticism, the Missouri House of Representatives urged major changes in the law. Its report recommended that pretrial evaluations should increasingly be made in urban facilities rather than at Biggs. It also suggested that criminal women be separated from mentally ill women who had not committed crimes. By June, the General Assembly had repealed the old law (202.010 RSMo 1969) and had passed a massive new law (202.010 and 202.110 RSMo 1978) that incorporated these changes as well as including clear definitions of mental illness and impairments that are not mental illness, and clear conditions for admission, release, and movement from one facility to another. However, patients convicted under the old law were not retried or reevaluated based on the new definitions, which created confusion.[49]

Nevertheless, the hospital put new treatment plans into operation and standardized job titles according to the new law. Joe Mangini, director of Biggs, reorganized the wards so that staff worked as teams. This replaced the old approach where, for example, a social worker with clients on wards 1, 4, and 9 could be teamed with different psychologists on each ward. The reorganization assigned patients to wards on the basis of their cooperative attitudes. The goal was to move patients through a six-level system, with staff votes and reviews at each step. Two self-governing wards housed the most responsible patients. Finally, nondangerous patients moved to the rehabilitation unit in the North Ward. There, patients again worked their way from

---

47. Luci Hess interview.
48. "Hospital Head Denies Mental Patient Forgotten," *Columbia Daily Tribune*, December 18, 1977, 1.
49. For a detailed explanation of the old law versus the new, see George Mazurak, "Patient History Sordid," *Columbia Daily Tribune*, May 9, 1988, 1.

a very secure ward to one with more freedom, including grounds and town passes. Two wards were created to treat chronic schizophrenics. Two wards treated the mentally retarded. A typical ward now consisted of twenty-five to thirty-five men, usually with two aides. A difficult ward—like the pretrial (admissions) ward—might need as many as six aides, while an easier ward might have only one. If there was trouble on a ward, aides could call "Code Orange" for assistance, and employees from other wards would come to help.[50]

As administrators and lawmakers addressed organizational problems, they also began to address the low salaries of personnel. In July 1978, physicians and nurses received up to 21 percent raises while social workers and other professionals received 11.6 percent. The increases brought some salaries, such as those for doctors and psychologists, in line with private-sector salaries. Maintenance workers had been reclassified as "skilled" and received 16.6 percent raises. Psych aides and laundry and dietary workers remained classified as "nonskilled" and got only 6.6 percent cost-of-living increases. Aides were still at the lowest level, and a few days after the announcement, twenty-two of thirty called in sick. Local 1810 of the American Federation of State, County, and Municipal Employees expressed displeasure at the salaries of the "unskilled" by voting to hold an informational picket.[51]

The salary issue had become more complicated. Since its beginning, the hospital had been Fulton's largest employer, but by the late 1970s a new employer began to compete for workers, when Union Electric started work on the Reform nuclear plant. UE paid more than the state and allowed workers to be outside rather than in the confines of the hospital. The combination of discontent over low wages, coupled with an alternative employer, led to a severe shortage of trained staff at the hospital. Soon, a rash of highly publicized deaths were at least partially attributed to staff shortage. The first came on May 5, 1978, when patient Michael Howard died after a violent struggle with aides. Then, on June 3, another patient, Louise Langley, was found floating in Stinson Creek after breaking away from staff. She had had enough time to remove her glasses and put them neatly on the bank before drowning. After the Langley death was ruled accidental, the Howard case was reopened against Dr. Ritterbusch's protest. Investigators discovered that one of the aides was on probation after being convicted of a 1975 stabbing.

---

50. Bill and Bessie Clevenger, interview by Brazos, summer 2003, tape recording in authors' collection. One ward likely to call Code Orange housed sex offenders, who made up 8 percent of the Biggs population and took 30 percent of staff time. See Herweg and Yow, "By Reason of Insanity," 21.

51. Most Missouri media covered the story; see, for example, "Hospital Employes, Union, Map Strategy," *Columbia Daily Tribune*, July 6, 1978, 8.

Despite the staff shortage, it now became official policy not to hire patient caretakers with felony convictions.[52]

On September 27, 1978, Biggs was short about twenty-five aides. On that day, patient James Simmons murdered psychiatric aide Robert Newsom as Newsom led twenty-three patients from breakfast. Simmons's weapon was a piece from the electric floor buffer that he had operated as a trusted, unsupervised worker. He also attacked another aide, Ron Shoaf, who was bringing up the rear of the line of patients. Shoaf said, "He just went berserk." Shoaf told the *Columbia Daily Tribune*, "They're always short of help . . . always asking people to work overtime . . . some work as many as 17 days overtime a month. . . . There isn't enough pay for the risk."[53] The Biggs Building was under constant public scrutiny. An article from the *Jefferson City News-Tribune*, reprinted in the *Fulton Sun-Gazette*, reported that the staff-to-patient ratio had risen to 2 to 1 at Biggs, and that care was $325 per day compared with $35 per day at state prisons.[54]

On May 1, 1979, Federal District Judge Elmo Hunter opened trial on count 1 of the suit filed against the hospital in 1972 on behalf of 315 patients. At the trial, Ritterbusch stated the need for two more psychiatrists, five or six social workers, three or four psychologists, and five or six clericals.[55] During the trial, another patient died; thirty-nine-year-old Lewis Logan's heart "suddenly stopped beating" after a struggle with aides. Investigators immediately questioned whether drugs had played a part in the death, and Fulton observers, including NAACP leader Jack McBride, noted the "pattern of violence" at the hospital.[56] The U.S. Department of Justice agreed to investigate.

In August, Judge Hunter found violations in Biggs's physical environment, individual treatment plans, visitation, telephone, mail privileges, and policies of seclusion and restraint. He wrote "drab and depressing surroundings can be harmful or countertherapeutic as patients may become withdrawn as a reaction to their environment." He also noted that additional money for staff "is highly desirable and would be the act of an enlightened legislature" and ordered improvements. More important, his

---

52. See "Beating Alleged in Death," *Columbia Daily Tribune*, June 4, 1978, 1; "FSH Patient Drowns in Creek," *Fulton Sun-Gazette*, June 3, 1978, 1; and Jim Herweg, "State Policy Change May Exclude Felons from Patient Care," *Columbia Daily Tribune*, June 16, 1978, 1.

53. "Fulton Patient Charged with Murdering Aide," *Columbia Daily Tribune*, September 28, 1978, 10.

54. Nancy Vessel and Julie Smith, "Home for the Criminally Insane," *Fulton Sun*, February 7, 1979, 8.

55. "Officials Say Biggs Treatment Is Adequate, Not Inhumane," *Columbia Daily Tribune*, May 10, 1979, 8.

56. "Legal Aid Society Wants Clay to Call Biggs Investigation," *Columbia Daily Tribune*, June 18, 1979, 4.

thirty-seven-page ruling noted that confining a patient without treatment "may condemn him to a lifetime of hopeless mental illness." Hunter suggested that daily treatment might be a part of a patient's constitutional rights, but he didn't find inadequate staff to be a violation of a patient's constitutional rights.[57]

However, Hunter's decision said that patients had the right to be moved away from Biggs when they were no longer dangerous: "Patients are placed in the Biggs Building because of their dangerousness. After the treatment staff has determined that aspect of a patient's behavior is no longer present, there is no constitutional justification for the continued massive curtailment of liberty inherent in confinement in Biggs." This backed up a U.S. Supreme Court decision of 1975 that nondangerous mentally ill persons had a "right to liberty."[58]

At the close of the 1970s, it seemed that some problems at the hospital would never be solved. There would never be enough money and never enough staff with adequate credentials and training. Staff exhaustion was already a reality, and the staff shortages meant that working extra shifts was mandatory if you were asked, a requirement known as "mandation." Patient deaths seemed abnormally high at Biggs where, between 1970 and 1980, there had been twelve: seven from heart or lung disease, one from collapse of the circulatory system, one from starvation, one unexplained, one unknown, and Logan's, which was still undetermined.[59]

Nor, as the decade ended, did the legislature seem to understand the pressing needs of the institution. The 1979–1980 Department of Mental Health budget requested thirty-one new staff members for Biggs and thirty-four for the Biggs rehabilitation unit. After long sessions, the House and Senate approved only eighteen of the sixty-five requested positions and added eighteen positions around the state to conduct pretrial evaluations. Governor Joseph P. Teasdale did not approve any of the requests.[60]

No doubt the hospital community welcomed some respite from the dramas of real life when a European film crew chose the decrepit North Ward and South Ward buildings as its set. Several staff members, patients, and students from the Missouri School for the Deaf were extras, and one nurse— Iris Owens—played a bit part in *The Price of Survival,* a film about a troubled employee who goes on a shooting spree.

Despite all the problems with the institution, in the Fulton community at large the image of the hospital was positive. Community volunteers were

---

57. "Judge: State Hospital Inmates Have Right to Treatment," *Columbia Daily Tribune,* August 12, 1979, 1.
58. "Some Insane to Be Released," *Columbia Daily Tribune,* June 27, 1975, 3.
59. "Answers Sought for Hospital Deaths," *Columbia Daily Tribune,* August 18, 1979, 2.
60. Herweg and Yow, "By Reason of Insanity," 39.

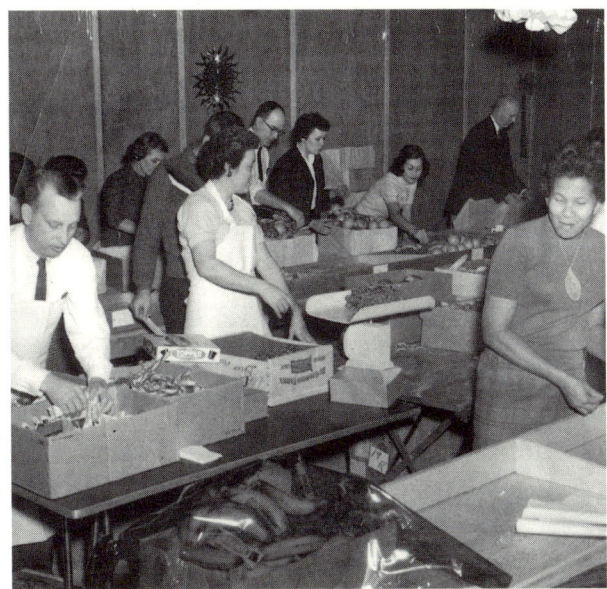

After the fire, and for several decades, volunteers renewed their commitment to the hospital. Here they fill gift boxes for the residents (Fulton State Hospital).

frequent hospital visitors and clubs from as far away as Williamsburg, twenty-five miles away, adopted wards. College fraternities and sororities helped with geriatric and youth programs.[61] One Fulton scout leader remembers:

> We used to go out and have parties for a ward in the houses on the north side of the drive—one of those. And that's one time when all my girls would show up. They were junior high age cadets. And (the patients) preferred when we'd do the songs and dances. I suppose people had bingo games out there all the time, but we'd go out and have parties.[62]

---

61. Among many articles on this subject, see "The Concerned Generation," *Kingdom Daily News*, December 17, 1973, 1.
62. Shirley Payne interview.

13

The Challenge of Youth, 1950–1991

By 1962, there were 175 children and adolescent patients under seventeen-and-a-half years old living in the South Ward, a building that dated back to the Civil War. Some youth were delinquents, but others came to Fulton because they were neglected, abused, abandoned, or could not adjust in foster homes, among the reasons. The 1962–1963 *Annual Report* documents 151 admissions (106 boys and 45 girls), and there were 76 discharges. Therapies included individual and group psychotherapy, play therapy, psychodrama, recreation, OT, industrial therapy, socialization classes, physical education, home economics, arts and crafts, music therapy, dance therapy, hygiene, religious discussions, church services, and ward meetings.

Years later, one patient wrote about his experience as an eighteen-year-old in 1960 at Fulton. He described the admission ward of thirty patients, who ranged in age from a ten-year-old epileptic child to a seventy-year-old farmer with depression:

> I was in a dayroom with rocking chairs lined against one wall. Across the room there was a piano in the corner, a television in the center and several library tables to my right. . . . Some of these people were obviously nuttier than fruitcakes, and I wondered just how dangerous they were.[1]

Teenage delinquents were a new population, and the staff worked hard to keep them busy, but teenagers are a restless group at best, and the writer describes the boredom of being locked up as well as the diversions that the

---

1. J. J. Maloney, "Shame Colored FSH Admission," *Fulton Daily Sun-Gazette* (reprinted from *Kansas City Star*), February 10, 1978, 1.

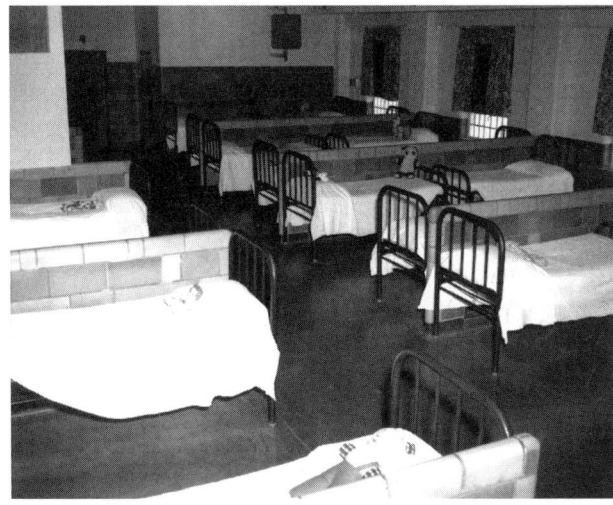

In this girls' dormitory in the old ward, circa 1956, children with a multitude of problems were crowded together (Fulton State Hospital).

patients found, including looking out the windows at female patients and playing checkers, dominoes, or cards. The teens, dealing with the rejection they felt from their families and their isolation from society, were anxious to find friendship and (particularly) romance. For a teenager in love, the hospital became "the right place to be," and loneliness was replaced with alternating times of separation and the excitement of reuniting.[2]

After he met a girl, the youth moved to an open ward and began to visit her regularly; he began to believe he had no worries. His parents sent money, and his living expenses were taken care of. His only obligations were to take care of himself and report for meals, take tests, and work with others to do the housekeeping. A sharp observer, he realized that staff also spent much of their time absorbed in the routine. Staff, however, had control of the patients. If a staff member turned in a bad report about a patient, the patient might be discriminated against by other staff and even punished. So it was safer to get along with the staff: "They develop dislikes and likes, fears and anxieties, and if they stay at the hospital long enough both groups become institutionalized in their own ways. . . . So, yeah, you end up playing checkers with them, or listening to them talk about their kids, their dogs, their farm, how frustrated and low paid they were."[3]

For the larger society, it was clear that delinquency and mental illness in young people were not going away. Since it was unfair and dangerous to keep juveniles with adults, new solutions were needed. In 1968, the Seven-

2. Ibid.
3. Ibid.

Volunteers from William Woods College were frequent visitors in the children's wards (Fulton State Hospital).

ty-fourth General Assembly appropriated $3,800,000 for construction of the Warren E. Hearnes Child and Youth Center, a six-building complex with a residential unit, schools for high school and younger children, a gymnasium, a recreational center, and an administration building. This was the first facility in the state specifically for youth, essentially a prototype juvenile center. It would also serve as a training center for child psychiatrists and special education teachers from the University of Missouri.

In the meantime, the children's unit struggled to find ways to make the hospital experience a time of positive growth for their young residents. At the end of the 1960s, the unit developed a foster grandparent program using federal "War on Poverty" funds with no expense to the state. Social worker Jane Bierdeman-Fike remembered, "You could get older people to come and spend time and be paid to take care of the children. And we had ... ten and fifteen grandparents that wanted to work. They were bused out by the SERVE bus [public transportation administered by Fulton churches] ... and spent time. We had one autistic child that nobody could do anything with except 'Grandma,' and she'd sit with him on her lap and she'd rock him, and that was what she did for him."[4]

Another informant remembered that when the foster grandparents were

4. Jane Bierdeman-Fike interview, July 1999.

there, the children's language improved a lot. There was one great big kid that followed a diminutive grandma around "Like a little puppy dog."[5] That legendary grandma was Mattie Perkins, the first foster grandmother, hired in 1968. She told an interviewer:

> When I was a girl, they called the state hospital the asylum. Only the employees understood the folks out there. Other people didn't visit the place much; they just put the patients out there and left them.... Some of the folks used to treat the Negro folk at the Hospital terribly. I know my folks were mistreated as though they were nothing and nobody. I saw things there that were horrid, but things are more humanitarian now. The law and Dr. Biggs, for whom the Biggs Building is named, were instrumental in bringing about a change, because when he saw someone mistreating my race, he saw to it that they didn't stay there.[6]

In June 1974, after federal spending cuts, the foster grandparent program, which paid $1.75 an hour to twenty persons, was discontinued. Dr. Elmer Jackson and Jane Bierdeman-Fike fought to continue the program, and they saved it. The foster grandparents stayed at Hearnes until 1991, when the youth program was moved to Mid-Mo.[7]

Dedicated in 1971, the Hearnes Center for Youth would serve the same thirty-four counties as the rest of the hospital, taking referrals from juvenile courts, schools, parents, and other agencies. The age limit was set at thirteen to sixteen years, with thirty beds for female patients and forty-five for males. Age, and not any category of problem, was the defining factor for residents of Hearnes, so by 1976, the population included a variety of juveniles who ranged from retarded and autistic kids to violent delinquents. For staff, the memories of working at Hearnes were poignant: "Before we went to all behavior-disordered youth, we had one ward that was just autistic.... I can still see one little boy.... He could twirl faster than you could imagine, then he would come right out of it and jump. All day long."[8]

Despite the challenges, the staff felt they had backing from the state for the accomplishment of great things:

> The administrations were Democratic in Jeff City, there was a lot of money nationwide—the tail end of the Kennedy stuff—and that campus was ideal . . . all one story . . . air-conditioned. Back in the education building, we had a full auto repair shop to teach the kids auto

---

5. Anonymous Fulton resident, interview by Brazos, tape recording in authors' collection.
6. "Autobiography of Mattie (Bagby) Perkins, 6-20-79," 3-4 (FSHA).
7. See "Foster Grandparent Plan Dropped," *Columbia Daily Tribune*, June 8, 1972, 2.
8. Jane Bierdeman-Fike interview, July 1999.

mechanics. There was a TV studio . . . that was kind of the "seat" of filming things for DMH. . . . It was like a little community almost. In addition to the three inpatient wards, we had a very large, active children's outpatient service . . . a day treatment program for the younger kids.

Children as young as three or four came to the outpatient center, and there was money to take the kids on outings to Six Flags amusement park and other places: "The seventies were the heyday."[9]

The financial support led to many new programs. One creative project of the staff at Hearnes was the "Condor" video series. Therapists and artists developed costumed characters and puppets to illustrate lessons in socialized living. The lessons included concepts such as how to drink from a cup or how to use utensils rather than one's hands to eat wet foods like stew. The programs were filmed in a studio in Hearnes, financed by a grant from the U.S. Department of Health, Education, and Welfare.[10]

One employee started working at Fulton in 1971 as a twenty-two-year-old aide; she eventually built a lifelong career at the hospital. She found her niche working at the youth center, back when youth were still housed in the South Wards: "It was great. I loved it. . . . I guess I just saw the kids as needy. . . . They'd never had homemade soup, or homemade spaghetti, or homemade macaroni and cheese. . . . They were very street smart, . . . but they didn't have that nurturing family." The children were there because of court order, "as in a case of incest, or because of abandonment; some were there for crimes. Robbery. One girl was there for attempted murder of herself." She remembers the patient mix as very diverse, with whites, African Americans, Native Americans, and others, and she was dedicated to them all: "I came early and I stayed late." She felt comfortable bringing her own children to the wards for visits. Like many of the staff, this worker wondered what the future held for the Hearnes kids: "I've seen a couple that work in hospitals in Columbia. One went into the military, a girl. Several of them are in Biggs, or were in Biggs. . . . I loved working with those kids."[11]

Staff brought their own ideas to work. Some ideas worked, and some did not. One aide came to the youth center with the intention of treating the kids as she had treated her own: "Beds had to be made practically military style—well, these kids had never made a bed." Every morning, the aide inspected the beds and never found them to suit her. The kids were on a merit-demerit system and were getting demerits every day for sloppy bed-making.

---

9. Tom Lezon interview.
10. The Condor tapes were preserved in the BetaMax format and in 2003 were kept in a hospital storage building.
11. Jamesetta Van Buren interview.

So one evening, two other aides held classes on how to make beds. Each of the kids practiced until they all had perfectly made beds, "all neat and tight." But "this created another problem." The kids didn't want to sleep in their beds and mess them up. The staff gave permission for one night to sleep on the floor. When the aide inspected, the beds were perfect. Then, the inspector had a new demand—she wanted nothing stored under the beds. Of course, there wasn't enough storage elsewhere in the rooms for the new rule to be practical.[12]

"Hearnes" soon became well known for its multidisciplinary approach. An unsigned manuscript in the hospital archive explains that most admissions were due to "Adjustment Reaction," or emotional disturbance due to conflict at home or in school. Some patients were brain-damaged or had learning disabilities. But, the manuscript notes, "Very few patients fall in the category of Personality Disorders":

> Within 72 hours of a child's arrival at the Center, he receives a diagnostic evaluation by the multi-disciplinary team. . . . An initial, individualized program is designed for the child to meet his emotional, social, physical, and special educational needs. Psychotherapy, both individual and group, psychopharmacology therapy, education which includes vocational education, activity and occupational therapies, speech therapies, etc., and all the representatives of the different disciplines work in a team fashion to provide the desired treatment for the patient.

The treatment goal was to discharge the patients back to their family and community, but other placement was often considered—to foster homes, group homes, or the Job Corps.[13]

The youth center was divided into three wards. The first ward, for admissions, was locked. There, newly arrived youth stabilized under staff observation. A second ward housed children who needed supervision, but these youngsters could earn points to go to activities. Third, there was an open ward, and some of these residents attended Fulton schools. Being strangers to the tight-knit community of Fulton teens, the Hearnes kids experienced social obstacles. In a town where everyone knew each other, it was easy to identify newcomers. Sometimes the young people from Hearnes were good students, while others were passive and sat in the back rows. Others disrupted the whole class. Whatever the behavior challenges, it was a commonly held opinion that the advantages of having the kids live in a stable environment outweighed any stigma. The stigma depended on the atti-

---

12. Ibid.
13. Introduction to unsigned manuscript (FSHA).

The Hearnes complex provided a safe school setting for juveniles who could not attend school in the community (Fulton State Hospital).

tudes of society, and some Hearnes high schoolers adjusted well enough to go to the Fulton High School prom.[14]

Some Hearnes children could be better served in family homes than an institution, so social workers began a cooperative program with the Department of Child Welfare to find placement in foster homes. Depending on their progress, some of these children eventually went back to their own families, but Nina Davis, who was director of youth services from 1977 to 1982, observed that their own families were often responsible for children's problems; also, "it's hard to keep a parent interested in a child when the child has caused trouble," she said.[15]

There were some children who could not be helped. One aide remembers a boy of about nine who "really hated his brother-in-law." She remembers taking walks with the boy, taking him to ball games, and feeling very comfortable with him. After he had been released from Hearnes and was out quite a while, he shot at his brother-in-law, and finally, in his twenties, he was admitted to Biggs.[16]

By the end of the 1970s, a new type of youth started coming to the center: "Street smart. Sexually active. They were just different." One aide left

14. Anonymous worker, interview by Brazos, tape recording in authors' collection.
15. Barbara Fairchild, "She Confronted the Challenges," *Fulton Sun,* July 20, 1991, 9.
16. Sparks interview by Brazos.

the hospital in the late seventies to go back to nursing school and came back to the children's ward in 1982: "It had completely changed. They were still needy, but they didn't have the same needs. I'm not sure I would have taken my children into the youth center, because you had child molesters.... It wasn't that way when I started."[17]

One Fulton resident who lived near the hospital came home one day to find that someone had broken into her house and stolen a ring. The police told her that she could not accuse anyone specifically, but they wondered if the thief had come from the open ward at Hearnes, where the children had "considerable freedom." Phoning around, she learned that on the day her ring disappeared, a young man from Hearnes had entered the back door of another neighbor's home. The neighbor, a Fulton junior high school teacher, knew the child was not local. The police searched the Hearnes Center and recovered the ring.[18]

In the mid-1980s, there was another effort to take patients out of the institution and move them back to the community, with continuing therapy. This movement could allow the state to reduce the costs of maintaining their collection of aged buildings. The North and South Wards, which were still housing adults, were slated for demolition. So as beds in Hearnes became available, adults were moved in. Hearnes's open floor plan meant there was contact between adults and the youth. One staff member recalled, "Even when they started bringing adult patients into the Hearnes complex . . . or just to use the canteen . . . there was always staff available to make sure there wasn't too much congress going on, because the kids like to move cigarettes off the adult patients."[19]

The education department was eliminated and a new agreement forged between Mid-Mo in Columbia and Fulton State Hospital. The younger children were sent to Mid-Mo, and the older were admitted to Fulton. At the same time, personnel numbers at Fulton again started shrinking. Also at the same time, a Columbia branch of Charter Behavioral Health System and some smaller private clinics were built. The campus, which had been so lively, became more and more deserted, until the last children left the Hearnes Center in 1991. When the population was down to ten children, half went to Burrell Children's Home in Springfield, Missouri; the other five went to Mid-Mo. The brief, bold experiment of the Hearnes Center was over. Families of children with disabilities like autism or cerebral palsy were now referred to one of eleven regional centers, where caseworkers helped families develop plans to keep the children at home.

17. Jamesetta Van Buren interview.
18. Mary Virginia Baker interview.
19. Tom Lezon interview.

14
Deinstitutionalization, 1980–1989

At the dawn of the 1980s, the hospital served thirty-four counties in northeastern Missouri. The Hearnes Center served the state's juveniles; other treatment centers were roughly divided into "acute" and "chronic," with special areas for aged patients. Patients with sudden (and perhaps fleeting) breaks with reality were admitted to "acute," while those with long-term mental illness went into "chronic." The Cremer Clinic was devoted to admissions, evaluation, and short-term treatments, and the hospital maintained several clinics and counseling centers in other communities. The Biggs Building still served the entire state for forensic admissions.[1]

The hospital was still self-sufficient, with its own food production, a power plant, wells, fire station, morgue, and medical staff. Doctors still did medical procedures on the campus. One nurse recalled working in the acute building in 1982: "One floor had nothing but eye surgeries . . . you were giving eye drops every half hour to somebody. Lots of IVs."[2]

The trend, however, was toward outpatient treatment, with a short term in the hospital and release with follow-up in the community. This eliminated the problem of "warehousing" patients who would never be released, but warehousing had been replaced by recidivism. A national study of admission records showed that while the length of stay for schizophrenia between 1978 and 1980 was thirty-two times less than it had been between 1886 and 1904, "the modern psychiatric hospital tends to keep patients for fewer days but does so at the apparent cost of a higher re-admission rate."[3]

---

1. Kenneth M. Johnson, ed., *Official State Manual, 1979–1980, James Kirkpatrick, Secretary of State* (Jefferson City: Von Hoffmann Press, 1980), 757.
2. Jamesetta Van Buren interview.
3. Richard Evenson, Richard Holland, and Dong W. Cho, "A Psychiatric Hospital 100 Years

Readmissions were expensive, and the financial situation was exacerbated when home counties refused to pay for their patients. Jack Morris, Missouri's assistant attorney general, noted that "conservatively" 95 percent of the bills were ignored: "Their rationale is that the state should pay for everything." On January 1, 1980, outstanding county bills amounted to $1,634,382.73.[4] To make matters worse, the hospital lost its Medicare-Medicaid certification in January 1980, so that 892 out of 1,017 beds were not qualified for those programs. The loss was partly because of inadequacies in staffing and record keeping. In the two years before the hospital regained accreditation, it lost $4.16 million. In 1984–1985, another loss of accreditation cost the hospital $3.3 million.[5] The Department of Mental Health later explained that the losses were probably less than that figure because most patients did not qualify for the federal programs.[6]

Critics of the hospital, including many in the media, reviewed the failures of Missouri's mental health system and revisited the Lewis Logan death of 1979 several times in 1980. Logan's heart failure had led to an autopsy that showed four hundred milligrams of Haldol—a medication fifty times more powerful than Thorazine—in his blood. While a hospital physician had ordered seventy-five milligrams, the drug company's recommended dose was much lower, five to ten milligrams per injection, not to exceed fifty milligrams per day. Four hundred milligrams by injection was equivalent to as many as eighty injections. The autopsy listed the cause of Logan's death as acute or chronic overmedication. Hospital spokesmen responded that Logan might have metabolized drugs differently than other people, meaning that the drug may have built up in his body over time. A review board said the death was from "natural causes."[7]

"If understaffing endangers any area of treatment," concluded *Kansas City Star* reporter Jim Herweg in his 1980 series on Biggs, "it probably is in dispensing medication. He noted that some professional staff members call the situation 'lunacy.'" Herweg, who had been working on the stories for a year and had gained remarkable trust and access to Biggs, had interviewed

---

Ago: A Comparative Study of Treatment Outcomes Then and Now," *Hospital and Community Psychiatry*, October 1994, 1021. Deinstitutionalization was hotly debated within the psychiatric community. As early as 1960, psychiatrist Thomas Szasz had written *The Myth of Mental Illness*, maintaining that there was no such thing as insanity and, therefore, no justification for locking people away. Szasz's critics were vocal and outraged, but he stuck to his arguments. When deinstitutionalization became reality, he was blamed for single-handedly creating the homeless population. In Missouri, however, and probably most states, the politics and economy of the early 1980s were more responsible for deinstitutionalization than were the writings of Szasz.

4. Herweg and Yow, "By Reason of Insanity," 39.

5. "Fulton Hospital Lost $7.6 Million, State Says," *Columbia Daily Tribune*, November 17, 1987, 12.

6. "Hospital Challenges State Audit," *Columbia Daily Tribune*, November 28, 1987, 1.

7. Herweg and Yow, "By Reason of Insanity," 40.

family members, staff, and even some of the most difficult patients. While his text skillfully brought together personal stories and policy, photographer Ann Yow's sensitive photographs brought the public inside Biggs for the first time. Rather than seeing monsters, readers of "By Reason of Insanity" saw people who had done monstrous things.[8]

As a result of Judge Elmo Hunter's ruling, the Biggs Building was being air-conditioned and walls were being built to divide dormitories into private sleeping spaces. A visiting room was being built, and the entire facility was getting a coat of paint. There were 255 men living at Biggs: 200 in the maximum-security unit and 55 in the rehabilitation unit in the ancient North Ward. Sixty-five percent of these patients were white; most were between twenty-six and thirty-five, and the average age was younger every year. About half of Biggs patients at that time were court-ordered "not guilty by reason of insanity." Of those, about half had "some form of schizophrenia." Of the other half of the total population of Biggs patients, 10 percent were sexual sociopaths convicted under the old statute, 7 percent were being held as incompetent to stand trial, and 2 percent were prisoners from other prisons who became insane during their incarceration. Another 12 to 15 percent were at Biggs for evaluation before standing trial. The balance of Biggs residents were transfers—problems—from other state mental institutions.[9]

"There are friendships, shared moments of happiness and discovery, arguments, occasional fights and lessons in tolerance and privacy . . . a system of interaction based on knowing each other so well that a single word can bring laughter or tears," wrote Herweg, describing "how truly complex life can be with 25 men who spend the bulk of their day in a room half the size of a tennis court." The Biggs sex offenders' ward quickly became a model, with director Dave Jannick assigned with the best staff, the best furniture, and a group of patients who were mostly white and literate. Herweg mused, "were Biggs to have a College Bowl, this ward would seat the winning team."[10]

During therapy with the sex offenders, every aspect of the patients' lives was examined. It was also important to the staff that the atmosphere was therapeutic in every detail. This led to many disputes about the hospital setting. At the time, the HBO television network was beginning to carry R-rated movies, and the staff maintained a lively debate about whether these should be allowed on the ward. While some maintained that the programs were too stimulating, others argued that, since the movies would be

8. Ibid.
9. Ibid, 6–8.
10. Ibid, 21.

In a Biggs Building bathroom, a row of toothbrushes (Fulton State Hospital).

part of their culture after release, the patients should see it on the wards where its effects could be discussed and controlled. In their quest to rehabilitate their patients, the therapists in the sex-offenders ward used all the techniques they could find, including an experimental program that took rape victim counselors to meet these sexual sociopaths to impress upon them the trauma that rape leaves.[11]

All in the hospital staff were anxious to try new things, and the mid-1980s saw another wave of experimentation in the search for cures. Some of these therapies attempted to bring fun and recreation to the ward. A pet dog was introduced on one ward as an experiment in "pet therapy." The maintenance staff built a doghouse and pen for him outside the exit door of the ward, but he spent his days inside. A Labrador retriever mix, "Labbie" was nearly full-grown when he started work, and the transition to having the attention of twenty or thirty people must have been difficult and confusing for him. Within weeks, he snapped at a nurse, and his position was terminated.[12]

Another positive program, which had better results, was Camp Wonderland, where the patients and staff enjoyed a week together in the outdoors. The camp, designed to serve handicapped individuals, was supported by Jaycees from all over Missouri. "Down here it doesn't matter who you are. We break all the barriers," Gail Bross, the 1992 camp director, told the *Fulton Sun*. Some campers came only for the day, but others stayed overnight. They slept in cabins, were awakened by reveille, and spent the day outside

11. "Counselors of Rape Victims Confront Sex Offenders in Hospital's Pilot Program," *Columbia Daily Tribune*, February 26, 1979, 8.
12. Brazos, notes on first draft of manuscript, 2002, in authors' collection, 3.

enjoying activities such as fishing, swimming, cooking, and taking care of each other.[13]

"We expect a lot more of them," Janie Smith, camp co-coordinator, told the *Sun:* "You see a real change in them. A lot of them haven't done things like this in years." In 1992, three groups of patients, ninety-four patients total, spent a September week at camp. Biggs residents were not eligible, and security was a primary concern at the thirty-five-acre camp, so staff members were assigned to each cabin, and security patrols circulated all night.[14] Susan Lindsey, camp co-coordinator in 1990, described the event as moving the hospital to the camp.[15]

While hospital personnel continued to try new therapies, lawmakers and the public were still debating the issues on many fronts: how should mental illness be defined, when should the government step up and offer help, and where is the line between nondangerous and dangerous behavior? One criminal trial drew particular public attention. The accused had killed his cousin in a gruesome, seemingly premeditated manner. Conviction of premeditated murder would have meant life in prison or the death sentence, but in pretrial evaluations, three psychiatrists found the defendant insane. A conviction of insanity would have kept the prisoner in Biggs for help with his mental illness. His attorney requested a trial by judge rather than by jury, explaining, "I knew no jury would accept a psychiatric defense. I think most juries think psychiatrists don't know what they're talking about and would throw it out." The judge, indeed, sentenced the man to Biggs. Public reaction was mixed, with one reaction summed up by the victim's twin sister: "How guilty can you be?" She continued:

> He got exactly what he wanted. He's always wanted to be in a mental hospital. Now he has it better than ever—all the drugs he wants, food and a clean bed. He's flying high in the sky. What kind of punishment is that? . . . I think we should scrap the mental illness option altogether. It's the biggest cop-out in the world . . . like saying, "Naughty, naughty boy. We'll take care of you."[16]

Stories about the hospital continued to stimulate the public imagination, especially in the town of Fulton. Patients with ground privileges had sexual experiences that became legendary. For example, the tunnels under the complex became well-known meeting places. It was said that they were even furnished with mattresses for the convenience of patients and even staff. A

---

13. Nancy O'Connor, "Camaraderie at Camp Wonderland," *Fulton Sun,* September 25, 1992.
14. Ibid.
15. Barbara Fairchild, "Summer Camp in September," *Fulton Sun,* September 2, 1990, 3.
16. Herweg and Yow, "By Reason of Insanity," 45–47.

physician created a stir when he wanted to put a trailer on the grounds for conjugal visits. Another wanted to buy vibrators for the women patients. Patients seemed to be able to find their own ways to create relationships, however. One female patient would call a taxi, sign off the ward, and go to meet one of the male Cremer Building patients.[17]

While the community was alternately shocked and delighted by the stories, the hospital staff tried to put the stories in perspective. They knew, after all, that sexual urges do not go away when a person becomes mentally ill. Surrounded by the combination of fact and rumor, worsened by the paralyzing state budget and the shortage of staff, Elva "Al" Anderson, hospital management assistant, sought community support. He focused on the financial picture when he addressed the local Chamber of Commerce in 1982. Three million dollars had been cut from the department's budget, a layoff had cut over two hundred jobs, a no-raise policy was damaging worker morale, and a group had been formed to study the feasibility of closing one of the system's five hospitals. The definition of mental illness had changed so that many chronic and elderly patients were now in outpatient care or in other facilities. Statewide, the Department of Mental Health inpatient census had fallen to 1,800. In 1970, it had been 10,000.[18]

Such policy decisions raised critical questions, according to Anderson. Would the state "roll over and allow the institution to turn into a people warehouse, which was incidentally the original concept 132 years ago," or would the institution continue to work with the mentally ill and "act as a haven of refuge for the hundreds of people that we housed that did not have mental illness"? There was ample reason to be concerned. The Department of Mental Health ordered Fulton State Hospital to admit and retain only mental health patients that required active mental health treatment and to place all others "appropriately." The staff was to reduce the number of patients from 1,200 to 650, moving others to "accreditable" space so that federal programs rather than the state could pay the bills. Social workers tried to find family members to take responsibility; in some cases, guardians were appointed for a patient. The guardians applied for Social Security or other benefits, then paid for patient care and needs.[19]

The hospital hoped that things would improve, of course. The old North and South Wards were slated for demolition. That would soon mean that other spaces could be modernized, adding 240 Medicare-funded beds to the

---

17. Teresa Scuderi, interview by Brazos, summer 1999, tape recording in authors' collection.

18. Elva Anderson, speech to Chamber of Commerce, February 18, 1982 (FSHA). Elva "Al" Anderson would step twice into the role of acting business manager. A much-loved citizen of Fulton, Al's involvement in the Fulton Art League theater productions and other local organizations made him the natural choice for hospital public relations.

19. Ibid.

facility. The move resulted in saving four thousand dollars per day for the state, as money moved from the federal program into the state's general revenue fund. And the legislature had promised to restore sixteen jobs for RNs and LPNs even though the reduction in patients meant that retiring workers were not replaced. The hospital was hoping for autumn accreditation by the JCAH. Anderson asked for community support and hoped that, by the night of the Chamber dinner in far-off 2118, the report would be that "the State Hospital is still serving the Kingdom [of Calloway] as well as the State . . . or closed its doors because treatment has advanced to the point that it has put itself out of business."[20]

Patients released to their home communities, however, found that services were lacking. As a result, mentally ill people were often set adrift, sometimes homeless and confused. In the downsizing process of deinstitutionalization, geriatric patients were placed in local nursing homes. Two Fulton women remembered visiting a nursing home where they visited people who had been moved from Fulton State Hospital. One patient wished she could go back to the hospital, where there were parties, movies, and therapy: "In the nursing home, there was nothing for her—and how many magazines could you read in a month?"[21]

Years before, a patient had written about these feelings:

> If you have never been closed away from the world for a long period of time you could never understand the courage needed to face it again—the fears that assail you—both real and imaginary. If you have in the past had a family to which you can no longer turn you clutch wildly in your imaginings hunting for a straw of security to which to cling. You say to yourself, "If I get a job outside and should lose it—where would I go? Would the hospital let me come back? Will the people I work with want to associate with me after they learn I've been in an institution? . . . You learn to doubt your own abilities—one minute you think you can conquer the world and the next you have no courage at all. For so long you have been told just where to sit and stand and what to do and how. All this discipline has a certain amount of good—but prolonged over the years it tends to make automatons

---

20. Ibid. When Barbara Brazos started at the hospital in 1983, she was advised not to get to know patients personally or to make them feel at home because the hospital was not their home, and they should not be made comfortable enough to consider that it was. Instead, they were to be looking forward to going somewhere else. This seemed contradictory, as Brazos was working on a ward of chronic schizophrenics, all of whom had been at the hospital longer than with their families, and there were no plans for them to go anywhere (Brazos, notes on manuscript draft, August 7, 2006).

21. Mary Virginia Baker and Shirley Payne interviews. The problem of untreated mentally ill people continued. A 1993–1998 study called PORT (Patient Outcomes Research Team), funded by the National Institute of Mental Health and the Agency for Health Care Policy and Research, found fewer than half of individuals with schizophrenia receive adequate care.

of one. You lose your initiative—you tend to become an unresisting speck in a great mass of humanity—you lose your identity and become just a shadow among shadows. And this is the perfect state into which institutions used to want to bring patients—they were much less trouble when thus docile.[22]

An aide during the period of deinstitutionalization explained it this way:

A lot of the patients there were there as youths, and were born there. That was their home. The staff was their family. I mean, they were just like family. They felt safe and secure. People that make these decisions somehow don't see the whole thing. You go thirty, forty years in one spot, and you have a thought process problem, you can't really cope with that . . . but they were downsizing.[23]

In the midst of all this change, on August 9, 1983, Superintendent James K. Ritterbusch died. A letter published in the *Kingdom Daily Sun-Gazette* called him "a kind, unassuming man" and called the loss a "blow to morale" that came at a low point in hospital history. Five state institutions were now without superintendents, due to retirements and resignations. Ali Ahmed was named Fulton's acting superintendent. He supervised an increasingly frustrated and demoralized staff. An August 17 letter to the editor complained about staff turnover, inept supervisors, and time devoted to administrative details. JCAH required a paper trail, acknowledged the writer, to prove "quality patient care." But, the writer pointed out, "Time spent writing about patients is time spent away from patients."[24]

Ahmed resigned after less than two months in office. In the interim, a legislative panel had been considering the numerous superintendent vacancies. When the lawmakers announced their decision, a headline in the *Kingdom Daily Sun-Gazette* informed readers: "Panel Wants Business Managers as Superintendents." Fulton's state representative, Gracia Backer, wanted a "person with a good knowledge of budgets and good communication skills." Five days later, FSH doctors made an announcement of their own: "Doctors want physician to head hospital."[25]

For those working in the hospital, the times were tense. John H. Mayfield, who had been the acting superintendent since October 5, was finally appointed superintendent on December 15, 1983. During the difficult job of downsizing, Mayfield had to make some tough decisions. One staff member recounted a Mayfield announcement in one staff meeting: "Today we're

22. Binkley, "They Help Us to Live Again," 3.
23. Norbert Giesing interview.
24. Anonymous letter, *Kingdom Daily Sun-Gazette*, August 17, 1983, 3.
25. *Kingdom Daily Sun-Gazette*, September 17 and 22, 1983, 1.

closing the acute hospital." The doctors asked him what to do with patients who were on IVs and could not be moved. Mayfield paused and said he'd think about it further.[26]

Missouri was not the only state suffering. According to Jane Bierdeman-Fike, "At one hospital in Michigan, they were told at ten o'clock that the hospital was going to close, and at four o'clock in the afternoon, all the patients had their baggage packed in garbage bags and whatnot and [were] sent out."[27]

By 1984, the American Psychiatric Association, which had been studying the effects of deinstitutionalization on the mentally ill, issued a special report, *The Homeless Mentally Ill*. It noted that the national system of state hospitals had held 559,000 patients in 1955, but only 132,000 in 1983. Exploring the effects of closing state hospitals, the study concluded, "Without this structure, many of the chronically mentally ill feel lost and cast adrift in the community—however much they may deny it." The study pointed out that even healthy people have trouble dealing with service bureaucracies, and that persons who are chronically mentally ill, often paranoid and delusional, give up, disappear from caseloads, and finally become homeless. "In the state hospitals . . . treatment and services . . . were in one place and under one administration. In the community the situation is very different."[28]

Former superintendent Donald Peterson summed up the problem: "The debate is who takes care of what patient. . . . The jails are filled with our ex-patients. Mostly harmless, but hungry, unable to hold a job. Behaving in a bizarre fashion, living out of brown paper bags, out of garbage cans, which I don't think is a step in the right direction." Peterson blamed legal aid societies and the American Civil Liberties Union. These organizations had changed commitment laws: "Laws make it impossible to commit a person unless the judge can be convinced that the person is dangerous to himself or others. Of immediate physical danger. Patients may take their cases back to court every 6 months." Peterson called the old laws "lenient" in getting commitment, allowing "early treatment, easy treatment. . . . It's difficult for a patient to get in the hospital anymore, to be committed."[29]

Fulton State Hospital, under deinstitutionalization, soon had a lot of empty buildings. In other communities, homeless shelters were set up or leases arranged with private corporations for halfway houses or group homes. These projects met with mixed success, including some outcry from communities that did not want to invite homeless people into their midst. In

26. Norbert Giesing interview.
27. Jane Bierdeman-Fike interview, November 15, 1999.
28. H. Richard Lamb, ed., *The Homeless Mentally Ill* (Washington, D.C.: American Psychiatric Association, 1984), 26, 57–58.
29. Donald Peterson interview.

The pre–Civil War North and South Wards came down in 1984 (Fulton State Hospital).

Fulton, the oldest and least useful of the buildings—North Ward and South Ward, constructed in 1851—were torn down in April 1984.

When an audit showed the hospital could save money by closing its pharmacy and using state pharmacists, it did so. It also sold its dairy—140 to 150 Holstein cows that handlers milked twice a day. The dairy had been an impressive operation where milk was pasteurized and homogenized on-site. The dairy had consistently been profitable and had supplied milk to other state hospitals, the Missouri School for the Deaf, and some prison populations. Despite the fact that it provided patient jobs and an income to the hospital, the legislative panel recommended that the dairy program be transferred to the Department of Corrections, leaving the hospital less self-sufficient and more connected with the Department of Corrections.[30]

In 1984, for residents of Columbia, the imagined threat from State Hospital patients on release became real when Dennis Smith and Willie Lyles attacked women in two separate, violent sex crimes. Both men had committed similar crimes before, pleaded insanity, and been treated and released by the hospital. Then, because Missouri had no system to track people after release, there had been no further therapy for either man. In these cases, the failure of the system was the failure of psychiatry to be able to guarantee a cure: "We just don't have the knowledge of human behavior to predict, without error, what a person is going to do," Superintendent Mayfield told reporters.[31]

---

30. "Auditor: Fulton Hospital Can Save Money," *Columbia Daily Tribune*, May 7, 1984, 2; "Fulton Hospital to Give Dairy Operation to Prisons," *Columbia Daily Tribune*, June 30, 1984, 25.

31. Christoph Szechenyi and Forrest Rose, "The Madness of the Mental Health System," *Columbia Daily Tribune*, August 19, 1984.

The prizewinning dairy herd at Fulton State Hospital was a source of local pride and provided milk for the institution, the Missouri School for the Deaf, and many other state facilities (Fulton State Hospital).

Incidents like these notably raised concerns for public safety but also prodded the state mental health panel to ask for fifteen million dollars to renovate and expand Fulton's facility, add eighty beds in the Biggs Building, and establish a clinical parole program to follow patients after release. The panel recommended that some of the improvements were to be paid by the Department of Corrections.

By June 1985, all but the most chronic patients were gone from the regular FSH wards. Downsizing meant that only the most resistant patients, those most unable to respond to therapy, remained in the hospital. These "chronics" were the most violent and dangerous as well.[32] The increased concentration of violent, chronic patients meant that staff were in more danger. One RN had a vertebra that healed out of place after one patient "whopped me upside of the head.... I was in a neck brace for over two weeks." She also remembers a patient who knocked off her glasses and stamped on them, and another incident where her knee was twisted. Another worker, feeling that the supervisor didn't care, said she didn't pursue treatment when she was hurt. Certain patients made most of the trouble.

32. Christoph Szevchenyi, "$15 Million Fulton Hike Sought," *Columbia Daily Tribune*, September 24, 1984.

The patient that "whopped" the RN hurt other staff, too, and also smashed someone's hand in a door, causing permanent injury. On November 29, 1987, the *Columbia Daily Tribune* reported that two security aides had contacted Representative Gracia Backer and U.S. Senator Roger Wilson to say that they feared for their lives. The department was able to answer most charges, but the lawmakers pointed to lack of funding and lack of leadership.[33]

Throughout the 1980s, the hospital seemed plagued by accusations, rumor, and scandals. The newspapers reported lost accreditation, sexual abuse, and an attempted suicide by hanging in Cremer. The latter incident involved a former Marine who had become mentally ill after being robbed and beaten in the service; he died two months after his attempted suicide from the injuries he sustained in the attempt.[34] Later, a nurse remembered that there had been confusion because the hospital had instructed that, in the event of a crime, no one should disturb a crime scene. However, two months earlier, the hospital had initiated "code blue" training, to educate staff on resuscitation and handling suffocation emergencies. A doctor, four nurses, and three security aides were accused of not rendering aid when they discovered the hanging. All left their jobs under the cloud of accusation.[35] Another hanging, in Biggs, took place two weeks later.

Amid these gloomy reports, John Mayfield moved to a new job in the Department of Mental Health on December 1, 1987. Bill Holcomb, a forensic psychologist, was named to replace him as acting superintendent, then superintendent. With all the problems Holcomb inherited, there were several rays of hope: A task force created by Mayfield had looked at all the options available for treating forensic patients and decided that a social-learning program (SLP) developed by Gordon Paul and R. J. Lentz was promising and affordable. The program seemed especially promising for the chronically mentally ill, the largest population now at Biggs and the population with the most recidivism. The task force contacted Dr. Neals Beck for ideas on programming. Beck, having met Dr. Gordon Paul, asked Paul to recommend any graduate students that might be interested in coming to Fulton. They recruited Dr. Tony Menditto, who had trained under Dr. Paul.[36]

Menditto arrived on September 6, 1988, and quickly set up the first SLP

---

33. "Hospital Employees Fear for Their Lives," *Columbia Daily Tribune*, November 28, 1987, 1.

34. Rudi Keller, "A Mother's Torment, a Son's Tragic Death," *Columbia Daily Tribune*, December 12, 1987, 1.

35. Rudi Keller, "Head of Hospital in Fulton Resigns," *Columbia Daily Tribune*, November 25, 1987, 1.

36. Anthony A. Manditto, "A Social-Learning Approach to the Rehabilitation of Individuals with Severe Mental Illnesses Who Reside in Forensic Facilities" (in press), 5.

ward. A second SLP ward was set up a few months later. Instead of "acute" or "chronic" wards, where individuals were grouped according to the estimated length of their stay, the new system brought together groups with common problems. In SLP, clients learned to set goals and receive tokens for achieving the goals. They could spend the tokens immediately or save them for larger purchases. SLP was dedicated to helping people "take back control of their lives," and "formulate goals and plans for pursuing them." In hospital language, the word "client" replaced "patient." Staff was trained to use "verbal praise, positive social attention, and material reinforcement" and to discourage "bizarre, aggressive, or rule-violating behaviors."[37]

Another ray of hope was the Chaplaincy program, directed by Rev. Richard Rummel, who had started as a hospital chaplain in 1968. Often, people with unique skills find themselves called to work with the mentally ill, and Rummel, in addition to his counseling duties, developed a personal strategy for working with reticent patients. He had learned to paint and draw as a young man, and he took his skill to the wards. Rummel completed two portraits a week, using watercolor, pencil, and colored pencil and working where other patients could see him. He found that, while he was focusing on a face, tension was released between him and the subject. He felt more connected to the patients and they, in turn, felt his caring.[38]

The Chaplaincy program was getting positive attention, not only for its caring but for its therapeutic effects. Rummel told the *Columbia Daily Tribune* that mentally ill people often have to put aside their hopes and dreams, and asked, "Can you believe in a loving God when you have to settle for less?" Rummel's coworkers echoed his opinions. Chaplain Bob Vegiard pointed out that "They don't all get better—someone has to love them." Chaplain Larry Jones pointed out: "The work takes a tolerance for the bizarre. But you need to recognize the person behind the illness with acceptance and love. . . . My belief is that the relationship itself is the healing vehicle." Bill Mosby, a pastoral counselor, mentioned that some patients just came to his office and sat quietly without speaking. One goal of the chaplains' office was to develop trust. "We're there to talk, not to say what we believe is the only thing," said Rev. Don Stassel.[39]

The Chaplaincy program had received a donation of pews and a cross in December 1987, which inspired the creation of a chapel in Biggs. One resident, an architect, agreed to design four stained-glass windows. The "Peace Window" features a dove, the "Lord's Supper Window" depicts a chalice, the "Word and Light Window" has a scroll, and the "New Life Window"

37. Ibid., 6–7.
38. Nancy O'Connor, "Callaway Portrait," *Fulton Sun*, July 13, 1990.
39. Deidra De Pree, "In Touch with the Mentally Ill," *Columbia Daily Tribune*, February 18, 1989, 7.

The stained-glass windows in the Biggs chapel depict typical Christian iconography except for a strand of barbed wire that runs near the top of this panel (McMillen photo).

pictures a lamb. The well-known and beloved Fulton artist Kathy Howser built the windows.[40]

The hospital, though newly downsized and more closely connected with forensics, had survived another decade and, as the 1980s ended, State Auditor Margaret Kelly revealed a new ray of hope for the future. While audits through the 1980s had revealed waste and inefficiency, giving lawmakers excuses to cut, her new audit demonstrated that the hospital had not lost as much federal money as formerly stated, and that other losses—such as overpayment for medical services, fraudulent use of sick time by employees, and excessive inventories of clothing and linens—could be fixed fairly easily.[41]

40. Barbara Fairchild, "Putting the Pieces Together," *Fulton Sun*, October 14, 1990, 3.
41. Rudi Keller, "Auditors Find Fault at Fulton," *Columbia Daily Tribune*, October 2, 1989, 8.

15

New Missions as the Century Turns, 1990–2000

The 1990s began on an optimistic note. According to a survey by the Department of Mental Health, 90 percent of Missourians believed that a person treated for mental illness could lead a normal life. Sixty-five percent said they would freely discuss treatment if they had used it. As if to underscore the new attitudes, besides covering bad news like the sixty-five-mile police chase of a patient who stole a nurse's car, the media covered success stories such as the former patient who worked with First Responders in Callaway County.[1]

The inpatient census had fallen so that Fulton now had only 511 patient beds, but in November 1990, the National Alliance for the Mentally Ill (NAMI) and the Public Health Research Group rated Fulton best of all eight publicly funded mental health facilities in the state. At the same time, the state system only received a score of 9 on a 25-point scale, and the mental hospitals 2 on a 5-point scale. Then, as the legislative session opened in 1990, Governor John Ashcroft announced there would be new budget cuts, perhaps as large as $1.5 million.[2]

The hospital tried to balance bad news with good, releasing positive images of the occupational therapy program. There was also hospital-wide de-

---

1. Janine Latue, "Picking Up the Pieces," *Columbia Daily Tribune*, February 23, 1990, 11. See also Joel Fahnestock, "State Hospital Patient Takes Car, Flees," *Fulton Sun*, June 22, 1990, 1.

2. George Mazurak, "Fulton State Hospital Administrator to Resign," *Columbia Daily Tribune*, October 6, 1990, 10; Paul Hicks, "Withholding Funds Could Hit Fulton Hard," *Fulton Sun*, August 3, 1990, 1. Created in the late 1970s, the National Alliance on Mental Illness (formerly called the National Alliance for the Mentally Ill) (NAMI) has served as a source of information and support for families of mentally ill people and to help families cope with difficult relatives at home or in other community living plans.

bate on becoming smoke-free. Superintendent Bill Holcomb explained that the hospital was committed to the "health of the whole person," and, using data gathered by C. Everett Koop, M.D., former surgeon general of the United States, announced that the hospital would be one of the first state complexes to insist that smokers "go outside."[3] Soon thereafter, Holcomb resigned to return to private practice. In his three years of leadership, he had increased public understanding by establishing a Community League and contributed a frequent column, "Mental Health," to the *Fulton Sun*, discussing issues like post-traumatic stress disorder, self esteem, child care, and drug use as well as policy at the hospital.

Steve Reeves, who had been assistant superintendent since 1989, became the new superintendent. While his academic training had led to his receiving an MBA, Reeves had spent his career in health care and was married to a social worker. Reeves's first days are remembered for his appreciation of ideas from the staff. As soon as he began work, he met in the break room with all staff members and asked for their ideas. One idea that came from the meeting was to make the physicians' cottages on the circle into group homes. That way, clients who were ready to move to independence could begin the transition close to the hospital where they felt secure. Reeves's tenure was also remarkable for his personal efforts to quell rumors and to reach the public. He established a rumor hotline soon after beginning his new job. Callers could ask anonymously about stories they had heard, beginning with the budget crisis of 1990. He also continued writing the column in the *Fulton Sun*. Reeves was also intimately familiar with hospital programs and finances. In his column he explained it straightforwardly: "To strengthen the treatment programs we currently offer and to maintain these programs in an era of shrinking financial resources—this is our challenge and my goal."[4]

Landmark legislation that passed in 1989 took effect in Reeves's first year as superintendent when the legislature passed a state licensing law for social workers. The requirements reflected the complexity of the problems handled in the profession. Jane Bierdeman-Fike, who had worked to pass the legislation, calls our state "one of the last" to have such a law. By 1999, all field supervisors and most of the other social-work staff held licenses. The new requirements also strengthened hospital ties with nearby William Woods University and the University of Missouri–Columbia. Bierdeman-Fike estimated that half the hospital's social work staff began as students from the University of Missouri and William Woods University in the hos-

3. "Occupational Open House," *Fulton Sun*, October 18, 1990, 5; Bill Holcomb, "Fulton State Hospital Is Instituting Smoke-Free Environment," *Fulton Sun*, August 8, 1990, 15.
4. Fred McDaniel (regional director of DMH), "Fulton State Hospital Hotline Quells Rumors," *Fulton Sun*, June 21, 1994, 4; Steve Reeves, "Fulton State Hospital Enters New Year with New Administrator at the Helm," *Fulton Sun*, January 9, 1991, 13.

pital doing fieldwork toward a degree. Bierdeman-Fink explained how the program eventually went full-circle: "Finally, [William Woods] hired one of my best supervisors, who later became head of that program, and got it accredited by the Council on Social Work Education, so it's one of the four hundred or so accredited undergraduate programs."[5]

While requirements for professional caregivers were being strengthened, new drugs came on the market to help the mentally ill to better manage their diseases. When the antipsychotic Clozaril was introduced, the drug and tests cost a minimum of nine thousand dollars a year. In November 1990, ten patients had started taking it. By October 1992, sixty-two were taking it. Clozaril brought dramatic improvement, but it was expensive because frequent blood tests were required to determine if it was causing side effects.[6] Weighing the benefits of using drugs that could cause debilitating side effects, one psychiatrist said,

> How long do you think a heart drug would be on the market if it had the same probability for serious adverse reactions that some of the psych meds do? The FDA would never approve a medication for hypertension that might cause diabetes or agranulocytosis. Only because we are treating a disease so terrible [as psychosis] are we allowed to use these drugs.[7]

For many patients, the new drugs have meant that they really can resume life in society. For others, the drugs have made life in the institution much more bearable and perhaps made it possible for them to be useful members of the group. One nurse told about a patient whom she knew for decades. From the middle 1930s, this patient was confined to a small room because of her violent episodes. All day long, this patient stood at her window and yelled in a booming voice that could be heard all over the ward. She was also physically powerful and was reputed to have torn an aluminum serving tray in half. Because staff could not handle her, she received her meals on a tray handed through a slim opening in the door and got a bath and a new mattress on Sundays if there was enough help. Thirty years later, this woman was on the geriatrics ward and receiving medication, including Thorazine. Someone had taken the time to teach her to make beds, and she

---

5. Jane Bierdeman-Fike interview, July 1999; Pat Mosher, "Students Get Experience," *Fulton Sun*, April 1, 1990, 3.

6. Jane Bierdeman-Fike interview, July 1999. Clozapine is classified by NAMI as an "atypical antipsychotic . . . for management of people who fail to respond adequately to standard antipsychotic drug treatment." Its side effects include "weight gain, sedation, anticholinergic side effects, seizures, danger of agranulocytosis [decrease in white blood cells], [and] sexual dysfunction," www.nami.org.

7. Jerome C. Peters, interview by Brazos, summer 2001, tape recording in authors' collection.

helped by making all the beds on the ward. She still stood at the windows, distressed, her lips moving, but she was no longer yelling.[8]

Despite the expense and side effects, researchers continued to develop drugs that were more specific in treatment of mental illness: Risperidone and Olanzapine treated schizophrenia; Prozac, Wellbutrin, and Paxil treated depression; Revia was shown effective in the treatment of alcohol and drug addictions. Along with the new medications, the social-learning program was proving itself. To run the SLP, staff is trained to observe clients regularly and mark a "Time-Sample Behavioral Checklist" hourly. Behaviors such as reading, talking to another, and participating in a group are noted as "appropriate," and behaviors such as responding to hallucinations, speaking incoherently, or being verbally abusive are labeled "inappropriate." When clients have stabilized their behaviors, they are provided with opportunities to work in sheltered workshops and to participate in social, recreational, and leisure activities, including games, sports, and crafts, all in preparation to allow the client to return to society at large. From maximum security in the Biggs Building, clients moved to intermediate security in Cremer, eventually receiving vocational training and earning a token paycheck or a credit card. Group home residents eventually learn to make budgets and live with considerable freedom.[9]

There was evidence as early as 1991 that this goal of independent living was achievable for SLP clients who learned to replace habits of mental illness with habits of mental health. In the words of one RN: "Now they have to buy the time to smoke, buy the cigarettes. It teaches the clients to take care of themselves again. . . . They kind of lose those skills. . . . They do their own laundry now. They work now. They start out earning tokens and they progress to where they actually earn cash. . . . It really does teach them to function more normally . . . To budget. . . . We have active treatment in the Social Learning Program."[10] A major challenge to schizophrenics is free time. Classes to teach social skills fill up some time, along with classes in "shaping," or blocking out the inner voices.[11]

A 1999 article by Paul Stuve and Anthony A. Menditto summarized a decade of making Fulton State Hospital "rehabilitation-ready." Their article, "State Hospitals in the New Millennium: Rehabilitating the 'Not Ready for Rehab Players,'" was published in *New Directions for Mental Health Services* and explains that the hospital had been ready for a change and that desire

---

8. Julia Davis interview.
9. Anthony A. Menditto et al., "Effectiveness of Clozapine and a Social Learning Program for Severely Disabled Psychiatric Inpatients," *Psychiatric Services*, July 1996, 46, 9–16.
10. Teresa Scuderi interview.
11. For case histories, see Mark Horvit and Brian W. Kratzer, "Lives in the Balance," *Columbia Daily Tribune*, September 4, 1998, 1–40.

As the mission increasingly focused on treatment of the criminally insane, security became a bigger issue (Fulton State Hospital).

for change was crucial to the success of SLP. The article credited staff for being willing to build teams of various professionals and to take on the roles of guides and teachers rather than caretakers.[12]

Despite its successes, SLP has had detractors. Some people are not helped by behavior modification, and critics have charged that the expense of SLP with its teams of observers drains other programs, making therapy less available for others. It has been criticized as a research program with handpicked clients and staff and is also criticized for its high cost—$267 a day in 1998.[13] And, as with other programs, SLP has had its failures. In 1992, Robert Lafferty choked and died while eating a meal of peanut butter, prunes, and bread. The meal was given to him because he hadn't earned enough tokens for a regular hospital meal; he had been served "repetitive evening meals consisting of peanut butter" even though he had choked before.[14]

"It was the peanut butter, not the program" that killed Lafferty, one staff member explained in 2003. Other clients had choked on the government-surplus peanut butter served at institutions. For Lafferty, the danger was extreme, as he did not chew his food and was under continual watch when he ate. Lafferty, at age forty-four, had lived at the hospital for twenty-seven years and was described by Luis Valdes, program coordinator, as "the lowest functioning I have ever treated."[15]

12. Paul Stuve and Anthony A. Menditto, "State Hospitals in the New Millennium: Rehabilitating the 'Not Ready for Rehab Players,'" *New Directions for Mental Health Services*, winter 1999, 35–46.
13. Horvit and Kratzer, "Lives in the Balance," 12.
14. "Patient Death Prompts Lawsuit," *Columbia Daily Tribune*, June 5, 1992, 12.
15. "Fulton Hospital Might Have Violated Standards," *Columbia Daily Tribune*, February 24, 1992, 8A.

For critics, the incident proved the faults of SLP, which, besides Fulton, was only practiced at institutions in Austin, Texas, and Chattahoochee, Florida.[16] Such intense scrutiny and criticism could have meant the end of the SLP, but staff could point to meaningful successes. Defending the program, the parent of a schizophrenic SLP participant told the *Fulton Sun*, "If the program is taken away, or modified in any way, I'm not sure what I'll do. . . . He's the nearest to his old self that he's been in 10 or 12 years."[17] The Department of Mental Health backed up the SLP, but the punitive dinners were discontinued.[18] Soon, SLP would be studied by teams from Texas and featured on nationally broadcast medical education program *psychLInk*. It was also adopted by the St. Louis State Hospital.[19]

The hospital was becoming predominantly forensic. This created a reshuffling of resources. Nevada State Hospital's twenty-five forensic beds were moved to Fulton, and Fulton's nonforensic twenty-five-bed acute care program was moved to Mid-Mo. Mid-Mo's twenty-eight-bed alcoholic program came to Fulton, and thirty geriatric Fulton patients were moved to nursing homes.[20] In 1991, the Hearnes Juvenile Center closed and, the same year, the legislature passed a bill allowing sale of most of the farmland, which had become a liability: "We will be able to cut back costs we have been paying for the past several years on the land and focus on our patients," Superintendent Steve Reeves told the press.[21] Soon the hospital also began providing innovative programs in drug rehabilitation for females and for Alzheimer's victims too ill for nursing homes or home care. The drug-rehab program, housed in the Cremer Building, served female inmates from the Department of Corrections.[22]

As the Department of Mental Health prepared to celebrate 150 years of mental health care in Missouri, it introduced a new vision statement that reflected the hopefulness for the future. To publicize and celebrate the new vision, the department produced a video introduced by Walter Cronkite, who had grown up near the St. Joseph State Hospital. The video featured

---

16. Steven Bennish, "Other States Pan Low-Grade Patient Meals," *Columbia Daily Tribune*, February 20, 1992, 1.

17. Joan Wallner, "Mother: Son Would Be Lost without FSH Program," *Fulton Sun*, February 26, 1992, 1.

18. Bennish, "Other States."

19. Joan Wallner, "Texas Group Studies State Hospital Procedures," *Fulton Sun*, October 4, 1991, 1. See also Stuve and Menditto, "State Hospitals in the New Millennium," 35–46.

20. Sean D. Hamill, "Reeves Confident FSH Will See Few Layoffs," *Fulton Sun*, August 10, 1991, 1.

21. Joan Wallner, "State Hospital Ready to Sell Dairy Farm, Acreage," *Fulton Sun*, November 15, 1991, 1.

22. See Sarah Baxter's articles, "Cremer Building Will House Drug Program for Female Prisoners," July 30, 1994, 1, and "FSH Provides Unique Alzheimer's Program," *Fulton Sun*, December 28, 1994, 1.

a panel led by Henry Guhleman who, after a long career in mental health care, observed that the notion of making clients the partners of the staff for treatment could not have been envisioned even forty years earlier.[23]

The Department of Mental Health outlined its goals for its clients, which included independence and productivity (helping clients to overcome thoughts about limitations); dignity and rights (putting individuals first, before the disability); and individualized services and choices (viewing the client as a partner in the treatment). Regarding staff, the department's major goal was familiar, dating back to the hospital's earliest days: motivation and training, even in hard-budget times. Because the programs owe their success to public awareness, the hospital rededicated itself to increasing public knowledge about mental illness. Public knowledge would lead to support, making the public a partner in the struggle. The supportive partnership is important when, for example, staff brings mentally ill individuals to public places. One ambassador for mental health issues was the pastoral counselor Bill Mosby, who made fifty-five presentations to community groups in 1995. Wearing a button that said, "Let's talk about mental illness," Mosby in his presentations focused on the stigma of mental illness and reminded listeners that illness is "not because they've sinned or done something terrible."[24]

In October 1992, at the insistence of Louise and Marshall Gillispie of the Alliance for the Mentally Ill of Springfield, the Fulton hospital made an effort to recognize and rehabilitate the cemetery with its one thousand graves. The Gillispies helped organize a remembrance ceremony and placed an iris, a symbol of forgotten people with mental illnesses, at an unmarked grave. The gesture, which launched a restoration of the cemetery, will "remind us that mental illness is no longer a single origin," said Marshall Gillispie.[25]

In 1995, NAMI launched its five-year Campaign to End Discrimination. They decided to emphasize three messages: Mental illnesses are brain disorders, treatment works and is affordable, and discrimination is wrong.[26] Part of the strategy of NAMI's campaign was that, as the public comes to understand that mental illness can strike anyone, more people will be willing to pay the cost for treatment. Indeed, treatment always depends on funding, especially funding for salaries. The hospital's Web page noted:

---

23. Department of Mental Health, "A Chance for Change: The Missouri Model" (video, 1992).

24. Jodie E. Jackson Jr., "Stigma Busters," *South Callaway Courier*, February 15, 1995, 1.

25. Joan Wallner, "Dedication Honors Forgotten Mentally Ill," *Fulton Sun*, October 15, 1992, 1. NAMI selected the iris as a symbol in part because that flower had been the subject of a famous painting by Vincent Van Gogh that was created while he suffered from mental illness.

26. "Spotlight" (Arlington, Va.: NAMI, 1994).

While in the fiscal years of 1996 and 1997 the legislature has been very responsible in funding additional revenues for the purchase of the new medications, continuation of increased funding is dependent on the economic health of the state. Also, to operate high-quality programs in psychosocial rehabilitation requires expertise in the specialty program areas. This requires FSH to search out and retain the highest quality clinicians available.[27]

As the twenty-first century begins, each ward of as many as thirty clients is attended by a professional team, including a psychiatrist, a social worker, and a nurse, all of whom meet each client upon admission. As the client settles into the intake ward, he meets other team members, including aides, speech therapists, and dieticians, who play an important role in ensuring that clients receive good nutrition but eat no foods that interact with their medications. Each team meets weekly for two months or so, enters information into the medical record, develops an individualized treatment plan, and decides which team member will take care of what aspects of client care.

Clients are put on wards according to the stage of their treatment. For example, a client begins on the "Intake" ward and might move to "Social Learning." Group therapy has become an important part of client care, including all kinds of group therapies guided by professionals such as psychologists, social workers, or nurses. Besides discussing aberrations or other social problems, there are meetings to discuss current events and education.[28]

Discharge planning is more complicated with forensic clients because there are more legal considerations as well as the considerations for the safety of citizens. In the mid-1990s, as had happened many times before, a sensational story broke into the news media when a schizophrenic man killed his parents in a St. Louis suburb. The victims, Jim and Nancy McBride, were a successful middle-class couple. Their youngest son, Matt, had been the boy that brought the family together with his joy and good nature. In adolescence, however, Matt had begun to believe that other people were controlling his thoughts. He began to hear voices. He blamed his parents for his problems and became convinced that the only way to get the voices to stop was to kill his parents. While medications helped, Matt resisted them. He entered institutions, was treated, stabilized with medications, and released. His delusions, which disrupted his life, did not cause enough violence to keep him in a hospital. Then, released too early from a St. Louis hospi-

---

27. Missouri Department of Mental Health, "History of Fulton State Hospital," www.dmh.mo.gov/fulton/history.htm. Hereinafter cited as MDMH, "History."
28. Ibid.

tal and convinced that the murder of his parents would prevent World War III, he broke into their house and stabbed them to death.[29]

The story might have been forgotten if it were not for the reaction of Matthew's brother Mark. Arriving at the scene, Mark overcame his shock and told reporters, "It wasn't my brother that did this. Schizophrenia did this."[30] Rather than resist the publicity, Mark began a campaign that led to passage of what became known as the "McBride Bill" in 1996. Signed into law on the anniversary of Nancy McBride's birthday, the law allows judges to order hospitalization of a mentally ill person based on patterns of behavior, including failure to take medication.

After the murders, Matthew was judged incompetent to stand trial and taken to Biggs. Months of depression were followed by his effort to understand his disease. Mark and a sister have made it clear to Matthew that they have forgiven him, and they visit him frequently. Psychologist Elaine Larson has taught him that people cannot read his mind and that the road to recovery will be long. Stabilized with a regimen of regular medication, Matthew's progress has allowed him to move to a setting of intermediate security.[31]

In 1998, *Columbia Daily Tribune* produced a forty-page insert about Biggs as a follow-up eighteen years after the 1980 story "By Reason of Insanity." Besides describing the wards and SLP, a group meeting, and life in a halfway house, the articles focused on three men in treatment. While medications were controlling most of the bizarre and violent behavior of the men, the article made it clear that "with the tiniest shift in your genetic makeup, just a few misfiring neurotransmitters, you could be plagued by disembodied voices, rendered helpless by your inability to unravel the tangled thoughts in your head."[32]

To increase employee satisfaction and retention, the hospital began to look for staff members whose ethnic and cultural backgrounds more closely parallel the clients'. For staff, this meant working next to people with different training and from a variety of places. One longtime staff member observed, "The farmers will stay here because they live here . . . but we're getting an inner-city mix, not only with clients but with staff." New employees come from St. Louis, Kansas City, New York, and elsewhere. Physicians and nurses are coming from foreign countries, including Brazil, Canada, England, and Asian countries.[33]

The religious diversity can be seen in "Topic: Overview of Specific Faith

---

29. Horvit and Kratzer, "Lives in the Balance," 34.
30. Ibid.
31. The McBride story has been documented in a film, *Before They Fall off the Cliff*, by St. Louis newsman Art Holliday.
32. Horvit and Kratzer, "Lives in the Balance," 17.
33. MDMH, "History."

Groups and Religions," a white paper produced in 1998 by the Chaplaincy Department. The department is responsible for making it possible for visits from leaders of various faith groups, recognizing each faith's teachings, commandments, taboos, oral traditions, and dietary requirements and for helping staff "respect prayer times and practices, holy days, and worship needs." The diverse population includes Protestant, Catholic, Jewish, Eastern Orthodox, Muslim, Buddhist, Hindu, Native American, Amish, and most other religions that exist in the nation. In addition, participants in the department needed to understand spiritual traditions such as Wicca and Tao, which were not yet part of the client population but whose numbers were growing in the overall Missouri population at the time.[34]

The hospital renewed its dedication to training its workforce, targeting employee needs, helping develop training programs, and advocating for zero tolerance for discriminatory behavior toward staff or clients. After talking to focus groups and surveying staff, the hospital adopted a program called "Winning Balance." In the program, staff members rate pictures of people on the basis of appearance only and then make up stories about the backgrounds of these people. The stories reveal how we all jump to conclusions about each other, and how wrong we can be. In the words of one RN, "We have to work together, and you are different from me . . . age is a factor, our backgrounds are different . . . it's just recognizing that people are different . . . each unique creatures . . . we have to work together."[35]

---

34. Robert C. Vegiard, "Topic: Overview of Specific Faith Groups and Religions," 1998.
35. Jamesetta Van Buren interview.

16

An Uncertain Future

By 2005, Fulton State Hospital was by far the largest state mental hospital in Missouri. The population had stabilized with 464 beds to serve the thirty-one-county service area of central Missouri as well as thirty-one counties in the southwest region, in addition to serving the forensic maximum and medium security mentally ill of the entire state. Indeed, forensic patients have become the dominant population, occupying the majority of the 201 maximum-security Biggs unit, the 175 beds in the intermediate-security Guhleman unit, and the 88 beds in the minimum-security psychiatric center at Hearnes. Emerging in the mid-1800s, an era when no external agencies except the state legislature observed its functions, the hospital today is accredited by the Joint Commission on Accreditation of Healthcare Organizations and certified by the Center for Medicare and Medicaid Services.[1] Federal monies are increasingly important in fulfilling the hospital's mission. According to one source, Medicaid spending on mental diseases accounted for "about 20%" of total expenditures in 1997.[2]

Many of today's challenges would seem familiar to administrators of the past. Overcrowding is still a problem; hospital census for much of 2005 was at 105 percent of capacity, with the minimum and intermediate security units reaching highs of 115 percent and 110 percent, respectively.[3] Many of the hospital structures are deteriorating and in need of an update; many are empty. The buildings—forty of them altogether—range from one built in

1. MDMH, "History."
2. Richard Frank, Howard Goldman, and Michael Hogan, "Medicaid and Mental Health: Be Careful What You Ask For," *Health Affairs* 22, no. 1: 101.
3. Felix Vincenz, interview with McMillen, June 25, 2005, tape recording in authors' collection.

The Hadley Building stands empty in 2006, but it still shows the care and attention to detail of the early builders (McMillen photo).

1860 to the most recent addition to the Biggs Building, completed in 1988. Over eight hundred acres have been transferred to other state agencies and the city or county or sold, but there are still over ninety acres of campus.

With 1,250 employees, the hospital is Fulton's largest employer by far, but the state budget, whether in 1855, 1905, or 2005, has never kept pace with fair compensation. Many Missouri mental health workers collect food stamps or use other government programs to get by. A March 2004 survey showed "The greatest number of state employees on welfare . . . work for the mental health department, consistently mentioned as having among the lowest-paid workers with the highest-stress jobs."[4]

Care for the mentally ill has come a long way since the early days, however. The landmark Social Learning Program, by treating schizophrenia by teaching individuals to replace bizarre habits with socially accepted habits, is one of Fulton State Hospital's proudest achievements. In addition to SLP, Fulton State Hospital uses rehabilitation strategies developed by the Boston Center for Psychiatric Rehabilitation for higher-functioning clients and cognitive behavioral programs for clients with severe personality disorders, including Dialectical Behavior Therapy, which, using psychotherapy and

4. "Data Reveal State Workers on Assistance: Missouri Pay Ranks 49th in the Nation," *Columbia Daily Tribune,* June 12, 2004, 5A.

group therapy, validates the clients' experience, suggests alternative ways to handle adversity, and helps them to learn healthy new behaviors.

Other important programs include a special program for individuals with co-occurring substance-abuse disorders, a group home transitional housing program, and Brandt Vocational Enterprises, a sheltered workshop that provides instruction in basic work skills, along with more advanced "work-hardening" opportunities in fairly independent work enclaves. Each of these programs focuses on building skills and on finding resources, assisting clients in the development of support systems so that they can live in the community despite their illnesses. For older patients who also have medical or physical impairments that require unique diagnostic approaches, the psychiatric center at Hearnes provides psychosocial rehabilitation.[5]

The Biggs Forensic Center offers inpatient services to patients from all over the state whose commitment to the Department of Mental Health is associated with major criminal offenses or who have demonstrated an intensity or frequency of dangerous behavior that rules out successful management in less-secure settings. Biggs's services include pretrial evaluations and restoration to competency as well as programs for individuals committed for long-term care and treatment. The Biggs Building also includes the Biggs Acute Treatment Program of forty-four beds (thirty male and fourteen female) operated jointly by the Department of Mental Health and Department of Corrections for inmates in need of acute inpatient psychiatric services provided by Biggs staff.

Treatment wards in Biggs include Social Learning, Cognitive Behavioral Rehabilitation, Psychiatric Rehabilitation, Competency Restoration, and Pre-Trial Evaluations. The goal is movement from the highly structured setting of Biggs to the less-restricted living in the Guhleman Forensic Center or some other Department of Mental Health facility. Guhleman is a 175-bed intermediate-security treatment facility for male and female patients. Its primary clientele are those who have histories of committing criminal offenses and are either committed by the circuit courts of Missouri or admitted under the authority of an appointed guardian. It serves as a "step-down" unit for the clients judged ready to leave the maximum-security setting of the Biggs Forensic Center, or a "step-up" facility for clients determined incapable of remaining in minimum-security or group-home settings. Guhleman Forensic Center also accepts commitments directly from the courts when the client's criminal behavior and current conduct make neither maximum-security nor minimum-security placement appropriate.

The Guhleman complex contains four areas. Guhleman East has three

---

5. MDMH, "History." Information in the next several paragraphs is outlined in this document.

wards, one of which is the coeducational Cognitive Behavioral Rehabilitation Program. Also in that building are various medical clinics (such as dentistry). Guhleman West contains two wards dedicated to the Psychiatric Rehabilitation Program and two wards devoted to the Social Learning Program. Each Guhleman ward houses twenty-five people. Also in Guhleman, the Cremer Activity Center houses a large activity and recreational area, a fitness center, a library, and a barbershop/beauty salon. Brandt Vocational Enterprises, named for Kay Brandt—a former RN and administrator of the hospital—consists of a vocational training center, a client and staff canteen, and administrative and clerical offices.

Brandt Vocational Enterprises (BVE) provides a wide variety of vocational experience, a critically important part of rehabilitation. Due to their severe and prolonged mental illnesses, many clients have never had a job or have unsuccessful employment histories. Thus, vocational services assist clients in developing work habits, skills, and vocational interests so that they may pursue employment or advanced vocational training in the community upon discharge. BVE has developed many strategies for helping clients achieve a satisfying work life. There are in-hospital sheltered workshops where clients can practice work habits and develop skills. Clients with more abilities, or who have made greater progress in their rehabilitation, work at more independent assignments in various departments.

The work ranges from very basic, repetitive work to difficult tasks with multiple steps or instructions. There are service projects for the community, such as cleaning the YMCA gym. And because the hospital, from its earliest years, has functioned as a small community, there are many tasks to do within the facility. Clients serve as client advocates, fulfill various support positions, and work at office jobs. They perform such tasks as sending out mailings, collating, developing weekly curfew notices, making customized buttons, shredding paper for recycling, working in the laundry, taking care of the recycling, working in the yard crews, washing cars, wrapping packages, and publishing the *Fulton Forum*, the hospital newsletter.

For those who can leave the campus, the hospital has contracts with Kingdom Projects, Inc., and other companies. KPI is a sheltered workshop in Fulton where clients learn a wide range of tasks in manufacturing, recycling, and janitorial work under supervision by KPI and hospital staff. For those who are ready to reenter community life, the Supported Employment Program finds employment. Each client is assigned a job coach to provide training and support and to function as a liaison between the client, the agency, and the employer. These workers need to be very independent in their ability and motivated to complete tasks and go to work. Sometimes the job is adapted to the client. The desired outcome is to provide well-paid work in an integrated work setting. Some clients work at the Department of Mental

Health in Jefferson City performing office assistance and janitorial tasks or working in the mail room.

In every job, each employed client is paid either by piece rate or by an hourly wage. The work program is approved by the U.S. Department of Labor; every two years, a recertification process takes place and a prevailing wage study is done, updating the piece rates and time studies. The BVE payroll is provided as part of the hospital's personnel budget, and the work centers provide enough income to pay for supplies and equipment.

In 2001, the hospital announced a strategic plan that named "shareholders" and "stakeholders." Shareholders are "those who share in our mission to provide services, such as employees, DMH Central Office, and the Legislature." Stakeholders include families, courts, community mental health centers, administrative agents, law enforcement agencies, the Department of Social Services, community hospitals, the Department of Corrections, Missouri Protection and Advocacy Services, the Missouri Mental Health Consumer Network, and institutes of higher education. Much of the 2001 strategic plan aimed at increasing employee satisfaction and retention. Among the goals were recruiting staff members whose ethnic and cultural backgrounds more closely parallel the clients', training the workforce, helping develop university training programs, and advocating for zero tolerance for discriminatory behavior toward staff or clients.

As has been the case through most of Fulton State Hospital's history, staff, especially psychiatric and security aides, are in short supply, and there is particular difficulty in filling male-only positions. The 2001 plan acknowledges the need "to ensure an adequate number of staff" through recruitment and the staff recognition and appreciation program. The hospital also acknowledges its duty to train future mental health workers. All Fulton State Hospital facilities serve as training centers for mental health professionals from the state's schools of nursing, social work, occupational therapy, and psychology. There is a psychiatry residential program with fellowships and pre- and postdoctoral programs in psychology.

In 2004, the plan was updated. Additional goals for the hospital now include greater participation by clients. Its strategies include seeking input from clients to create a culture of nonviolence, asking clients to help develop orientation materials for newcomers, and seeking client input to develop a welcoming atmosphere in the treatment team meetings.[6] The goal of nonviolence is particularly elusive; on March 30, 2005, there was another patient killed in Biggs. In spite of the dangers, or perhaps because of the dangers, the goal at the hospital is still to find strategies that will guarantee safety to all without the use of physical restraints.

6. Master Strategic Plan, January 7, 2004 (FSHA).

An Uncertain Future

The Hyde Building, photographed in 2006, is a testament to the architects and builders of its time, although it is one of many buildings on the campus that are now unused (McMillen photo).

In 2004, budget problems at the Department of Mental Health meant that the executive leadership of the hospitals in the central region was consolidated. Felix Vincenz, the CEO of Fulton at the time, became the CEO of two other state facilities as well. His new obligations include the Mid-Missouri Mental Health Center in Columbia and the Southwest Missouri Psychiatric Rehabilitation Center in El Dorado Springs. The organizational changes have had an impact on all members of the executive team. The responsibilities of the quality improvement director, human resources director, and chief financial officer of Fulton State Hospital have also been expanded to include the other two facilities. Each facility has a unique mission and size, creating distinctive challenges. To ensure that there is no interruption in day-to-day activities at Fulton, the quality improvement officer, Marty Martin, became the chief operating officer in the summer of 2005, the first woman to hold such a high position at the hospital. In 2006, Robert Reitz replaced Felix Vincenz as CEO. Vincenz has moved to the Department of Mental Health's central office as director of facilities operations.

Looking back on his years at Fulton, Vincenz ticks off his accomplishments: Developing minimum-security and intermediate-security settings, integrating LPNs and RNs into coverage responsibilities and thereby professionalizing the delivery of nursing care, developing more collaborative working relationships with the various unions at the hospital, hiring consumer advocates and expanding the hospital's commitment to patient rights and patient empowerment, and initiating a facility-wide commitment to the safety of both clients and staff. One interest of Vincenz, the development of a "treatment mall," has not been possible due to competing priorities and budgetary shortfalls. Such a facility would look and feel like a shopping mall, providing access to rehabilitative services in a centralized location easily accessible to clients from multiple residential areas, as well as other everyday services such as a barbershop, a bank, and a post office. The experience of leaving the ward to access treatment would provide a more normalized experience for patients, while providing for more efficient and effective deployment of staff with unique skills.[7]

Unfortunately, a variety of challenges make planning for the future an uncertain business at best. Some laws have changed to make commitment to state mental health facilities easier, while others make release more difficult. Prison populations have risen, and critics such as the National Alliance on Mental Illness (NAMI) remind us, "It is easier for a person with a severe mental illness to get arrested than to get treatment. . . . More than 10% of all inmates . . . in prisons and jails suffer from schizophrenia, bipolar disorder, or major depression. This is nearly 4× the number of people with these illnesses being cared for in hospitals."[8]

Despite increased admission pressures, the hospital is responsible for keeping the public safe and cannot recklessly discharge clients to the community or refuse individuals in need of inpatient care in secure settings. Without close attention to public safety issues, the hospital's future ability to provide treatment will be jeopardized or impaired, shifting mentally ill clients to other state agencies, and resulting in potentially increased cost and further reduction of public safety. At the same time, there is a familiar dilemma for clients after inpatient care in the facility: How does one deal with the stigma of having been institutionalized, and get back into community life? The hospital has pledged to increase public awareness through education, including presenting information to schools and service organizations: "This education," according to the strategic plan, "must be ongoing, up-to-date, and from all levels of individuals dealing with mental illness (clients, family, professionals, and administration)." A hospital goal is to develop understandable written materials and a better advocacy program for clients

---

7. Felix Vincenz interview.
8. S. M. Morris, H. J. Steadman, and B. M. Veysey, "Mental Health Services in United States Jails: A Survey of Innovative Practices," *Criminal Justice and Behavior* 24 (1997): 3–19, cited online in NAMI of Massachusetts, "Mental Health Facts," www.namimass.org/facts.htm.

and families. In 2006, the Department of Mental Health invited interaction from the public when it launched a Web site and invited public comment from "families, guardians, providers, and other interested persons."[9]

On the positive side, medications have become increasingly specific in treatments, leading to greater treatment success. According to the National Association for Mental Illness, the treatment success rate for bipolar disorder stands at 80 percent, for major depression, 65 percent, and for schizophrenia, 60 percent. Yet the benefits of these cures are often lost when mentally ill people become homeless and unable to access the medications. Government aid such as Supplemental Security Income has been cut to the point where recipients cannot afford to rent modest efficiency apartments. The nation's sizable homeless population—estimated at 600,000—contains, by one estimate, 200,000 severely mentally ill persons. Nearly 50 percent of individuals with severe mental illnesses receive either Social Security Disability Insurance or Supplemental Security Income; thus mentally ill people are among the lowest income households in the country, earning probably only 24 percent of the income of average households.[10]

Low-wage earners have the additional problems of lacking health insurance and little job security. Confusion, anger, and irregular work habits can result in job loss. NAMI estimates that "an 85 percent to 90 percent unemployment rate exists among individuals with severe mental illnesses":

> The cost of severe mental illness to the United States economy is staggering. The price tag for direct treatment costs, including hospitalizations and medications, is $67 billion. The indirect costs that come from inadequate and even denied treatment are an even bigger drain: *Annual Cost:* $63 billion in lost productivity, including $11 billion in Social Security Disability Insurance benefits to 1.3 million persons and $11 billion in Supplemental Security Income benefits to 2 million persons.[11]

Their estimate adds an annual "$12 billion in lost productivity due to premature death, including suicide" and "$6 billion to incarcerate more than 250,000 persons with mental illnesses in jails and prisons."

There is no doubt the future holds many improvements in mental health care, and the hospital will always strive to provide the latest medications and strategies. It is estimated that one out of every four individuals will need some type of treatment for a mental illness in his or her lifetime. While medications and advanced therapies play a leading role in rehabilitation, con-

9. MDMH, "History"; Missouri Mental Health Task Force, www.dmh.mo.gov/mmhtaskforce.
10. NAMI of Massachusetts, "Mental Health Facts."
11. Ibid.

tact with friends and family contribute greatly to the healing process. The hospital welcomes visitors who want to help as volunteers or who are simply interested in learning more. At the same time, the hospital is a busy place and security is high, so visitors must call in advance to arrange a visit. A panacea cure, as history has proven, is elusive. Yet Fulton State Hospital's quest to end mental illness, and its quest for a sensitive and workable approach to the treatment of the mentally ill, will continue.[12]

Our Philosophy

MISSION
Rehab and Recovery
We partner with people who have the most serious mental disorders, as they reclaim their lives and progress toward the community, by offering them treatment and rehabilitation in a manner consistent with both individual and public safety.

VISION
Creating Hope through Excellence

VALUES
Each of these values represents the attitudes and behaviors that we, as employees, care about and live by:

Partnership
We believe in partnership
—among clients served, their families & friends, staff & community providers
—with the City of Fulton and the other communities we serve
—that stresses communication across all levels of the organization
—that bridges cultural differences that might otherwise divide us
—that supports & maximizes the range of available choices for our clients

Responsiveness
We support an array of services
—that are accessible
—that are tailored to individual needs and goals
—that are effectively linked to the community
—that enable clients to succeed

12. MDMH, "History."

Integrity
We expect ourselves
—to deliver the best possible outcomes effectively and compassionately
—to provide the tools, training & resources needed by staff to do their jobs safely and well
—to use funds responsibly & to be good stewards of the public trust
—to recognize & celebrate excellence in all our staff
—to provide the follow-up & transition services necessary for community success
—to advocate tirelessly for those who struggle with mental illness, developmental disability, or substance abuse/addiction
—to be accountable to those we serve

Dignity
We recognize the aspirations of our clients
—for respect & dignity
—to fulfill hopes for growth & change
—to achieve a balance among choice, personal responsibility & socially acceptable behavior
—to live as they choose within the limitations of the legal system & public safety

Empowerment
We value clients' ability
—to direct their lives & act on their own behalf
—to use their individual talents & resources
—to improve the quality of their lives
—to work toward their own personal recovery.[13]

---

13. Missouri Department of Mental Health, "Our Philosophy," www.dmh.mo.gov/fulton/philo.htm.

Fulton State Hospital Administrators

Superintendents (Chief Executive Officers)

Turner R. H. Smith	1851–1865
Rufus Abbott	1865–1867
Charles Hughes	1867–1872
Turner R. H. Smith	1872–1885
W. R. Rodes	1886–1888
LeGrand Atwood	1889–1893
R. S. Wilson	1893–1897
J. T. Coombs	1897–1901
W. L. Ray	1901–1902
J. W. Smith	1903–1905
Porter E. Williams	1905–1909
George Williams	1909–1913
Marion Oley Biggs	1913–1927
E. T. McGough	1927–1931
D. H. Young	1931–1933
R. C. Fogley	1933–1935
Ralf Hanks	1935–1939
J. R. Bunch	1939–1943
Charles Carter Ault	1943–1947
William J. Cremer	1947–1956
Alfred K. Baur	1956–1962
Louis Belinson (acting)	1962
Donald Peterson	1962–1976
Richard Jacks	1976
James Ritterbusch (acting)	1976
James Ritterbusch	1977–1983
Ali Ahmed (acting)	1983

John Mayfield (acting). 1983
John Mayfield. 1983–1987
William Holcomb (acting) 1987
William Holcomb. 1988–1990
Stephen Reeves. 1991–1999
Felix Vincenz 1999–2006
Robert Reitz (acting) 2006–

Chief Operating Officer
Anthony Menditto 2003–2005
Marty Ann Martin 2005–

Business Managers
C. O. Atkinson 1878–1888
W. H. Smith 1889–1893
William Lloyd. 1893–1899
L. W. Summers. 1899–1907
S. P. James. 1907–1909
J. F. Smith 1909–1913
James E. Moore 1913–1917
Charles M. Wilson 1917–1921
Joseph E. Elliott 1921–1925
T. E. Dunphy 1925–1927
J. J. Corey 1927–1933
James H. Harris 1933–1935
Paul Culver. 1935–1939
Charles S. Turner. 1939–1943
Edward Wilson 1943–1945
J. B. Groner. 1945–1950
Edwin J. McKee 1951–1956
Robert Seaman. 1956–1976
Mike Benzen. 1977–1988
Elva Anderson (acting) 1988–1989
Stephen Reeves. 1989–1990
Elva Anderson (acting) 1991–1992
J. Ken Lyle Jr. 1992–

Index

Abbott, Rufus (superintendent), 43–44, 45, 46, 49
Abuse of mentally ill at FSH. *See* Investigations; Violence
Abuse of mentally ill before asylums, 4–5, 6, 7, 8, 14–15, 25
Accreditation, 186, 187, 205, 209, 210
Acock, Robert E., 11, 12
Addiction. *See* Mental illness, diagnoses
Administration Building: fire at original, 161; new in 1958, 163, 167; and cutbacks, 188. *See also* Buildings
Admissions, 22–24, 41, 45, 48, 65, 99, 100, 112, 191–92, 204
Adolescents. *See* Juveniles
African Americans: segregated, x, 6–7, 47, 113–15, 199; racism, xii, 168, 170–71; slavery, 122; Elmer C. Jackson, 165; desegregation, 168, 170–71; Miss Willie Samson Edwards, 170; Black Muslims, 185; Mattie Perkins, 199
After-care, 89–91. *See* Therapy
Agency for Health Care Policy and Research, 210
Agricultural Labor. *See* Self-sufficiency; Therapy
Ahmed, Ali (acting superintendent), 211
Aides: attendants, 158; psych aides, 169, 180, 191, 192, 193, 200, 201, 202, 232; security aides, 215, 232; mentioned, 158, 179, 225
Alcohol and Drug Abuse Program (ADA), 179, 181, 212, 221

Alcoholism. *See* Mental illness, diagnoses
Allopathic Therapy. *See* Therapy
Alzheimer's Disease. *See* Mental illness, diagnoses
American Federation of State, County, and Municipal Employees, 192
American Journal of Insanity, 20
American Journal of Psychiatry, 20
American Medical Association, 181
American Psychiatric Association, 20, 90, 152, 181, 212
American Psychoanalytic Association, 91
Anderson, Elva (Al): as spokesman, 209–10; as acting business manager, 240
Andrews, Gregg, xv
Annual Reports: 1953–1954, 151; 1962–1963, 156; 1959–1960, 165; 1968–1969, 177
Anthony (patient), 124–27
Architectural Design of Asylums. *See* Asylums
Artificial fever. *See* Therapy
Ashcroft, John (governor), 218
Assistant Physician(s). *See* Management
Association of Medical Superintendents of American Institutions for the Insane (AMSAII), 20, 67, 68
Asylum, Fulton: proposal, 4–6, 9; rationale, 4–9, 14–17; site selection, 4, 9–13; legislative debates, 6, 9–11, 13–17; construction, 13, 16, 25; architectural design, 13–14, 28. *See also* Buildings
Asylums: national movement, xiii, xiv; as

242 Index

place of refuge, 177; end of era, 188. *See also* Institutions, other Missouri; Institutions, other places
Atkinson, C. O. (business manager), 240
Atlas Portland Cement Plant, 127–29
Attendants/nurses before 1940. *See* Management
Attitudes about mental health. *See* Public perceptions
Atwood, LeGrand (superintendent), 239
Ault, Charles Carter (superintendent), 239

Backer, Gracia (state representative), 211
Bailey, William H., 60
Ballew, George, 97
Banking system for patients' spending money, 147, 179, 181
Battie, William, 7
Baur, Alfred K. (superintendent): hired, 156–57; policies, 159–62, 165–67; retired, 168
Beck, Neals, Dr., 215
Belinson, Louis (acting superintendent), 239
Bell, M. F. (architect), 67, 74–75, 104, 108
Bell, Ovid, 138
Bellamann, Henry, 137–39
Bellamann, Katherine, 139
Benton, Thomas Hart, 3
Benzen, Mike (business manager), 240
Berry, Evelyn (volunteer supervisor), 162
Bierdeman-Fike, Jane (social worker): hired, 170; and desegregation, 170–71; and treatment policy, 172, 175, 184; and foster grandparents, 198–99; and deinstitutionalization, 212; and social work education, 219, 220
Biggs, Marion Oley (superintendent), 79, 80, 84, 87, 96, 107, 110, 199, 239
Biggs Building: staffing, 158, 166; serves entire state, 165, 178, 204, 228–32; and Dr. Peterson, 171–74; and chaplains, 180, 216–17; and violence, 184–85, 193, 194, 215; reorganization, 191, 206, 214; and journalists, 205, 208; chapel, 216–17; and SLP, 221–23, 226; mentioned, 200, 202, 207, 208. *See also* Forensics
Binder, Elsie, 86

Bingham, Eliza Thomas (patient), 120–24, 127
Bingham, George Caleb, 120–24
Binkley, Vesta (patient), 142–43, 163–64, 210–11
Bipolar disorder. *See* Mental illness, diagnoses
Board of Managers, State Eleemosynary Institutions, 80–82, 84, 93. *See also* Management
Bond, Christopher "Kit" (governor), 186
Boone County, 10
Boonville, Missouri, 122, 123
Boston Psychiatric Hospital, 92
Brandt, Kay, R.N., 189, 191
Brandt Vocational Enterprises, 230–31, 232
Bratkowski, Henry, Dr., 189
Bratton, Louis (maintenance worker), 132–34, 161–62
Bross, Gail, 207
Brown, B. Gratz (governor), 72, 109
Brown, Doris (nurse), 152
Budgets: hospital, xvi, 187, 188, 194, 199, 209, 232, 233; buildings and grounds, 168–69, 186, 218; patients' personal, 181, 221. *See* Finances
Buildings: early (pre-1940) construction, 17, 29, 34, 37, 64, 65, 66, 69, 70, 75, 93, 94, 103, 104, 106, 109, 110, 113, 114, 115; early (pre-1940) repair and renovation, 25, 28, 33, 35, 45, 55, 62, 63, 67, 69, 103, 104, 106, 108, 115. *See also* Administration Building; Biggs Building; Budgets; Chapel; Cremer Building; Dairy; Farm; Geriatrics; Guehleman Forensic Center; Hyde Building; Medical (Hospital) Building; North Ward; South Ward; Warren E. Hearnes Child and Youth Center
Bunch, J. R. (superintendent), 239
Burrell Children's Home, 203
Businesses, patient-owned, 181–83
Business Managers, listed, 240

Callaway County: and hospital development, 10, 12, 36, 38, 42–43, 56, 60; fires in, 161; Chamber of Commerce, 209–10; First Responders, 218
Camp Wonderland, 207–8

Canteen, 147, 159, 160, 203
Carnival, 147, 160, 165, 166
Case histories, 24, 26. *See also* Paperwork
Cause. *See* Mental illness, causes
Cave, Harriet (nurse), 186
Cemetery, 33, 34, 162, 224
Census, patient, 132, 150, 159, 165, 178–79, 218, 228, 234
Cerletti, Ugo, 95
Chapel: original building, 70; held in several buildings, 157, 163; in Biggs Building, 216–17
Chaplains, 158, 162, 174, 180, 184, 185
Chariton County, 10, 12
Chase, George (chaplain), 184–85
Chiarugi, Vincenzio, 7
Chief executive officers: listed, 239–40
Chief operating officers: listed, 239–40
Children. *See* Juveniles
Civil War: prewar reforms, ix, 5–6; coming of, 38–39; impact on Missouri, 39–44;, impact on asylum, 40–43; Union damage to asylum, 44, 114–15; mentioned, 160, 163, 177, 190, 193, 213
Civil Works Administration, 108
Clark, John P., 56, 61
Clark, Thaddeus, 153
Clay, Henry, 4
Clients, xii, 216, 227, 234, 236; as partners, 224. *See* Patients
Clinical Pastoral Education Program, 157–58, 180, 184
Club, the, 169–70
Code Blue, 215
Code Orange, 192
Cole, Brooks Ann, 161
Cole County, 10
Columbia, Missouri, 203
Columbia Daily Tribune, xvii, 187, 193
Communities, xii, 175, 179, 186, 204, 210, 212, 236; health clinics, 186, 232; hospitals, 137, 232
Condor the puppet, 200
Conference of Officers of State Eleemosynary and Penal Institutions of Missouri, 86
Connolly, John, 22
Constitution, State of Missouri, 137, 145, 149

Convulsive Therapy. *See* Therapy
Coombs, James T. (superintendent), 79, 80
Cooper County, 10
Corey, J. J. (business manager), 240
Cornell, Hiram, 56, 59–60, 61, 73
Costs: private patients, 23, 24, 41, 100, 130; indigent patients, 23, 64, 91, 100; per patient, 165, 178, 179. *See also* Finances; Purchasing practices
Council on Social Work Education, 220
Court system. *See* Judicial system
Cremer, William J. (superintendent), 146–51, 239
Cremer Building, 209, 223, 230
Cremer Clinic, 204
Criminally insane, 63–64, 108–10, 115, 148, 157, 158, 174, 178, 208, 221. *See also* Forensics
Cronkite, Walter, 223
Culver, Paul (business manager), 240
Cure rate: predicted pre-1940: 8, 26–28, 51–52, 63, 64, 67–68, 70, 77, 99, 100–101
Custodial care, 5, 14, 48, 68–69, 70, 90, 102

Dairy: sale of, 213; mentioned, 75, 190, 214
Dances. *See* Recreation
Davis, Nina (nurse), 158, 202
Deaths: at FSH, 33–34, 63, 148–49; 184- 85, 192, 193–94, 205, 222; suicide, 172, 192, 215. *See also* Violence
Deinstitutionalization, 204–17 *passim*
Delay, Jean, 154
Delinquents. *See* Juveniles
Deniker, Pierre, 154
Dentistry, 159, 190, 231
Depression. *See* Mental illness, diagnoses
Deutsch, Albert, xii
Diagnoses. *See* Mental illness, diagnoses
Discharge plans, 180, 181, 186
Dix, Dorothea, 15
Dixon, Missouri, 126
Dockery, Alexander (governor), 80
Doctors, medical. *See* Physicians
Donnell, Forrest C. (governor), 135–37
Donnelly, Phil M. (governor), 137
Downsizing. *See* Deinstitutionalization

Dress code, 166–67
Drug abuse. *See* Mental illness, diagnoses
Drugs. *See* Medications; Therapy
Dunavant, E. W., 114–15
Dunphy, T. E. (business manager), 240
Duval, Addison: as director of Division of Mental Diseases, 167

Earle, Pliny, 67–68
Eckerhart v. Hensley. See Judicial system
Education: for nurses, 69, 86–88, 152, 203, 232; for staff, 134–35, 224, 232; for patients, 157, 159, 174, 221; for public, 165; for social workers, 170; for juveniles, 201, 202. *See also* Research and professional development
Edwards, John C. (governor), 3, 13
Edwards, Miss Willie Samson, 170
Electricity, power plant, xiii, 133, 134, 135, 145, 150, 181, 204
Electroconvulsive Therapy (ECT) (Electroshock): experimental, 95, 140; at Fulton, 142–43, 159, 171, 172, 191. *See also* Therapy
Eleemosynary Act of 1921, 80–82; Board, 130, 137, 140
Elliott, Joseph E. (business manager), 240
Employees: shortages, xvi, 140, 149, 158, 179, 186, 192, 193, 194, 205, 232; policies, 20–22, 132–37; 158, 169, 217, 219, 232; wages, 132, 140, 147, 150, 169, 186, 187, 192, 224, 229; honored, 163, 166, 188; suggestions from, 219; mentioned, 175, 177, 211, 226, 227, 229. *See also* Employment of mentally ill; Management
Employment of mentally ill, 15, 130, 151, 184, 185, 188, 190, 214, 230–31, 235
Epifanio, Giuseppe, 95
Epilepsy. *See* Mental illness, diagnoses
Escapes, 159, 173, 175
Ettmueller, Gustav, 70
Evans, H. D., 81
Evans, Tom (assistant superintendent), 188–89

Factory output. *See* Self-sufficiency; Therapy

Families: affected by mental illness, x, xii, 179, 180, 186, 188, 209, 210; finances, 23, 24, 77; as part of treatment, 232, 234, 235, 236
Farm, xi, 15, 75, 190; land sold, 223. *See also* Food; Therapy
Federal Emergency Relief Administration, 103, 108, 110
Ferenczi, Sandor, 91
Ferguson, Jack, 155
Finances: and state, 4, 9–14, 16, 28, 34–35, 40, 44, 45, 46, 47, 51, 64–65, 71, 77, 78, 81, 85, 88, 105–8, 186–88, 209, 214, 215, 218, 219, 229; and families, 23, 24, 77; and counties, 23–24, 41, 45–46, 63, 64, 65, 77, 78, 79, 88, 100, 110, 209; and U.S. government, 199, 209, 217, 228, 235; mentioned, 5–6, 179, 209. *See also* Budgets; Canteen; Costs
Findley, June, 98–99
Fire: protection, 69, 107–8, 115; old Administration Building, 161–62; brigade, 161, 204; standards, 186
Fogley, R. C. (superintendent), 239
Food: production, 15, 134, 146, 147, 148, 150, 190, 204, 223; service, 99, 125, 132, 133, 134, 141, 135, 173, 192, 208; rationing, 140, 187; dietary workers, 192, 225; stamps, 229
Forensics, 174, 178, 190, 204, 215, 222, 223, 225, 228, 230. *See also* Biggs Building; Social Learning Program
Foster grandparents, 198–99
Foster homes, 202
Foucault, Michel, xiii
Fox, Richard, xiv
Francis, David (governor), 74–75
Frazer, T. R., 90, 96
Freeman, Walter, 95–96
Freud, Sigmund, 91, 140
Friendships, 182, 197, 206, 236
Fry, Mrs. J. E., 98
Fulton, City of: 12–13, 18, 20, 36–38, 40, 42, 73, 74, 106, 107, 175, 229, 236; public schools, 170, 199, 201–2; police, 203
Fulton Female Academy, 37
Fulton Forum, 231

"Fulton State Hospital: A Guide," 179–81
Fulton Sun (Sun-Gazette), 140, 148, 158, 169, 189, 193, 207–8, 219, 223

Galbraith, Ralph, 180
Gamble, Hamilton (governor), 40
Gambling at FSH, 181
Gamwell, Lynn, xv
Gannon, Dr. Patrick (psychiatrist), 187
Gender, differences in treatment, xii, 28, 29, 30, 34, 64, 65, 92, 96, 97, 100, 101, 102, 112, 113, 146, 147, 223, 230
Geriatrics: building, 167, 174, 178, 181, 190, 195, 209, 210; mentioned, 162, 220, 223
Gilbert, Joan, 124
Gildea, Edwin P., 153
Gillispie, Louise and Marshall (advocates), 224
Goffman, Erving, 183
Governors of Missouri: Thomas Reynolds, 3; Meredith Marmaduke, 3–6, 9; John C. Edwards, 3, 13; Austin King, 14; C. H. Hardin, 19; Claiborne Jackson, 39–40; Hamilton Gamble, 40; Silas Woodson, 65; B. Gratz Brown, 72, 109; David Francis, 74–75; Lon V. Stephens, 75, 79, 80; Alexander Dockery, 80; Forrest C. Donnell, 135–37; Phil M. Donnelly, 137; John M. Dalton, 168; Joseph P. Teasdale, 194; John Ashcroft, 218; mentioned, 169
Graveyard, 33, 34, 162, 224
Greenblatt, Milton, 92
Grob, Gerald, xiv, 69, 90
Groner, J. B. (business manager), 240
Group homes: as part of therapy, 186, 212, 219, 221. *See also* Therapy
Guardians, 130, 209
Guehleman, Henry, 224
Guehleman Forensic Center, 230–31
Guehleman Unit, 228

Hadley Building, 105, 113, 167, 229
Halfway houses, 212
Hall, Milton J., 42, 45
Hanks, Ralf (superintendent), 103, 111–12, 239

Hannibal, Missouri, 129
Hardin, Charles H. (governor), 19
Hardin, Mary, 19
Harding, Chester, Jr., 42
Harris, James H. (business manager), 240
Harris, Thomas, 19, 114
Hawkins, M. C., 14, 15, 16
Health insurance, 235
Hearnes Building. *See* Warren E. Hearnes Child and Youth Center
Hensley, Duane: as director of Department of Mental Health, 188
Herweg, Jim, 205–6
Historians, xi, xii–xiv
Hockaday, John, 114
Holcomb, William (superintendent), 215, 218, 219, 240
Holmes, Oliver Wendell, 96–97
Homelessness, 186, 210, 212, 235. *See also* Deinstitutionalization
Homeopathic therapy. *See* Therapy
Horner, M., 12, 15, 16
Hospital (Medical) Building, 132, 133, 158
Hospital Highlights, 142–43, 149, 163
Howard, Michael: death of, 192
Howard County, 10
Howser, Kathy, 217
Hughes, Charles (superintendent), 47, 48, 49–51, 52, 54, 55, 56, 57–61, 64–65, 71, 72, 75, 80, 109, 110, 239
Hughes, Jas. M., 11, 12, 15, 16
Hughes, John, xiv
Humor, 147, 151, 160, 161
Humphrey, Wesley, 56, 61
Hunter, Elmo (judge), 185, 193, 194, 206
Hyde Building, 190, 233
Hydrotherapy. *See* Therapy

Indigent patients. *See* Costs
Institutionalization, xiv, 145, 182, 183, 197
Institutional labor. *See* Self-sufficiency; Therapy
Institutions, other Missouri: St. Louis, 46, 48, 62, 223; St. Joseph (#2), 63, 80, 81, 170, 189, 223; Nevada (#3), 81, 86, 187, 223; Farmington (#4), 81, 98, 113, 170; Mid-Missouri Mental

Health Center (Mid-MO), 176, 190, 199, 203, 223, 233; Southwest Missouri Psychiatric Rehabilitation Center, 233
Institutions, other places: South Carolina, xiv; Rhode Island, 6; Connecticut, 6, 8; New Hampshire, 6, 8; Vermont, 6, 8; Massachusetts, 6, 8, 87, 92; Germany, 7; Williamsburg, Virginia, 7; France, 7, 8; Pennsylvania, 7, 8, 31, 50, 89, 90; Great Britain, 7, 8, 32; New York, 7–8, 67, 90; Ohio, 8, 13; New Jersey, 8, 16; Indiana, 13; Minnesota, 168; Boston Center for Psychiatric Rehabilitation, 229
Insulin shock therapy. *See* Therapy
Integrity, 237
Intermediate security, 228, 230
Investigations, 53–54, 55, 57, 61–62, 106, 185–86, 193, 215. *See also* Accreditation
Iowa-Missouri boundary dispute, 3

Jacks, Richard (superintendent), 188–89
Jackson, Claiborne (governor), 39–40
Jackson, Elmer C.: as first African American doctor at FSH, 165–66
Jails, as alternative to asylum, 144
James, S. P. (business manager), 240
Jameson, W. Ed., 108
Jameson's Ford dealership, 136
Jamison, C. W., 75
Jannick, Dave (psychologist), 184, 206
Jefferson City, Missouri, 161, 166, 171, 199; *News Tribune*, 193
Jenkins, Solomon, 13, 16
Joint Commission on Accreditation of Hospitals (JCAH), 172, 181, 186–87, 210, 211, 228
Jones, Larry (chaplain), 216
Journal of Nervous and Mental Diseases, 76
Judicial system: placing patients, 148; and sex offenders, 167; not guilty by reason of insanity, 176, 191, 208; *Eckerhart v. Hensley*, 185, 193, 194, 206; pretrial evaluation, 191, 230; juvenile court, 199; and deinstitutionalization, 212; as stakeholders, 232
Jung, Carl, 91

Juveniles, 156, 159–60, 165–67; 176, 186, 195, 196–203 *passim;* Children's Code, 160; Children's Unit, 198; juvenile court, 199; diagnosis of, 199, 201, 203; Matt McBride, 225–26

Kansas City, Missouri, 122, 153
Kansas City Star, 152
Karr, Jay, 137–38
Kelly, Margaret (state auditor), 217
Kesey, Ken, 189
KFAL-KKCA, 175
Kingdom Daily News, 188
Kingdom Daily Sun-Gazette, 211
Kingdom of Callaway, 134
Kingdom Projects, Inc., 231
Kings Row, 137–39, 144
Kirkbride, Thomas, 13, 68
Kitchen. *See* Food
Klaesi, Jakob, 95
Koop, C. Everett (U.S. surgeon general), 219
Kraepelin, Emil, 76

Labor, patient. *See* Employment of mentally ill; Therapy
Laboratory procedures, 159
Lafferty, Robert: death of, 222
Langley, Louise: death of, 192
Larkin, Lew, 152
Larson, Elaine (psychologist), 226
Law: enforcement, x; and women, 128–30; federal, 136; sex offenders, 167; lawsuits, 185, 193; legal definitions of insanity, 191, 208; and racism, 199; and deinstitutionalization, 212. *See also* Judicial system
Leeper, John, 19
Legal Aid Society. *See Eckerhart V. Hensley*
Lehrman, Nathaniel, 154
Lenoir, W. B., 61, 74
Lentz, R. J., 215
Lima, Almeida, 95
Lincoln, William, 20
Lincoln University, 171
Lindsey, Susan, 208
Lischway, Bernie (chaplain), 180
Lloyd, William (business manager), 240
Lobotomy. *See* Therapy

Logan, Lewis: death of, 193, 194, 205
Lost Weekend, The (film), 139
Low-bid system, 15
Lykins, Mattie, 122
Lyle, J. Ken, Jr. (business manager), 240
Lyles, Willie: and sex crime, 213

Maintenance, 187; maintenance department 134, 192. *See also* Buildings
Management (before 1940): Board of Managers, 17–20, 24, 29, 31, 41, 42, 46, 53–54, 55–64, 70–74, 76, 79, 87, 105, 107, 108, 110, 114; matron, 18, 19, 20, 45, 46, 71, 99; steward, 18, 19, 20, 45, 56, 62, 71, 73–74, 81, 83; superintendents, 18, 19, 24, 62, 71, 76, 82, 83, 239; treasurer, 18, 19, 106, 114–15; governor, 18, 55, 60–62, 71–74, 75–76, 79; attendants/nurses, 20–22, 30, 31, 46, 49, 50, 69, 77, 85, 86, 87–88, 99; assistant physician(s), 20, 44, 58, 59, 61, 64, 82, 93; nutritionist, 20, 98–99; Eleemosynary Act of 1921, 80–82; health supervisor, 82, 93; business managers, listed, 240. *See also* Board of Managers, State Eleemosynary Institutions; Governors of Missouri
Mangini, Joe, 172, 191
Maries County, 126
Marmaduke, Meredith (governor), 3–6, 9
Martien, James, 56, 60
Martin, Marty Ann (chief operating officer), 233, 240
Mass media: books, 137–39, film, 139–40, 144, 145, 148, 150; reporting 1956 fire, 161; viewed in Biggs Building, 206–7
Matron. *See* Management
Maudsley, Sir Henry, 111
Maximum security, 174, 178, 206, 228, 230. *See also* Forensics
Mayfield, John H. (superintendent), 211–12, 213, 215, 240
McBride, Jack (Fulton NAACP representative), 170, 193
McBride Bill, 225–26
McCandless, Peter, xiv
McElheney, William, 12, 13, 15, 16

McGough, E. T. (superintendent), 239
McGready, Theodore, 33
McKee, Edwin J. (business manager), 240
McReynolds, Bill: and token economy, 190
Medical (Hospital) Building, 132, 133, 158; pharmacy, 155, 213
Medicare/Medicaid. *See* United States government, financing
Medications: purgatives, 30, 31, 50, 80, 181; before 1940: 31, 48, 49, 50, 69, 80, 95, 96; after 1940: 143, 155, 171, 172, 180, 181, 188, 201, 208, 213, 221, 225, 235; Epsom salts, 143–44; Chlorpromazine, 153; Thorazine, 153–54, 205, 220; pharmacy, 155, 213; Haldol, 205; Clorazil, 220. *See also* Therapy
Medium security. *See* Forensics
Melcher, S. H., 72–73
Menditto, Anthony, Dr., 215, 221, 222; as chief operating officer, 240
Mental illness, causes, 26–27, 49, 52; 66, 76, 89, 90, 99–102. *See also* Mental illness, diagnoses; Mental illness, duration; Therapy
Mental illness, diagnoses: epilepsy, 52, 96, 97, 110–11; inebriation, 52, 102, 110–11; utromania, 129; monomania, 129; schizophrenia, 140, 142, 143, 154, 178, 204, 210, 221, 223, 225–26, 229, 234, 235; depression, 172, 190, 191, 234, 235; alcoholism, 176, 179, 221; psychotic, 178, 183; paranoia, 178, 212; catatonic, 185, 190; retarded, 191, 199; legal definitions, 191, 208; autistic, 198, 199; post-traumatic stress disorder, 219; substance (drug) abuse, 221, 223, 230; bipolar disorder, 234, 235. *See also* Juveniles; Mental illness, causes; Mental illness, duration; Therapy
Mental illness, duration: chronic, 140, 158, 181, 184, 188, 191, 204, 209, 210, 212, 214–15, 216; acute, 140, 159, 204, 212, 216. *See also* Mental illness, causes; Mental illness, diagnoses; Therapy

248 Index

Mental illness, therapy. *See* Therapy
Merit system, 136, 144
Metrazol therapy. *See* Therapy
Mid-Missouri Mental Health Center (Mid-MO). *See* Institutions, other Missouri
Minimum security. *See* Forensics
Minor, James, 19
Mission statement, 236–37
Missouri, state government finances. *See* Finances
Missouri, state government patronage. *See* Patronage
Missouri Association for Mental Hygiene, 90
Missouri Association for Social Welfare (MASW), 144, 145, 153, 161
Missouri Attorney General, 205
Missouri Board of Charities and Corrections, 88, 89, 98, 110
Missouri Colony for Feeble-Minded, 81
Missouri Department of Child Welfare, 202
Missouri Department of Corrections, 174, 213, 214, 223, 230
Missouri Department of Health and Public Welfare, Division of Mental Diseases, 137, 156, 165, 173, 186; becomes Department of Mental Health, 176, 186
Missouri Department of Mental Health: shareholder/stakeholder, x, 232; created, 176, 186–87; budget, 194, 205, 233; and patients, 209, 224; mentioned, 174, 215, 218, 223, 230, 235. *See also* Finances
Missouri governors. *See* Governors of Missouri
Missouri School for the Deaf and Dumb, 11, 38, 44; School for the Deaf, 170, 194, 213, 214
Missouri State Archives, xv, 32
Missouri State Constitution, 137, 145, 149
Missouri State Hospitals, other. *See* Institutions, other Missouri
Missouri State Legislature: importance of, ix, x, xv, and finances, 130, 137, 148, 153, 169, 170, 173, 191, 194, 197, 198, 220, 211, 218, 219, 225, 228, 232
Missouri State Official Manual, 140, 165, 178, 179
Missouri State Penitentiary, 11
Moberly (Missouri) Monitor, 123
Mohatt, Kay, 184–85
Moniteau County, 10, 12
Moniz, Egas, 95
Moore, James E. (business manager), 240
Morgue, 136, 190, 204
Morris, Jack (assistant attorney general), 205
Mosby, Bill, 216, 224
Muller, Max, 95
Murder. *See* Deaths; Violence
Museum Hall, 66
Music therapy. *See* Therapy

Naming of hospital, ix, 176
National Alliance on Mental Illness: data from, 218, 224, 234, 235
National Association for the Protection of the Insane and the Prevention of Insanity, 68
National Committee for Mental Hygiene, 68, 90
National Institute of Mental Health, 183
Nevada, Missouri, 128
Newsom, Robert (psychiatric aide), 193
New York Hospital. *See* Asylums
Nichols, Orfa: and fire, 161
No-hostage policy, 173
North Ward: in use, 160, 190, 191, 194, 203, 206, 209; torn down, 213
Nurse-Patient Relationship, The (film), 154–55
Nurses: education of, 59, 86–88, 152, 203, 204, 207, 210, 215, 232; as oral history informants, 134, 143, 147, 169, 174, 220, 227; as caretakers, 141, 143, 154–55, 158, 180, 190, 191, 225; psychiatric nurse, 154; in charge of ward, 168; supported policy, 170, 186; mentioned, 72, 140, 179, 189, 192, 214, 226, 233, 234
Nursing homes, 179, 186, 223
Nutrition, 20, 98–99

Oabe, F. C., 75
Occupational therapy. *See* Therapy
Ohio Lunatic Asylum. *See* Institutions, other places
Olasky, Marvin, xiv
Omnibus State Government Reorganization Act, 186
Ophthalmologist, 196
Ordover, Nancy, 97
Orientation, x
Outpatient care, 179, 204, 209
Overcrowding: before 1940, 29, 32, 47, 49, 63, 65, 88, 98, 103–4, 111, 115. *See also* Census, patient
Owens, Iris (nurse), 194

Paperwork: records, xv, 119, 120, 162, 188, 205
Parades: in 1930, 104; in 1955, 141; in 1976, 188
Parker, E. R., 73
Parole, 89, 219
Pastoral setting. *See* Therapy
Patients: and privacy, ix, 119–20; warehousing of, xi, 121, 146, 204, 209; records of, xv, 119, 120, 162, 188, 205; treatment of, before asylums, 4–5, 6, 7, 8, 14–15, 25; admissions of, 22–24, 41, 45, 48, 65, 99, 100, 112, 191–92, 204; case histories of, 24, 26; by state and national origin, 77, 101, 112; and parole, 89, 219; after-care for, 89–91; rocking chairs for, 109, 152; and ward life, 146, 181–84, 196–203; and patients' rights, 176, 185, 234; on leave, 178; and discharge plan, 180, 181, 186; trial visits, 181; ground privileges, 181, 208; and employment, 184, 185, 188, 230–31; definitions codified in law, 191, 208; empowerment of, 237. *See also* Forensics; Juveniles
Patients' rights: *Eckerhart v. Hensley*, 185, 193, 194, 206; mentioned, 176, 185, 234
Patronage: in hiring, 19, 71–76, 79–82, 88, 102; ended, 135–37, 144, 153
Paul, Gordon, 215
Pennsylvania Hospital. *See* Institutions, other places

Peterson, Catherine, 176
Peterson, Donald (superintendent): hired, 168–70; and racism, 170–71; policies, 171–74, 185; and community, 176–77; and juveniles, 186; retirement, 187–88; and deinstitutionalization, 212; listed, 239
Pet therapy. *See* Therapy
Pharmaceuticals. *See* Medications
Physical therapy. *See* Therapy
Physicians: before 1940, 29, 123–24, 130; treating mental illness, 123–24, 136, 142, 158, 180; and Medical (Hospital) Building, 132, 133, 158; and shortages, 140, 158, 186; cottages for, 175, 219; and medical procedures, 180, 189, 190, 204, 205, 212; and pay, 192
Pinel, Philippe, 7, 8
Politics. *See* Finances; Governors of Missouri; Missouri State Legislature
Polk, James K., 4
Population of FSH. *See* Census, patient; Overcrowding
Preventive care and outreach, 68, 89–91. *See also* Outpatient care
Price, Sterling, Jr., 53
Privacy, patients', ix, 119–20
Private patients, 23, 24, 41, 100. *See also* Costs
Production. *See* Self-sufficiency; Therapy
Professional development. *See* Research and professional development
Progressive era, xiv
Psychiatrists, 152, 153, 154, 156, 157, 172, 225, 232; psychiatric nurses, 154; psychiatric social workers, 174; forensics, 174, 208. *See also* Physicians; Therapy
Psychoanalysis. *See* Therapy
Psychodrama. *See* Therapy
Psychologists, 158, 173, 174, 179, 180, 183, 184, 189, 192, 215, 232; psychological testing, 172
Psychotherapy. *See* Therapy
Publications of Fulton State Hospital. *See* Annual Reports; *Fulton Forum*; "Fulton State Hospital: A Guide"; *Hospital Highlights*

Index

Public Health Research Group, 218
Public perceptions: of institution, 25–26, 49, 78, 79, 137–40, 151, 183, 196–97; of mental illness, 119, 120, 123, 126, 129–31, 156, 176, 183, 196–97, 224. *See also* Investigations; Mass media
Public Works Administration, 103
Purchasing practices, before 1940, 56–58, 59–60, 61–62, 71–72, 81. *See also* Costs; Finances
Purgatives/emetics/laxatives. *See* African Americans, racism; Medications

Ralls County, 129, 131
Ray, W. L. (superintendent), 80, 113, 239
Recidivism. *See* Relapse
Recreation: carnivals, 147, 160, 164, 165, 166; at Biggs, 159, 173, 174; and volunteers, 162–64, 174, 195, 198, 236; Camp Wonderland, 207–8; mentioned, 171, 180, 196, 210
Recreational therapy. *See* Therapy
Reed, Preston (Missouri state senator), 37
Reeves, Steve: as business manager, 240; as superintendent, 219, 223, 240
Rehabilitation. *See* Therapy
Reil, Johann, 7
Reitz, Robert (acting superintendent), 240
Relapse, 183, 204–5, 215
Religion, 124, 196, 216, 226. *See also* Chaplains
Research and professional development: before 1940, 20, 69, 70, 81–82, 86–87, 88, 90, 91, 92–93
Restraints: use of, 15, 25, 31, 46, 48, 49, 50, 69, 121, 158, 159, 169; desire to end use, 232. *See also* Therapy
Reynolds, Thomas (governor), 3
Rice, Nathan L., 60
Richardson, W. H., 19
Ritterbusch, James K.: as surgeon, 172, as superintendent, 189–90, 192–93, 211
Robertson, W. W., Rev., 37
Rodes, W. R. (superintendent), 67, 239
Rogers, Ruth, 157

Rogers, William, 157, 158
Rollins, James S., 121, 122, 124
Rummel, Dick (chaplain), 180, 216
Rumors, 175, 219
Rush, Benjamin, 19, 22, 67

Sakel, Manfred, 95
Saline County, 10, 12
Schizophrenia. *See* Mental illness, diagnoses
Schools, Fulton Public, 170, 199, 201–2
Scull, Andrew, xiii
Seaman, Robert (business manager), 156, 240
Seaman Field, 134
Seclusion. *See* Therapy
Sedation. *See* Therapy
Self-sufficiency: electricity, xiii, 133, 134, 135, 145, 150, 181, 204; farm xi, 190, 223; patient labor, 8, 9, 30, 31, 50–51, 67–69, 80, 83–85, 105, 130, 157, 184; dairy, 75, 190, 213, 214; food production, 134, 141, 146, 147, 148, 150, 190, 204, 223; morgue, 136, 190, 204; end of, 213; mentioned, x, 15, 132, 133, 134, 150, 151, 204. *See also* Therapy
Service area (zone of service), 165, 228
Sesquicentennial, ix
Sewage, 34, 55
Sexual disorders, 206–7, 213; laws, 167, 191; psychopathy, 185; abuse, 215
Sexual experiences at FSH, 208–9
Sheltered workshop, 174, 221
Shidy, Hamilton, 58, 59, 61
Shoaf, Ron (aide), 193
Shorter, Edward, xiv, 68
Silbey, George, 19
Skin: infectious diseases, 167; test, 180
Smith, Dennis, 213
Smith, J. F. (business manager), 240
Smith, J. W. (superintendent), 83, 239
Smith, Janie, 208
Smith, Kline and French, 154
Smith, T. R. H. (superintendent), 19, 20, 22, 24–29, 30–32, 33–34, 35, 41, 44–46, 48, 49, 62–64, 65–67, 69, 71, 77, 78, 114, 123–24, 239

Smith, W. H. (business manager), 240
Smith, William, 97
Snake Pit, The (film), 139–40, 144, 148
Snelson, John, 19
Socialization, 196, 221
Social Learning Program (SLP), 215–16, 221–23, 225, 226, 229, 230
Social workers: psychiatric, 158, 174; education of, 170, 232; mentioned, 143, 175, 190, 219–20, 225
South Ward: in use, 160, 190, 194, 196, 200, 203, 209; torn down, 213
Southwest Missouri Psychiatric Rehabilitation Center, 233
Spa Therapy. *See* Therapy
Spellbound (film), 139
Springfield, Missouri, 203, 224
Staff. *See* Aides; Employees; Management; Nurses; Physicians; Psychiatrists; Psychologists; Social workers
Stassel, Don, Rev., 216
Stephens, Lon V. (governor), 75, 79, 80
Sterilization, 96–98
Stevens, Chas., 56
Steward. *See* Management
Stewart, A. C., 60
Stigma. *See* Public perceptions
St. Joseph, Missouri, 223
St. Louis, Missouri, 10, 165, 168, 170, 189, 223
Strategic plan, x–xi, 232
Stuve, Paul, 221, 222
Suicide, 172, 192, 215
Summers, L. W. (business manager), 240
Superintendents: listed, 239–40
Surgery, 29, 69, 92–93, 94, 95–96, 108, 158, 159, 171, 172. *See also* Physicians; Therapy
Swon, E., 74
Szasz, Thomas, xiii–xiv, 21, 26, 68, 205*n*

Tartaglino, Francis J., 173, 174
Telephone system, 88
Texas annexation, 4
Therapy: Labor (work as therapy), 8, 9, 30, 31, 50–51, 67–69, 80, 83–85, 105, 130, 157, 184; and restraints, 15, 25, 31, 46, 48, 49, 50, 69, 121, 158, 159, 169, 232; in pastoral setting, 17, 28–29, 45, 65, 67, 83; drug therapy before 1940, 31, 48, 49, 50, 69, 80, 95, 96; hydrotherapy, 50, 91–92, 172; allopathic, 79–80, 83; homeopathic, 79–80, 83; Occupational Therapy, 84–85, 159, 180, 196, 201, 218, 232; after-care, 89–91; psychoanalysis, 90, 91, 144; physical, 91; spa therapy, 91, 121; convulsive, 95; Electroconvulsive (ECT) (electroshock), 95, 140, 142, 143, 159, 171, 172, 191; lobotomy, 95–96, 158, 171, 172; X-rays, 140; Metrazol, 140–42; insulin shock, 140, 141, 152; artificial fever, 140, 142; music, 144, 159, 163, 174, 180, 196; psychodrama, 156, 196; vocational, 157, 221; sedation, 159; subshock insulin, 159; seclusion, 169; outpatient care, 179, 204, 209; recreational, 180, 196, 221; group homes, 186, 212, 219, 221; token economy, 190; psychotherapy, 196, 201, 229; pet therapy, 207; group therapy, 225; psychosocial, 230; mentioned, 158, 180, 212, 214, 225, 235, 236
Thomas, Lewis, xiv
Thomas, W. D., 106
Thomas, William, 56, 60, 61
Tissot, S. A. A. D., 67
Tokens: as reward, 190, 216, 221, 222. *See also* Therapy
Tomes, Nancy, xv, 26
Treasurer. *See* Management
Treatment plans, 191
Treatment units (teams), x, xi, 189, 201, 222
Treatment. *See* Therapy
Truman, Harry, 149
Tuberculosis care, 105, 113, 167, 180
Tunnels, 134, 135, 149, 182, 208
Turner, Charles S. (business manager), 240

Ulett, George: as state director of Mental Health, 168, 173, 176, 186; goals of, 178, 188
Union Electric, 192
Unions, 192, 234
United States government: mental health

policies, xiv; financing, 137, 179, 186, 198, 205, 209, 215, 228; rejections of troops for mental illness, 168; military, 168, 179, 215; Dept. of Justice, 193; Supreme Court, 194; Dept. of Health, Education, Welfare, 200; Surgeon General, 219; FSH employee use of benefits, 229; Department of Labor, 232
University of Missouri, 11, 145n, 219–20; Hospital, 176
University of Missouri–St. Louis, 189

Valdes, Luis: and SLP, 222
Values, 236
Vegiard, Bob (chaplain), 216
Video, 177; "Condor" series, 200
Vienna, Missouri, 124
Vincenz, Felix: quoted, xi–xii, 166; as chief operating officer, 233–34, 240
Violence: episodes in hospital, 148–49, 184–85, 192, 193–94, 205, 222, 232; dangerously ill, 158; suicide, 172, 192, 215; and larger society, 175, 213, 225–26; Code Orange, 192; juveniles, 199, 225–26; culture of nonviolence, 232; mentioned, 22, 25, 49, 154, 155, 169, 172, 214. *See also* Deaths
Vision, 236
Visitors, 8, 89, 147–49, 165, 236
Vocational therapy. *See* Therapy
Vocational training, 221
Volunteers, 162–64, 174, 195, 198, 236
Von Meduna, Ladislas, 95

Waggoner, Jacob, 23
Waggoner, Mary, 23
War, xii. *See also* Civil War; World War II
Waraich, Gus, 149
Warden, J. L., 70, 93
Warehousing patients, xi, 121, 146, 204, 209

Warren E. Hearnes Child and Youth Center (Hearnes), 198–203, 204; Hearnes Building adapted to other use, 228, 230
Washington University, 168
Watts, James, 96
Weakley, William, 97–98
Weber, William, 53
Wells, Robert W., 6–9
Westminster College (Fulton College), 37–38, 162, 189
Willard State Hospital, 67
Williams, George (superintendent), 86–87, 91–92, 107, 111, 239
Williams, John, 53
Williams, Porter E. (superintendent), 103, 239
William Woods University, 219–20
Wilson, Charles M. (business manager), 240
Wilson, Edward (business manager), 240
Wilson, R. S. (superintendent), 69–70, 83, 109, 239
Wilson, Roger (U.S. senator), 215
Woodson, Silas (governor), 65
Worcester State Hospital, 87
Works Progress Administration, 108
World War II: GI bill, 134; reserve funds, 137; created shortages, 140, 145, 148, 149, 165; mentioned, xvi, 168
Wortis, Joseph, 95

X-rays, 140, 180. *See also* Therapy

Young, D. H. (superintendent), 79, 80, 110, 239
Youth. *See* Juveniles
Yow, Ann, 206

Zinn, Howard, xii–xiii
Zone of service, 165, 228